THE
GREATEST
COMEBACK

THE STORY OF BÉLA GUTTMANN

THE
GREATEST
COMEBACK

FROM GENOCIDE TO FOOTBALL GLORY

DAVID BOLCHOVER

Biteback Publishing

First published in Great Britain in 2017 by
Biteback Publishing Ltd
Westminster Tower
3 Albert Embankment
London SE1 7SP
Copyright © David Bolchover 2017

ISBN 978-1-78590-139-3

10 9 8 7 6 5 4 3 2 1

A CIP catalogue record for this book is available from the British Library.

Set in Adobe Caslon Pro

ʹ Printed and bound in Great Britain by
CPI Group (UK) Ltd, Croydon CR0 4YY

To the memory of my parents and grandparents

CONTENTS

Introduction ix

Chapter 1: The First Escapes 1
Chapter 2: Years of Defiance 23
Chapter 3: The Big Apple 45
Chapter 4: Learning the Ropes 63
Chapter 5: Dodging Death 85
Chapter 6: The Survivor Returns 119
Chapter 7: The Italian Jobs 137
Chapter 8: Latin Lessons 159
Chapter 9: Conquering Europe 185
Chapter 10: Retention 203
Chapter 11: Fading Out 219

Conclusion: Reflections 251
Béla Guttmann's Career: Timeline and Achievements 259
Acknowledgements 263
Select Bibliography 269
Index 275

INTRODUCTION

At the Prater stadium in Vienna on 23 May 1990, the illustrious Portuguese football team Benfica was due to take on Italian giants AC Milan in the European Cup Final. Shortly before the game, Benfica's greatest ever former player, Eusébio, took a trip to the Jewish section of the city's Central Cemetery. There he prayed before the grave of the man who, three decades earlier, had plucked him from obscurity and propelled him to international stardom. Kneeling beside the tombstone, he beseeched his dead mentor to lift a famous curse.

In May 1962, Béla Guttmann's Benfica had beaten the great Real Madrid 5–3 in the Olympic stadium in Amsterdam to claim their second successive European Cup. Their final two goals were scored by Eusébio, the twenty-year-old phenomenon known as the 'Black Pearl'.

But after the match, the club's very realistic prospects of long-term European domination were thrown into disarray. The board of directors rejected Guttmann's continued demands for a pay rise, pointing to the absence of any such provision in his contract. As was his wont throughout his turbulent career, the deeply charismatic and innovative coach departed in fury. He is said to have told

his erstwhile employers that they would not win another European trophy for one hundred years.

Eusébio's supplication of 1990 came to nothing. Milan beat Benfica 1–0. Indeed, as of 2016, Benfica have appeared in eight European finals since 1962, and lost every single one – an eventuality, based on an even chance of winning each, with a probability of 1 in 256, or 0.4 per cent.

Such is the curse of Béla Guttmann. His powerful presence looms as large in death as it did in life. His statue greets Benfica fans as they walk through gate 18 of the club's magnificent Estádio da Luz in Lisbon. More than 500 years after the Easter weekend in which 3,000 Jews were massacred in that city in a prelude to the Portuguese Inquisition, one of their number stands tall once more. He proudly clutches the two European Cups that have eluded his thirty-two successors, a constant, mocking reminder to the Benfica faithful of what might have been if their stubborn and short-sighted directors had properly valued his managerial genius.

It would be hard to imagine a modern-day football club refusing to meet the seemingly reasonable demands of a coach who had presided over such glorious success. But Guttmann and Benfica both paid the price for his novelty, the ability he demonstrated throughout his career to smash tradition and then remould it.

While few now question the huge influence of the coach on team performance in football or other sports, the prevailing opinions of 1962 would have been very different. Despite the achievements of the likes of Herbert Chapman, who led Huddersfield Town and Arsenal to repeated success in England in the 1920s and 1930s, the now widespread cult of the coach was then still some way from being firmly established.

Béla Guttmann was the first of a kind, an international superstar football coach who eked every last drop of effort and tactical advantage from his teams, before José Mourinho or Pep Guardiola

were even born. 'He was ahead of his time,' says António Simões, another of his Benfica stars, thrown on to the world stage by his mentor at the tender age of seventeen. 'Mourinho says the same things today that Guttmann did more than fifty years ago.'

So when he gambled, Benfica sent him packing, labouring under the naive impression that there were plenty more where he came from.

• • •

To fathom the legend that is Béla Guttmann, we must first pay close attention to the time and place which this remarkable man came from: the immensely vibrant and creative society of Jewish central and eastern Europe as it entered its very final phase before almost total annihilation. In the football sphere, just as in so many others, the impact of this Jewish population was extraordinarily disproportionate to its size.

Guttmann was born in the last year of the nineteenth century, in the Hungarian capital Budapest, to Abráhám and Eszter Guttmann. His first notable footballing success was at MTK Budapest, a club founded by Jewish businessmen and subsequently associated strongly with its predominantly Jewish players and supporters. In a starting eleven that included six Jews, he then scored on his debut for the Hungarian national team against Germany in 1921.

Everything appeared rosy for Guttmann, but his success on the pitch was to be clouded by political events off it. Unsettled by the murder of thousands of Jews in the Hungarian White Terror, he decamped to the all-Jewish and Zionist football club Hakoah Vienna. It was to be one of twenty-one moves across international borders in the playing and coaching career of football's Wandering Jew, the founding father of a now globalised game.

It was at Hakoah that Guttmann reached the pinnacle of his playing career, winning the Austrian championship of 1925, the first

fully professional league title race in mainland Europe. But Gutt-mann's experience during his five years at the club was in no way confined to on-field glory.

Hakoah (the Hebrew word for 'the strength' or 'the power') was much more than just a successful team; it was a potent symbol of Jewish national pride, both in Vienna and throughout the entire Jewish world. Founded by a group of Austrian Zionists, the club's espousal of Jewish assertiveness and feisty self-reliance, and its re-jection of timid assimilation into Gentile society, chimed with a large section of Jewish youth who sought a vestige of dignity amid a constant torrent of abuse, intimidation and violence. 'A people who get used to being insulted are lost,' said Robert Stricker, one of Hakoah's founders.

Despite the intense loathing they attracted on and off the pitch, Hakoah sought no accommodation, standing toe to toe with hostile opponents in an often febrile and physically intimidating atmos-phere. Embodying the spirit of 'muscular Judaism', a phrase con-ceived by the Zionist activist Max Nordau, the players sported a large Star of David on their shirts in collective defiance of a world riddled with hatred of Jews since time immemorial.

Guttmann and his teammates travelled the world, enjoying sus-tained success on the pitch, and fêted by mass crowds of adoring Jewish fans wherever they went. In Poland, they provoked civil unrest after defeating the country's finest. In the United States, they attracted one quarter of a million spectators to their tour games in 1926, at one game breaking a soccer attendance record that had stood for half a century. West Ham United became the first English team to be defeated on home soil, dismantled 5–0 in their own stadium a few months after reaching the FA Cup Final. The then mighty Slavia Prague were beaten at home for the first time in more than a decade.

Viewed in retrospect, these glory years at Hakoah were to be the

last hurrah, one of the very final sources of joy for a people that was soon to be ravaged in the inferno that accounted for two of every three European Jews. At least thirty-seven members of the wider Hakoah sports club were murdered, including seven of its footballers. With Guttmann himself serving as its last coach before the Nazis marched into Vienna, the club was disbanded, the records of its achievements expunged from the history books.

Up to 600,000 of Guttmann's fellow Hungarian Jews, including his sister and elderly father, were also murdered. In a 54-day period in the spring and early summer of 1944 that plumbed the depths of hell, fully 435,000 of them were transported to extermination camps, the overwhelming majority to Auschwitz, at a rate of more than 8,000 a day – with one Jew put to death every eleven seconds.

The voracious Nazi machine eliminated at least eighteen Béla Guttmanns and nineteen Béla Gutmans, not to mention four Béla Guttmans, ten Bella Gutmans and three Bella Guttmanns. Legend has it that our hero, Béla Guttmann the football man, managed to avoid the Holocaust by decamping to neutral Switzerland. But as with many details about Guttmann's life, the truth is rather more noteworthy than we have been led to believe.

He was in fact in Hungary throughout 1944, somehow surviving the devastation all around him. For months, he lived like a rat in a dingy attic near Budapest, while thousands of his fellow Jews in the immediate vicinity were being dragged off to be murdered. He subsequently escaped from the gruelling humiliation of forced labour on the eve of a planned deportation and almost certain death, thereafter rebuilding his life to quite astonishing effect.

We don't have to be brilliant psychologists to believe that Hakoah's brash contrariness, or Guttmann's double fleeing from persecution and the obliteration of his world, were all important determinants of his future character. Bullish, argumentative, outspoken, distrustful, itinerant, iconoclastic, impulsive – Guttmann

was the archetypal outsider who knew the establishment would never accept him, but who scorned their judgement and ploughed his own furrow regardless.

• • •

Béla Guttmann's life story is the epitome of human triumph in the wake of adversity, the prime sporting example from a generation of inspirational Holocaust survivors who cast off the horrors of the past to achieve great personal success. A little more than a decade and a half after the extermination camps were closed down, denoting the end of an era in which much of Europe wanted him and his people dead, Guttmann ended up lifting the most prestigious sporting prize in that very continent. From the death pits of Europe to champion of Europe in little more than sixteen years.

This book is therefore not just an examination of a man whose influence on the football world resonates to this day, but of one of life's great survivors. It was Iain Dowie, the former British professional footballer turned pundit, who coined the term 'bouncebackability', referring to the ability of certain sporting personalities or teams to recover from negative circumstances and forge success. In this respect, is there anyone who can match Guttmann?

'In life, I was down more than I was up,' he said during his final years; some statement for a man who won twelve major titles throughout his distinguished playing and coaching career. But he was right, nonetheless.

Aside from this human story of resilience set against a dramatic footballing backdrop, Guttmann's life also symbolises something far broader, in two ways reflecting the hugely colourful but tragic span of Jewish history.

He lived in fourteen different countries, with several stints in some, mirroring the peripatetic nature of Jewish populations

throughout the ages. Hungary, Yugoslavia, Austria, the United States, the Netherlands, Romania, Italy, Argentina, Cyprus, Brazil, Portugal, Uruguay, Switzerland and Greece – all of these countries benefited from Guttmann's presence at some stage, and just as with virtually every country in the world, each has a captivating, often harrowing, Jewish story to tell.

Guttmann's life story of near-death and renewal also echoes the Jewish experience of the twentieth century in particular, of surely the most astonishing national comeback in human history.

The Jewish nation was on the floor in 1945. Abandoned to their fate by the world's hatred or indifference, six million of its people lay dead, including more than a million of the children who embodied its future. Tens of thousands of survivors languished in internment camps, with many more roaming around Europe seeking lost loved ones, only to be met on many occasions with yet more hatred and violence at the hands of their former neighbours.

But just three short years later, in 1948, the state of Israel was founded, the first Jewish sovereign state for almost two millennia. In May 1961, as Guttmann's Benfica took to the field against Barcelona in Bern to claim their first European Cup, the Jewish state that had already successfully defended itself in wars against its own neighbours was at that very time prosecuting Adolf Eichmann, one of the principal Nazi masterminds of the Holocaust, in a Jewish court with Jewish judges in its ancient capital of Jerusalem. For the Jewish nation, as for Guttmann, the world had turned on its head, only this time for the better.

You shouldn't therefore expect a conventional biography of a great sports coach with a compelling personality who led a fascinating life and heavily influenced the direction of modern-day football, although this is certainly a story well worth telling in its own right. Throughout the book, most notably at the start of each chapter, the symbolism and background of Guttmann's life will feature strongly,

with the biographical story placed within the context of the Jewish history of either the time or the place in which he finds himself. This background also underlines Guttmann's phenomenal achievement, emerging as a winner against all the odds.

One final point before the story begins. This is also very much a book about Europe. Guttmann's life straddled two contrasting visions of Europe that correspond with its conflicting history – one of barbarism and genocide, and one of beauty, wonder and romance, of balmy May evenings in magnificent cities, where great players would stretch every sinew before joyous crowds in a bid to win football's holy grail, the European Cup. At a time of renewed and escalating tension in that continent, as the last remnants of once-great Jewish communities pray in their synagogues and study in their schools behind high wire fences and armed guards, the story of Guttmann's life asks the question: which of these visions will triumph in *our* times?

CHAPTER 1

THE FIRST ESCAPES

'Here comes the Jew!' shouted the concierge of the Budapest apartment block as József Baumgarten approached. A crowd appeared from nowhere, chasing the First World War veteran to his home on the third floor.

Finding the apartment locked, he quickly ran into a neighbour's house. The mob broke down his door anyway, set about beating up his younger brother, Zsigmond, and threatened to hang his grandmother. In his subsequent statement to the Jewish Legal Aid Office, Baumgarten recounts the story about what subsequently happened on that August day in 1919:

My brother fled to the apartment of the neighbour Béla Rotling and closed the door. The crowd ran after him – a day labourer named János Putnik ... who was the gang's leader and who beat my brother most severely, broke the window above the door. In this way, the crowd entered the apartment. Here they began to beat my brother again. A few minutes later I heard a loud noise. My brother was lying dead on the ground floor (of the building's inner courtyard). Whether he jumped or was thrown out of the window, I do not know.

Jószef Baumgarten himself was eventually beaten so badly that he was

hospitalised for six weeks. Putnik was arrested, only to be released after three days.

This episode offers a snapshot of the White Terror, which bullied, beat and murdered Jews throughout Hungary between 1919 and 1921, the years immediately following the end of a war in which around 10,000 Hungarian Jews had died fighting for the Austro-Hungarian army.

The White Terror was a savage reaction to the brief but brutal rule of the Hungarian Soviet Republic, led by Béla Kun from March to August 1919. Even beforehand, the search for a scapegoat to blame for the country's humiliating defeat in the First World War, not to mention the continuing success of Jews in economic and cultural life, had served to nourish anti-Semitism. The prominence of Jews (most of whom had previously converted to Christianity) in the overthrown Communist government, including the half-Jewish Kun himself, was the additional catalyst which ensured that anti-Jewish violence would be the bloody centrepiece of the White Terror.

Orchestrated by Admiral Miklós Horthy, the commander of the counter-revolutionary National Army, and by his sadistic henchman Pál Prónay, White Terror units rampaged through the countryside, moving from village to town in the hunt for Jews. In Marcali, six Jews were hanged in August 1919; in nearby Csurgó, where the sixty-five Jewish families had lost thirteen men in the war, seven of their number were massacred in September; that same month, a unit armed with hand grenades and machine guns sought out and murdered all the Jews in Diszel; in November, eight Jews – two teachers, two lawyers, a banker, a merchant, a student and a printer's apprentice – were hacked to death in Kecskemét. The litany of murder was to continue unabated, with Budapest becoming the focus of the attacks in 1920 after the National Army had taken control of the capital. In total, some 3,000 Hungarian Jews are believed to have been murdered in the onslaught.

The new government's legal framework followed a similar pattern. In

1920, the Hungarian Parliament passed the so-called numerus clausus law, the first anti-Semitic law in post-First World War Europe. No new students, the law stipulated, should be accepted to universities unless they were 'loyal from the national and moral standpoint', and 'the proportion of members of the various ethnic and national groups in the total number of students should amount to the proportion of such ethnic and national groups in the total population'. The law was clearly targeted at Jews, and had its desired effect. The proportion of Jews at the Budapest Institute of Sciences collapsed, for example, from 34 per cent in 1913 to 8 per cent in 1925.

The frightened and disoriented Jewish community responded in time-honoured fashion, professing their loyalty and patriotism, and using rational forms of argument in an attempt to persuade an irrational enemy that they shouldn't hate Jews. The Israelite Congregation of Pest made a declaration:

> *The Congregation wishes to state that for every single Communist there are at least a thousand Hungarian citizens of the Jewish faith who in both peace and war faithfully served the Hungarian fatherland and nation, and in the mournful period of proletarian dictatorship suffered beyond endurance, and stand just as far from the erroneous doctrines of Communist morality as anybody else.*

Twenty-five years later, in the face of yet another incarnation of the longest hatred, the credibility of this policy of reasoned persuasion against bigotry was to perish in the gas chambers and ovens of Auschwitz, along with many of its former proponents. Horthy, meanwhile, who died an old man in Portugal in the 1950s, was reinterred in Hungary in 1993 amid much pomp and ceremony, and labelled a 'patriot' by the sitting Prime Minister.

• • •

If we are serious about understanding Béla Guttmann,* we cannot ignore the seismic change in his immediate environment during his most formative years. The Budapest into which he was born on 27 January 1899, teeming with happy and flourishing Jewish life, was an altogether more tranquil place than the one he fled from twice as a young adult, both during and after the White Terror.

At close to 170,000, the number of Jews then represented a quarter of the total Budapest population. What's more, these Jews were enjoying a golden period, in the main accepted by the majority population and living free from state discrimination. The Budapest-born Jewish historian Raphael Patai wrote that:

> in no period in their long history did Hungarian Jews feel as much at home in the *haza* (fatherland), as much at one with their Christian Magyar compatriots, as much part of the great national endeavour … as in the half-century between their emancipation and the end of World War 1.

In December 1867, a few months after Hungary had been granted full internal independence within the framework of the Austro-Hungarian Empire, its Parliament had abolished all laws that denied Jews civil and political rights. Primarily due to the removal of legal obstacles to their settlement in cities, Jews immediately flooded into Budapest, mostly from the nearby countryside. In just three decades, the size of the Jewish population of the city had quadrupled. By Guttmann's birth, of all the cities in Europe, only Warsaw had more Jews.

The burgeoning community enthusiastically embraced the process of Magyarisation (or Hungarianisation) introduced by the

* The surname is spelt *Guttman* on his original birth certificate. It seems that the family started using the more Germanic double 'n' during his youth.

Hungarian government in a bid to unify an ethnically disparate nation that now included many Slovaks, Croats, Germans and Romanians, as well as Jews.

Linguistic preferences highlight this trend. In the mid-nineteenth century, the overwhelming majority of Budapest Jews had spoken German as their first language. But by the turn of the century, a similar majority listed Hungarian as their mother tongue. (Two-thirds of Budapest Jews, however, remained completely fluent in the two languages, a capability that enabled Guttmann, although instantly recognisable as an outsider by his trademark heavy Hungarian accent, to integrate easily into Viennese life in later years.)

Jews eagerly professed their loyalty to the Hungarian nation, a move welcomed by the local Magyars, who sought to tip the balance in their own favour against the non-Magyar minorities. In this way, Hungarian Jews were no different in the perception of their environment, and in their resulting calculations, from many of their counterparts in the western half of Europe. They sensed that an unwritten social contract between them and the host nation was on offer: Jews would be free from persecution if they professed Jewishness to be a religion only, and dropped the associated national, cultural and linguistic baggage.

After the first Zionist Congress was held in Basel in 1897, prominent Hungarian Jewish leaders from across the religious spectrum queued up to voice their disapproval of the nascent nationalist movement.

Lipót Lipschitz, president of the Orthodox Intermediary Office, proclaimed that 'in judging Zionism, the Orthodox are unanimous with the Jews who belong to the progressives'. He continued: 'They, too, condemn this rash movement, which sins against both patriotism and religion. The Magyars of the Jewish faith want to thrive here at home; they have not the slightest intention of founding a Jewish state in Palestine.' It was a stance that angered and

disappointed Theodor Herzl, the founder of political Zionism, who had been born and brought up in Budapest, leading him to refer to Hungary as 'the withered branch on the tree of world Jewry'.

Ambitious Jews mimicked the dress and customs of upper-class Hungarians, with a disproportionately high number even taking to the gentlemanly pursuit of duelling when slighted. Between 1881 and 1919, an estimated 45,000 Hungarian Jews changed their name to something less conspicuously Jewish. Every year, several hundred even took the opportunity to convert to Christianity.

The community as a whole drifted slowly and contentedly towards full assimilation into Hungarian society. In 1900, fewer than one in ten Jewish bridegrooms in Budapest married outside the faith, but this percentage trebled in just fifteen years as the children of migrants to the city threw off what many viewed as the shackles of tradition.

Professional, commercial and artistic success abounded. Jewish Budapest squeezed all available potential from its newly acquired freedom, and bubbled with energy. Nearly 60 per cent of lawyers and doctors in the city were Jews, and around half of all journalists, with an even higher proportion at the most influential newspapers and journals. Jewish entrepreneurs powered the city economy – two-thirds of self-employed business people were Jews. The fields of literature, academia and the arts were all packed with Jews, who thus played a key role as the cultural gatekeepers of the Hungarian nation.

In short, the Budapest into which Guttmann was born was, to a very large extent, a Jewish city, one that unsurprisingly earned the sobriquet 'Judapest' among Europe's perennial army of anti-Semitic detractors. It was also a Jewish city that felt itself utterly at ease in Hungarian society, considered itself insulated from the pogroms taking place in what seemed a distant world farther east, and was blissfully unaware of what was soon to befall it. If you had convened

an audience of Budapest Jews in the early years of the twentieth century, Guttmann's family included, and told them what they would soon experience, they would have thought you were mad.

Trusting the outside world, they were soon to learn, was a very naive thing to do.

• • •

Béla Guttmann's early life was in some ways typical of the wider Jewish experience in Budapest at the time, but was nevertheless not entirely conventional.

His parents, Abrahám and Eszter (née Szántó), were part of the huge influx of other Hungarian Jews to Budapest in the late nineteenth century, in their case from the north-eastern part of the country, from two small villages (Tiszaújhely and Kisbégány) that now form part of Ukraine. At least one of Béla's two elder siblings was born in Tiszaszalka, another small village in eastern Hungary. It seems therefore that Abrahám and Eszter were comparatively late migrants to Budapest, arriving shortly before Béla's birth in 1899.

From the sketchy details of his early life, we can also surmise that the young Béla's upbringing will have been substantially less religious than that of his parents. This reflected a growing Magyarisation, and the relative secularism of Budapest Jews compared to the outlying Hungarian provinces of Eastern Hungary which clung on, more stubbornly, to the rituals of traditional Judaism and the Yiddish language.

His name, Béla, for example, was typical of those given to Jewish children of his generation, popular among the general non-Jewish population, but standing in contrast to his own parents' biblical Hebrew names. The same could be said for his elder sister Szerén, his elder brother Ármin and his younger brother Ernő.

The first seeds of Guttmann's sense of outsiderness, later to be heavily reinforced by bitter experience, may well have been sown in his very first years. Budapest was at the time divided into ten districts, with Jews in the main choosing to live in voluntary ghettos in a small area of the city, where they could be surrounded by friends and family and communal facilities. The Guttmann family, however, lived in the working-class district of Kőbánya, where only 1 per cent of Budapest Jews lived. It neighboured the areas of Erzsébet-város and Terézváros, which, by contrast, thronged with more than 100,000 Jews. The children were brought up as Jews amid Gentiles, separated from the many other Jews who lived in the same city.

Moreover, the family's social status and relative poverty were at variance with the norm of middle-class affluence. At the time of Béla's birth, Abrahám worked as a clerk in a lamp factory. Later on, he veered in an unusual direction, setting up a dance school with his wife Eszter. It was a career choice far removed from the traders and intellectuals who dominated Budapest Jewish life.

In his last years, Béla recalled that he often went around as a youngster 'with empty pockets and a hungry stomach', a long-held memory that helps to explain his constant striving for better contracts and more financial security in later years.

●　●　●

A Jew born in 1899 in central or eastern Europe didn't, when viewed in retrospect, have the greatest life prospects. But Guttmann was certainly more fortunate than those born a few years before him. The official conscription age for the Austro-Hungarian army in the First World War was twenty-one years, rendering Guttmann too young for a war that ravaged the Hungarian nation. The country's total number of casualties (killed or wounded) was more than 350,000, constituting an almost incredible 93 per cent of its entire

armed forces. Jewish Budapest was no exception to this suffering, with 4,000 of its men killed. Few families within the community would have remained unscathed.

Free from such military constraints and uninterested in conventional study, Guttmann initially followed his parents' chosen career, qualifying as a dance instructor at the age of sixteen. As we shall see, the qualification allowed him to supplement his sometimes modest earnings as a football player. Certainly, his dancing ability was a pointer to the poise and balance that was to characterise his later life as an elegant, ball-playing centre-half.

Guttmann's attraction to football was very much in keeping with the time and place of his upbringing, with the Jewish community playing as dominant and influential a role in the sport as it did in so many other spheres of life. A British import, football had started to take off throughout continental Europe since the turn of the century, and Hungary embraced it with particular enthusiasm. Several of the great Hungarian clubs of the future, such as MTK, Ferencváros and Újpest, were formed as early as the late nineteenth century, even before the establishment of various giants of the modern era, such as Real Madrid, Inter Milan or Bayern Munich.

The Hungarian league (known as Nemzeti Bajnokság) was formed in 1901, and the sport immediately became highly fashionable within the capital. The Hungarian-born historian John Lukacs writes that:

> by 1910, soccer was popular enough that famous actors and actresses were game to appear on the field, in order to start off an important match by punting the ball; there exists a photograph of the elegant Lord Mayor of Budapest, István Bárczy, in a top hat and Prince Albert coat, kicking off the ball with great verve and an agreeable smile.

Guttmann's first club was Törekvés, a small outfit in his local

Kőbánya district of Budapest, and a breeding ground for many who would later become top players, often abroad. He joined Törekvés at the age of eighteen in 1917, featuring in the same squad as his elder brother, Ármin, who was not only a fellow footballer but had also followed the family tradition in training as a dance teacher.

Béla helped the team to a creditable third place in the twelve-team premier league in 1918. Indeed, by the spring of 1920, his performances had become sufficiently impressive to attract interested scouts from other clubs. The Guttmann brothers, however, had other ideas. They put football aside and travelled 300 kilometres south to Újvidék, now Novi Sad in Serbia, to set up a dance school.

We can attribute two reasons for a move that has been wholly absent from previous commentary on Guttmann's life. First, the murderous assault on Jews was fully evident in Budapest by 1920. Although Újvidék had been part of Hungary for several decades, the post-First World War settlement had placed it within the new republic of Yugoslavia, rendering it immune from the White Terror. Yet, at the same time, there were still many Hungarian-speakers in the city to make up a sizeable potential market for the Guttmann brothers. They could make some money there without worrying too much about who was walking up behind them in the street.

Second, financial reward from football was negligible. Although clubs did make small, illicit payments to players, football was an amateur sport in continental Europe until Austria, where Guttmann was by then playing, introduced the first professional league in 1924. At any rate, it is interesting to note that Guttmann was by no means committed to a career in football in young adulthood.

In early 1921, the Guttmann brothers did eventually decide to return to Budapest, where the incidence of beatings and murders of Jews in the streets and cafés of the capital had subsided somewhat since the previous year. Although the dancing school

business had been going well, Béla's head was turned by an offer from the all-powerful MTK Budapest, who had identified him as a replacement for their centre-half, Ferenc Nyúl, a recent signing for Hagibor Cluj in Romania, one of the many Jewish clubs that were springing up in Europe at that time.

Guttmann would have found it difficult to turn his nose up at an opportunity to join a team that had just won four successive championships. It was a major career break, and it was here that he was first to experience the sweet taste of footballing success that he was to enjoy over a span of forty years.

But before this success materialised, his first big opening in football had almost fallen flat on its face. When the Guttmann brothers returned to Budapest, they were twice hauled in front of the disciplinary committee of the football association to explain their time in Újvidék. With earnings from football prohibited, they first had to prove that they were deriving income from another source, their dancing school. They admitted that they had played for the local club Újvidéki, but satisfied the committee that they had participated only in friendly matches.

Back in Budapest, however, a scandal erupted when some players from Pécs recognised Béla as a former teammate. Although Pécs (in the south of the country) was then under Serbian military occupation, it was considered part of Hungarian territory, and was still under the jurisdiction of the Hungarian Football Association. The players claimed that in September 1920, while he was living in Újvidék, Guttmann had played for Pécsi MFC in a lower league game. This was a clear contravention of the regulations, as players were not allowed to play for two teams in the country in one season (Béla was now playing for MTK).

MTK were threatened with a points deduction, and Guttmann with a ban of up to two years for lying to the disciplinary committee. When challenged about the indiscretion, Guttmann's defence

rested on the good will of the committee. He told them that he simply 'forgot to disclose' his solitary appearance.

This incident was to mark the first of a very long list of brushes with authority in a football career that spanned almost sixty years. On this occasion, the committee took a tolerant view, with both MTK and Guttmann remaining unpunished.

• • •

MTK stands for Magyar Testgyakorlók Köre, the Circle of Hungarian Fitness Activists. Founded in 1888, the club's name belies the club's Jewish origins, which accounts for the extreme racist abuse its few remaining supporters still suffer to this day, and offers a clear example of how the Budapest Jewish community of the era sought to assert its Hungarian credentials.*

Indeed, the culture of MTK was a far cry from the forceful Jewish nationalism of Guttmann's next club, Hakoah Vienna. The Jewish businessmen who founded and financed MTK were motivated by practical, rather than ideological, concerns. At a time when aristocratic sports clubs excluded Jews and pursued genteel sports such as fencing and horse-riding, the founders envisaged that MTK, by contrast, would be a place where 'everyone, without discrimination, had a chance to pursue the "latest" sports at a high level'.

But whatever image the club sought to project, the public (non-Jewish) perception was very different. In the popular imagination, the two clubs that vied for supremacy in Hungarian football during the first three decades of the twentieth century represented two distinct ethnic groups: German (Ferencváros) and Jewish

* MTK crowds are now sparse (an average of fewer than 1,500 people), but the fans are still mostly Jews.

(MTK). Any game between the clubs is even now still known as the Örökrangadó, the eternal rivalry.

Ferencváros was founded in 1899 in the Budapest district of the same name, then inhabited by people from the city's working class and lower middle class, often of German descent. The club is still known locally by its nickname, Fradi, which recalls the German name Franzstadt that was commonly used for the district at the time of the club's founding, rather than by its official Hungarian name, Ferencváros.

As the two clubs battled it out on the pitch, they engaged in a parallel confrontation off it, vying with each other to prove how Hungarian they were. The founders of Ferencváros decreed that the team's colours should be green and white, two of the colours of the Hungarian flag, believing this to be a clear signal that their club was more authentically nationalist than its rival with the 'M' for Magyar in its name.

For its part, MTK erected a new 20,000-capacity stadium in 1912 on a Budapest boulevard conveniently named Hungária. Fourteen years later, after Guttmann's departure, the club even took advantage of this (possible) coincidence by temporarily changing its name to Hungária.

Despite MTK's best efforts, one club's bid for Magyarisation, for acceptance within the wider society, was clearly more successful than the other's. Ferencváros were frequently described as a team with a fighting spirit, representing the Hungarian soul, whereas MTK's game was thought to be based on intelligence, on footballing brain. As the Hungarian sociologist Miklós Hadas puts it, 'At the beginning of the century, the concept and connotations of the "Fradi-heart" implied a sensitive, good-hearted, compassionate, enthusiastic petty-bourgeoisie who felt Hungarian, as against the coldly calculating, business-like, alienated big bourgeoisie of foreign origin – MTK.'

These generalisations stuck, despite the fact that the players of both teams came from a similar working-class and lower-middle-class background, and that Ferencváros also had a substantial number of Jewish players. (Around a quarter of their players in the first three decades of the century were Jews, compared to more than half of MTK players: one indicator of the extent of Jewish participation and influence in Hungarian football.) As anti-Semitism became a more powerful phenomenon, erupting in full force around the time Guttmann signed for MTK, so the confrontation between the two teams became increasingly viewed as a battle between the cunning Jew and the honest Gentile.

• • •

MTK's image as a clever and sophisticated footballing team was not without foundation, but in reality this owed just as much to British influence as to Jews.

Just before the First World War, central European football had begun to differentiate its style, focusing on short passing, rather than the dribbling, the physicality and the long, hopeful punt up-field, which all marked the game played in England, the country where football originated. The central European passing style was itself influenced by the methods practised in Scottish football, which for some decades had believed itself to be a cut above the Auld Enemy of England, stressing a more technical and aesthetic approach to the game.

MTK's highly charismatic Jewish president, the businessman Alfréd Brüll, who led the club throughout its glory days and until its forced dissolution in 1940 and his own eventual murder in Auschwitz, made a calculated decision to import this style, appointing several British exponents of the passing game as his head coach. The first was a Scot, John Tait 'Jacky' Robertson, who took

the reins in 1911. His two-year stay clearly made a profound impression, with a later obituary commenting that 'it was often said by leaders of the game in Austria and Hungary that it was Jacky Robertson who laid the foundations of the cultured style of football played there'.

But the man who made by far the most significant impression on MTK was a Lancastrian by the name of Jimmy Hogan.

Hogan, a former inside forward for Burnley and Bolton Wanderers, was a firm believer in the Scottish school of football. Just before the First World War, he had worked as coach of the Austrian national team together with Hugo Meisl, a Czech Jew brought up in Vienna, of whom we shall see more later.

The unlikely pair spotted a major strategic gap in a sport that had largely spurned cerebral input and overlooked the potential impact of on-field tactics and organisation. They 'believed that movement was necessary, that too many teams were too rigid and so predictable,' writes Jonathan Wilson in his history of football tactics, *Inverting the Pyramid*. 'Both believed that it was necessary to make the ball do the work, that swift combinations of passes were preferable to dribbling.'

Their dreams of Olympic Games glory with Austria, however, came to an abrupt end at the onset of war. Initially arrested as an enemy alien, Hogan was eventually rescued from the footballing wilderness by MTK, who pulled the necessary diplomatic strings with the Austrian authorities to appoint him as coach in 1916. He stayed for just two seasons, leaving eighteen months before Guttmann's arrival, but his enduring impact on the culture and style of MTK and Hungarian football was incalculable.

Hogan was a revolutionary, a coach decades ahead of his time. Once ensconced in Budapest, he sought a blank canvas of enthusiastic and talented young players whom he could inculcate with his preferred style of play through a relentless and meticulous

training schedule. It was a strategy, later followed by other great managers* such as Matt Busby and Alex Ferguson at Manchester United, designed to perpetuate success by institutionalising a system that could withstand the exit or ageing of individual players. 'The basis of modern football in this age must be built around the holy trinity of handling the ball, fitness and constructive tactics,' he said.

Hogan's approach was also characterised by an unprecedented attention to players' diet, and by an obsessive focus on the minutest detail – the state of the pitch or the position of the sun – which might somehow present his team with a narrow advantage.

Brüll's original foresight and Hogan's vision paid handsome dividends. MTK won the league in both seasons Hogan was coach, and for the next seven seasons after he left.

Jews dominated the MTK team during these golden years. Aside from Guttmann, there were men such as József Braun, the half-back discovered by Hogan, who represented Hungary twenty-seven times before perishing in a forced labour camp in 1943, aged forty-two; Gyula Feldmann, the full-back who went on to coach several major European clubs, including MTK itself; and two sets of brothers, all four Hungarian internationals – Vilmos and Adolf Kertész, and Kálmán and Jenő Konrád.

Under the coach Béla Sebestyén, a Jew who had played for MTK and the Hungary national team for several years, Guttmann helped the club to stroll to the championship in 1920/21, with just one defeat and nine goals conceded in twenty-four games, and with eighty-two goals scored (mostly by the fearsome striking trio of György Orth, György Molnár and the great goalscorer Imre Schlosser). The season also boasted a double conquest of fierce

* I have used the terms 'coach' and 'manager' interchangeably throughout this book. 'Manager' is still the term most commonly used in the UK.

rivals Ferencváros, with Guttmann playing in the 3–1 home victory in front of 30,000 overjoyed fans.

Despite what was to be only a year-long stay at the club, the Hogan-inspired MTK experience looks like it had a major effect on Guttmann's later approach to management.

As he was to show at Benfica several decades later, Guttmann went out of his way to identify young talent and make it thrive. An emphasis on short passing and ball skills was, for him, a basic imperative. 'If the original founders of football had wanted players to focus on headwork,' Guttmann once said, 'they would have named the game headball, not football.' He was perpetually searching for the extra detail, the 1 per cent, which could turn a game his way. And, like Hogan, he insisted on maximum fitness through rigorous training sessions, and that his team adhere to a strict code of discipline in their lifestyles.

In being swayed by the ideas of the English pioneer, he was far from alone. Under the direct or indirect influence of Hogan, a whole generation of Hungarian coaches, many of them Jews, were later to shape the direction of European and world football.

In fact, we can trace a direct link from Hogan to MTK players to the dominance of one of the greatest international teams the world has ever known, the Hungarian national team of the 1950s, known locally as the 'Aranycsapat' (Golden Team). The head coach of the team that trounced England twice and shook up the entire world of football throughout this era was Gusztáv Sebes, who played for MTK in the late 1920s, several years after Hogan and Guttmann had left the club.

'We played football as Jimmy Hogan taught us,' Sebes once said. 'When our football history is told, his name should be written in gold letters.' Sebes's assistant coach was Gyula Mándi, a Jew who played at MTK with Guttmann and earned thirty-two international caps for Hungary as a half-back.

The extraordinary impact of ex-MTK players was felt far beyond Hungarian borders. The flourishing of what now is commonly regarded as the greatest footballing nation in history, Brazil, owes much to two MTK Jews: Izidor (Dori) Kürschner and Béla Guttmann. Kürschner played for MTK before Hogan arrived and then managed the team for a year when the latter returned to England in 1918, introducing new European training methods and the fashionable W-M tactical formation to a still naive footballing culture when he coached Flamengo, the Rio de Janeiro club, just before the Second World War.*

Guttmann himself used the later 4-2-4 formation (four defenders, two midfielders and four attackers, a later adaptation of W-M), at São Paulo in the late 1950s. According to Jonathan Wilson, his combination of this system with a direct, attacking style was pivotal, forming 'the tactical basis for the gloriously fluid teams of Pelé, Jairzinho and Garrincha', which were to win the World Cup three times in four attempts from 1958 to 1970.

It is not difficult to see why Guttmann and the other MTK Jews, marginalised or even despised by so many in Hungary and Europe in general, identified with Hogan's ideas so strongly, and were such eager learners.

The Lancastrian was very much an outsider. He was an innovator whose ideas were rejected by the old-school establishment of the Football Association in his home country, but who was nevertheless labelled a traitor in England for devoting so many years to coaching foreigners. Hogan's open challenge to the prevailing orthodoxy will have sat comfortably with the 'disputatious people', as the British novelist Howard Jacobson, among others, likes to describe his fellow Jews.

* The W-M formation consisted of three full-backs, two half-backs, two inside forwards, two wingers and a centre-forward.

It was a perfect match: the analytical teacher and the Jewish students from a culture that prized shrewd brain over mindless brawn.

As well as the specific footballing wisdom, Guttmann and the others will also have learned important life lessons from Hogan's lasting imprint on MTK – the value of continuous progress and self-improvement, the dangers of complacency, and the outsider's obligation to work far harder than the clubbable insider to achieve success. The perfectionist and industrious Hogan once said that 'the coach who does not study commits the same mistake as the winemaker who, attracted by the beauty of the fruit, leaves it to die on the plant'.

Guttmann's restlessness throughout his later coaching career may well have derived in part from Hogan's obsessive belief in perpetual education. When the dynamic process of mutual learning between player and coach dissipates, when there is little new to absorb from one another, it is time to move on.

• • •

Guttmann's successful season at MTK was rewarded with a first international cap, in June 1921. He even scored in a 3–0 victory over Germany in Budapest. As befitting the era, eight of the starting XI were MTK players, and six were Jews, including the Ferencvarós half-back Zoltán Blum.

Interestingly, the selection of Guttmann and his Jewish teammates came in the immediate aftermath of the White Terror. It is perhaps testament to the Jewish dominance of the sport that even the surrounding extreme anti-Semitism could not stop them being picked. The Hungarian national team needed its Jews. It was only after a humiliating defeat at the Paris Olympics of 1924, as we shall see later, that the surrounding prejudice seeped more obviously into football.

But the atmosphere was certainly still nasty enough for Gutt-mann, and for thousands of Budapest Jews of his generation, to seek pastures new. Given their bilingual capability, and what Tibor Frank, in his book *The Double Exile*, refers to as the 'deep German embeddedness of Hungarian culture', the vast majority opted for German-speaking environments. Berlin, with an intellectual atmosphere considered by many émigrés to rival that of pre-war Budapest, was by far the most popular initial destination, before many eventually sought sanctuary in the United States as the climate worsened.

For Jewish footballers, however, Vienna held more appeal. It was there that Meisl and Hogan had first put their new thinking into practice, and where the revolutionary phenomenon of football tactics was now a central topic of conversation among the predominantly Jewish intellectuals who frequented the city's many coffee houses. And there was a football club by the name of Hakoah Vienna that was starting to make waves, with its combination of footballing excellence and vigorous Jewish self-confidence. Hakoah can have appealed only to a curious and ambitious individual who had just witnessed the degrading horrors of the White Terror unfold around him.

The intimidating climate of Jew hatred was not, however, the only reason for Guttmann's departure. A new coach had arrived at MTK, Herbert Burgess, formerly a player at both Manchester City and Manchester United, and Guttmann found himself out of favour. Ferenc Nyúl had returned after a year in Cluj and had started to dislodge him from the centre half-berth in the team, with Guttmann making just four league appearances in the first few months of the 1921/22 season.

It seems strange that a player who was to prove such an asset and attract such rave reviews in Vienna should be discarded in this way. We can certainly speculate that the club's narrow escape from

punishment over his undisclosed appearance for Pécsi MFC would have hardly endeared him to his employer.

Furthermore, a serious scandal over illegal payments to supposedly amateur footballers erupted in Hungarian football during this winter. Although Guttmann was not himself implicated, several of his MTK teammates were indeed punished. Rather than wait to be brought to heel by an investigation that may well, given the prevailing environment, have developed anti-Semitic overtones, Guttmann simply packed his bags and left.

The day after Béla Guttmann's twenty-third birthday, 28 January 1922, the Hungarian-language Viennese newspaper, *Bécsi Magyar Újság*, itself founded by recent émigrés, announced his transfer to Hakoah. 'We don't have to stress the fact that Hakoah has won a first-class player with Guttmann,' said the report.

In a footballing sense, he was moving from one centre of excellence to another, less than 250 kilometres away. But if he was expecting a more sedate setting in which to ply his trade, he was very much mistaken. In a Jewish sense, Guttmann was moving from the Budapest frying pan into the Viennese fire.

CHAPTER 2

YEARS OF DEFIANCE

Attempted assimilation, reawakening of identity, personal success, false sense of security, exclusion, capture, defiance, murder. With these words, we can summarise the life of Fritz Löhner-Beda, co-founder of the all-Jewish, Zionist sports club, Hakoah Vienna. With these words, we can summarise the lives of so many of his Jewish contemporaries, and of so many Jews of so many eras.

Born as Bedřich Löwy in 1883 in eastern Bohemia, in the modern-day Czech Republic, he moved to Vienna with his family as a young boy, where his surname was changed to the less Jewish-sounding Löhner. His parents may have wanted to pass unnoticed into Gentile society, but Löhner-Beda (Beda being his later pen name) was clearly in no mood to be similarly bashful. While still at school, he wrote satirical verses ridiculing Jews who were attempting to assimilate into Austrian society. At university, he joined the Zionist student association Kadima (the Hebrew word for 'forwards').

In 1909, at the age of twenty-six, he combined his love of football and pride in his Jewish identity to establish Hakoah. Löhner-Beda was not one to look backwards to a past of Jewish weakness and impotence.

He was as prominent in his chosen career as he was within the Jewish

community of Vienna. Originally a lawyer, and then a writer of satires and sketches for newspapers, he became one of the best-known librettists in the Viennese cultural powerhouse of the 1920s, writing and producing several popular operettas.

Like 300,000 other Jewish men, he served in the Austro-Hungarian army in the First World War, emerging as an officer. With this very considerable cultural and military contribution, Löhner-Beda lived his dual existence, an assertive Jew living in an increasingly hostile society.

By 1938, that fragile balance, which countless Jews have struggled to maintain throughout the ages, had become an insurmountable contradiction. Almost immediately after the Anschluss (the Nazi German annexation of Austria), he was shut out of the Austrian music scene, and many of his non-Jewish friends and colleagues distanced themselves from him. He was sent to concentration camps in Dachau, and then Buchenwald, where for three years he tried as best he could to organise cultural activities. His defiance and stubborn optimism were encapsulated in the Buchenwald anthem he composed while an inmate:

'O Buchenwald, we don't complain and wail,
and whatever our future may be,
we still will say Yes to life,
for some day the day will come when we are free.'

For Löhner-Beda, that day never arrived. On 4 December 1942, and already gravely ill, the 59-year-old found himself in the workcamp Monowitz, part of the Auschwitz complex. Raul Hilberg, in his comprehensive history of the Holocaust, The Destruction of the European Jews, *takes up the story:*

A party of I. G. Farben dignitaries passed by. One of the directors pointed to Dr. Löhner-Beda and said to his SS companion, 'this Jewish swine*

* I. G. Farben was a German chemical industry conglomerate, notorious for its role in the Holocaust. It worked with the Nazis to produce large quantities of Zyklon B to murder millions of Jews and other 'undesirables'.

could work a little faster'. Another director then chanced the remark, 'If they can't work, let them perish in the gas chamber.' After the inspection was over, Dr. Löhner-Beda was pulled out of the work party and was beaten and kicked until, a dying man, he was left in the arms of his inmate friend, to end his life in I. G. Auschwitz.

It was in this way that this highly cultured man, who did so much to bring Hakoah Vienna to adoring Jews throughout the world, met his end in the freezing wastes of Poland at the hands of smirking murderers. The only consolation was that he probably died without knowing what had happened to his family. Three months earlier, on 31 August 1942, his wife, Helene, and daughters, Liselotte and Evamaria, then thirteen and fouteen years old, were deported from Vienna to Minsk, where their party was herded into specially altered gas vans, and murdered.

• • •

Béla Guttmann, fleeing the racism of his native Hungary, signed for Hakoah Vienna thirteen years after the club's founding.

He joined a team in the ascendant, but one that had not yet reached its pinnacle. The next four and a half years until he departed the club in 1926 marked not just the height of Guttmann's playing career, but also the outstanding and most prestigious demonstration of Jewish team success in the history of sport. This was not a team, it must be emphasised, made up of players who just so happened to be Jews or, as was the case with MTK and several other European clubs until the Holocaust, happened to have many Jewish followers or administrators. Everything about this team – its origins, its name, its kit, its ethos, its supporters – exuded Jewish national spirit. Jewishness was hewn into the Hakoah soul.

Prominent among Löhner's co-founders were Ignaz Hermann Körner, a dentist and activist, who managed to escape murder by

fleeing to what was then Palestine in 1938, but who died in poverty in Tel Aviv six years later; and Robert Stricker, a firebrand public speaker who was to be elected to the Austrian Parliament as the only representative of the Zionist Jewish National Party in the 1919 general election, and was later to be murdered in Auschwitz at the age of sixty-five.

These men had been inspired by the ideas of Max Nordau, who had founded the World Zionist Organisation in the late nineteenth century together with the acknowledged father of modern-day political Zionism, Theodor Herzl, who, like Guttmann, had been raised in Budapest and made the journey to Vienna, where he wrote his most influential tracts.

Nordau was a once-assimilated Jew who, as with so many of his generation, embraced Zionism in the aftermath of the Dreyfus affair, in which a young Jewish officer was wrongly convicted of treason by a French court. According to this new perspective, there was no point in Jews obsequiously currying favour with the Gentile establishment in any given society; there might be respite from persecution, even golden periods, but the end result was destined to be repeated again and again, in a continuous and miserable loop. Only a Jewish homeland, with Jewish self-governance and control, could arrest this cycle.

Nordau coined the term 'muscular Judaism', advocating that Jews should abandon the past of anxiety and introspection and instead become bolder, stronger, sprightlier, physically and intellectually fit. 'In the narrow Jewish streets,' he wrote, 'our poor limbs forgot how to move joyfully; in the gloom of sunless houses our eyes became accustomed to nervous blinking; out of fear of constant persecution the timbre of our voices was extinguished to an anxious whisper.'

Another influence on the Hakoah founders would have been the fallout from the 1903 pogrom in Kishinev, then the capital of Czarist Bessarabia and now of independent Moldova. In an orgy

of killing, pillage and rape, forty-nine Jews were murdered, 500 wounded and 1,300 homes and businesses destroyed.

It was not the pogrom itself that made the effect of Kishinev so powerful; Jews were already depressingly accustomed to many similar stories, and would become yet more so in the ensuing years. What was so electrifying was the conjunction of the event and a particular Hebrew poem entitled *Ba'ir Hahariga* (In the city of slaughter) by the young Zionist Chaim Bialik, which was unsparing in its condemnation of what he believed to be Jewish submissiveness in the face of the braying mob. The poem's message reverberated throughout a Europe in which the Zionist idea had started to catch fire within households, shtetlekh* and cities, not least in the great Jewish centre of Vienna.

'*Of Hasmoneans lay, with trembling knees,*
Concealed and cowering – the sons of the Maccabees!'

And so it was at this highly charged moment in Jewish history that the Hakoah football team, wearing the blue and white colours of the Jewish national movement and a large Star of David on their shirts, first marched with head held high into the Vienna of 1909. A city, let us not forget, which then boasted a virulently anti-Semitic mayor, Karl Lueger, a man who desired liberation from 'the shameful shackles of servitude to the Jews', a man who was himself a major influence on one of Vienna's then citizens, a young twenty-year-old by the name of Adolf Hitler.

We cannot say for sure how this turbulent environment, and Hakoah's robust response to it, affected Guttmann during his young adult years. But it seems safe to say that only a Jew with eyes and ears switched off, and a heart and soul of stone, would remain the same person afterwards. Those rebellious and argumentative traits

* A shtetl (plural: shtetlekh, Yiddish) was a small town with a large Jewish population, many of which existed in central and eastern Europe before the Holocaust.

that we were to see so often later in Guttmann's life are likely to
have been heavily influenced by this extraordinary period.

• • •

Hakoah Vienna was a sports organisation, not simply a football
club. The swimming club was also very well known, as was its
wrestling division, which won 127 international titles between 1929
and 1934. Mickey Hirschl, a son of kosher butchers, won the gold
medal in the heavyweight category of the 1932 European Wrestling
Championships, and two bronze medals at the Los Angeles Olym-
pics of the same year.

The march of history was to ensure that this was to be Hirschl's
last Olympics. Together with three Hakoah swimmers – fifteen-
year-old Ruth Langer, seventeen-year-old Judith Deutsch and
eighteen-year-old Lucie Goldner – Hirschl refused to join the team
representing the still independent Austria at the 1936 Olympics in
Berlin, latterly known as the Nazi Olympics.

In a letter to the Austrian Olympic Committee, the teenage
Deutsch offered up a stirring example of the Hakoah spirit, writing:

> I protest … as a Jew I cannot participate in the Berlin Olympic
> Games. My conscience does not allow me. This is a personal deci-
> sion and is not to be contested. I completely understand that I am
> giving up my rights to participate as the Austrian contestant in the
> Olympic Games. I sincerely hope you will understand this decision
> and not pressure me to change my mind.

For their principled moral stand against Nazism, the Austrian
sports authorities rewarded the young swimmers with a two-year
ban from participating in all sporting events. (The Austrian author-
ities waited until Deutsch was seventy-six before they recanted.

'Perhaps we are apologising too late, but better now than never,' wrote the President of the Austrian Parliament in 1995.)

Other Hakoah sports included handball, table tennis and fencing. The club also provided a forum for social interaction among young Jews, with regular dances and music evenings. But it was in the realm of football that Hakoah was really to make its name, not just in Austria, but throughout the entire world.

• • •

From 1909 to 1920, the football club made its way from the Austrian fourth division to the first. In the first two seasons in the top flight, they performed creditably, finishing fourth in 1921 and second in 1922, Guttmann's first (half) season. It was in 1924/25, however, the season in which the Austrian league turned professional, when everything finally clicked into place in the domestic sphere.

Driven on by 18,000 boisterous fans at their home games in the heavily Jewish Leopoldstadt district of Vienna, and bolstered by eight goals each from forwards Max Grünwald and Moritz Häusler, Hakoah won ten and drew six of their twenty games to claim the league title.

The almost unbelievably dramatic denouement of the championship race would have made modern football commentators explode with screams of excitement, with footage repeated time and time again on sports channels for years and decades to come.

Hakoah started their third-last game of the season, away at Wiener Sport-Club on Saturday 6 June 1925, knowing that victory would bring the title. Towards the end of the game, with the score standing at 2–2, Hakoah's Hungarian-born goalkeeper Alexander Fabian, then considered one of the greatest in the world, broke his arm after being challenged by an opposition striker. Football was still several decades away from the introduction of substitutes,

so Fabian put his arm in a sling and swapped positions with a teammate.

Seven minutes after the injury, and nine minutes from the end of the game, the Hungarian international striker Ernő Schwarcz laid the ball into Fabian's path in the opposition penalty area. The one-armed goalkeeper-turned-striker shot weakly towards goal, but the ball was deflected by a defender into the back of the net, thus sealing the title and prompting wild celebrations and laudatory tributes. One commentator declared joyfully that 'Jewish dignity and Jewish self-confidence are indeed in good hands now; the ludicrous caricature of the bandy-legged, timid, contemptible Jew is already an anachronism'.

It was at Hakoah, Guttmann would later say, that his playing career really started to take off. He was a mainstay and fulcrum of the championship-winning team. Indeed, the combination of his footballing and negotiation abilities was to make him the highest-paid player at the club for this historic season, and the equal highest paid in the entire country.

The team played in the 2-3-5 formation, which was popular throughout the football world until the 1940s. Also known as the 'pyramid formation', the structure involved two full-backs, three half-backs and five forwards. As he was to do throughout his career, Guttmann played in the centre half-back (often known as centre-half) position, a pivotal role in the pyramid, fulfilling a crucial dual function. The centre-half would have to launch his own team's attack, but also blunt the threat of the opposing team's centre-forward, usually one of their most dangerous players. A Hakoah coach, Arthur Baar, later recalled: 'He supplied the attack with accurate passes (he often pointed out that the striker received the ball to the exact centimetre), but he also performed great deeds in defence.'

Baar also noted his professionalism and focus on fitness, doubtless picked up at MTK. 'As a player, Béla Guttmann really didn't

need a coach,' wrote Baar. 'When he came to training, he ran a number of laps, did some sprints, then performed a number of other disciplines to better his condition. Even then, his great talent as a coach shone through.'

Guttmann's small, slight frame belied a fierce competitiveness and refusal to give ground, deeply embedded within the culture of Hakoah, which were also to mark his future managerial career. An article in the Hakoah club magazine of February 1926 emphasises that 'his temperament dominated the team more than any other ... he was fighting to the end with clenched teeth'.

In at least one incident, the will to win spilled over into violent outbursts. In a tempestuous encounter in 1925 against rivals First Vienna, who were to finish third in the title-winning season, a fight erupted between opposing players.

Guttmann had clashed repeatedly during the game with Leopold Hofmann, a star player of the era who was to go on to play in the Austria team that reached the semi-final of the World Cup in 1934. In the melee after the final whistle, Guttmann sought out his opponent and hit him hard. 'The Vienna man was so hurt by a punch in the face that he was bleeding from the mouth and nose,' reported the *Neue Freie Presse*, a Viennese newspaper. A highly charged crowd invaded the pitch, and Guttmann was duly suspended for several games. 'My opponent was criticising my religion so I spat at him,' he recalled nonchalantly many years later.

Stylish artistry accompanied his combative character. He read the game intuitively. After his debut in March 1922 against Hertha Vienna, the newspaper *Wiener Morgenzeitung*, a German-language Zionist newspaper, waxed lyrical. He played a game 'rarely seen in Vienna', the report said, and 'his tactical understanding and his awareness brand him as a centre-half of class'. Later reports repeatedly describe his almost telepathic and highly productive on-field understanding with the inside forward Max Grünwald.

Hakoah practised a sophisticated style of play similar to that honed by Jimmy Hogan and MTK a few years before. The similarity is no coincidence. Hogan had played alongside the Scot Billy Hunter between 1909 and 1912 for Bolton Wanderers. Quite who influenced the other is open to debate, but Hunter certainly brought his ideas to bear during his short tenure as Hakoah coach from 1923 until 1925, and was no doubt another major influence on Guttmann's future approach to coaching. Working alongside Arthur Baar, Hunter drummed home the passing philosophy to his charges.*

Hakoah were in a unique position to showcase this brand of football. Few teams from any country would have played abroad in the 1920s, and certainly not frequently. The European Cup (now the UEFA Champions League), the cross-border club competition in which Guttmann was to build his legendary managerial reputation, was only inaugurated in 1955. It was simply because Hakoah was an overtly Jewish enterprise, with fans located far and wide, that the team was able to serve so often as an example of this distinctive regional style to foreign audiences.

When Hakoah played in England or the United States, two destinations among their many international tours, the spectators and media were especially admiring of their exotic system of play.

After the game against West Ham United in September 1923, when Hakoah demolished the hosts 5–0 a few months after the London team had appeared in the first FA Cup Final at the newly built Wembley stadium, the *Daily Mail* was fulsome in its praise. The newspaper's article pointed to the team's:

scientific football ... no exhibition of brute force, no kick and rush – they had no time for that. Instead their players worked tremendously

* According to Hakoah rules, players had to be Jews, but there was no such limitation for coaches.

well together without relying on long passes. They passed the ball smoothly and made good use of space. They were able to control the moving ball; unlike them, the West Ham players had feet of lead.

George Kay, West Ham's captain who watched the game from the stands, was similarly effusive, marching into the visitors' dressing room after the game and declaring, 'You are the best team I have ever seen, and believe me, I have seen hundreds of games of football.'

In 1926, the *New York Times* hailed Hakoah's 'intricate pre-arranged system of passing', for 'soccer is a game which requires the footwork of a danseuse'. The visitors' distribution was regarded as 'perfection and artistry in their highest stages'.

In central Europe, where the style of football was more similar, it was Hakoah's pugnaciousness that was more likely to draw attention. After games in Berlin and Leipzig in 1924, the Munich-based *Fußball*, considered one of the leading German sports newspapers of the day, remarked that 'Hakoah had helped to do away with the fairy tale about the physical inferiority of the Jews'.

• • •

The team needed that fighting spirit, often literally. Hakoah's success was achieved in the midst of unremitting hostility within Austria.

'No one likes us, we don't care' goes the song of the supporters of Millwall, the football team from south-east London, in response to sustained criticism of hooligan behaviour among a section of their number. An openly Jewish team in Vienna of the 1920s would have attracted a scale of dislike that would be utterly beyond the experience of the modern football fan, complete with his obligatory victim complex. Glasgow Celtic versus Glasgow Rangers in Scotland, Boca Juniors versus River Plate in Argentina, Fenerbahçe versus Galatasaray in Turkey. By comparison, these supposed

enemies are just playing at animosity. Most of Hakoah's many fans, throughout central and eastern Europe, were soon to be murdered.

Fanatical racism against Jews was already very much in evidence at Hakoah matches during Guttmann's time at the club. In 1923, for example, the co-founder and then president of Hakoah, Ignaz Hermann Körner, was physically attacked not by a random fan, but by a player from the opposing team, WAF (Viennese Soccer Association Club). Soon afterwards, at a match against Ostmark Vienna, crowds converged on the Hakoah spectators, spitting and throwing stones. Players were routinely the targets of racist insults on and off the pitch. In November of that year, *Wiener Morgenzeitung* railed against the repeated incidents:

> People who abide by the rules of common decency and manners in everyday life become brutal terrorists at Hakoah matches … What went on in the game between Admira and Hakoah, for instance, is quite simply beyond belief. There was a veritable orgy of verbal abuse, including the repeated use of the words 'Jewish pig' (Judensau), and wild threats could be heard from all sides. Scarcely a match takes place at which the Hakoah players are not insulted and threatened in the basest manner. At their own ground in Krieau (a part of Leopoldstadt), a whole team of mounted watchmen is needed to keep the hordes of spectators at bay.

To safeguard the security of players and fans alike, Hakoah employed its own boxers and wrestlers as a self-defence force. The coach Arthur Baar later recalled with pride that 'since the wrestlers knew no mercy, anti-Semitic attackers were often sent home with bloody skulls'. The team themselves proudly defied the pervasive Jew hatred and no doubt harnessed it to motivate themselves to great feats on the pitch.

The public reaction to the most high-profile Jewish event to take place in Vienna during Guttmann's time at the club clearly illustrates

the ugly atmosphere. On the eve of the Fourteenth World Zionist Conference, held at the Vienna Concert Hall in August 1925 just a few weeks after Hakoah's title triumph, widespread anger against the government for allowing the Zionists to meet in the city erupted into violent demonstrations. In the vicious riots, scores of police, demonstrators and counter-demonstrators were injured, and two killed.

Repeated bomb threats disrupted the conference. Delegates and Zionist leaders were taunted and threatened as they rode alongside a police escort from their hotel to the concert hall, which had to be surrounded by three cordons of police as the conference speeches were delivered.

● ● ●

Hakoah embarked on their many foreign tours for several reasons. They provided much-needed funds to help the club sustain their success in the Austrian league through recruiting top-class players. Hakoah also wanted to promote their belief in Zionism and their vision of Jewish athletic prowess, as well as to test themselves against top-class opponents. Their growing worldwide Jewish support ensured large attendances, and made Hakoah welcome guests for those running the finances of the clubs they visited.

Indeed, the tours were not just notable for on-field victories but also for the exhilaration of thousands of Jewish fans emboldened and liberated by the demonstration of the club's conspicuous self-confidence and its success against Gentile opponents. The peak of this worldwide achievement and excitement was reached during Guttmann's time at the club, in the prelude to, and immediate aftermath of, Hakoah's dramatic league title success.

The experience of Arthur Markowitz, who later became a journalist and author in South Africa, was typical. Interviewed for a book on Jewish sport that was published in the early 1960s, he

recalled how, as a youngster of ten or eleven, he and his friends cycled through the night from Mitau (also known as Jelgava) to Riga to be able to see Hakoah play, a distance of some 50 kilometres:

> We got there at early dawn and stood in the queue for hours to make sure that we would get into the ground. When we got in we were enthralled at the near-perfect precision of this team of stars. Fabian in goal, was compared with the superb Spanish keeper, Zamora, who is rated one of the greatest goalkeepers of all time, and the centre-half Guttmann, left-winger Eisenhoffer, right-winger Neufeld and inside-forward Grünwald were all familiar names even in homes where sport, until then, had been of lesser interest.*

Hakoah's notorious victory against an admittedly depleted West Ham team at Upton Park, said to be the first victory by a foreign team on English soil, was inspired by a hat-trick by Alexander Neufeld, a right-sided player. Like Guttmann, Neufeld had been born in Budapest in 1899 and then represented Hungary at international level. After signing for Hakoah from Ferencváros in 1919 in his own escape from the White Terror, he had rebelled against the prevailing fashion and changed his surname from Nemes to the more Jewish-sounding and presumably original family name.

In May 1924, with two further goals from Neufeld, Hakoah defeated Czech giants Slavia Prague 2–1, the first time the latter had been beaten on home turf in more than a decade. In a dramatic return fixture in Vienna the following year, at the height of their prowess three months after the championship win, Hakoah recorded perhaps their most dramatic win, recovering from a 5–1 deficit to win 6–5, with a last-minute winning goal by the forward Siegfried Wortmann.

* The Jews of Jelgava, numbering around 2,000, were wiped out in one weekend in the summer of 1941, shot into pits that they had been forced to dig. There were no known survivors.

The Hungarian national team selectors had clearly been taking note of Guttmann's personal performances, recalling him to play in the Olympic Games in Paris soon after the win in Prague. With the World Cup not to appear for the first time until 1930, the Olympics was then the leading football tournament for national teams.

Perhaps those same selectors had not kept so close an eye on how Guttmann's temperament was developing within the unique atmosphere of Hakoah. Guttmann was angered by the fact that the Hungarian football association had not spent the necessary money on ensuring that the players were properly prepared for such a major tournament.

He and his teammates travelled on wooden benches in a third-class train carriage to Paris, and then were consigned to a noisy, rat-infested city-centre hotel which prevented rest and sleep. No training pitch had been organised, and the first practice session took place in a field with no changing facilities. In a fit of rebellious anger, Guttmann hung dead rats on the doors of the rooms of the football association officials.

The team went out in the second round in a shock 3–0 defeat to rank outsiders Egypt. The match would go down in national history as Hungarian football's 'Mohács', a reference to a sixteenth-century battle in which the Hungarian army succumbed to the forces of the Ottoman Empire. The reaction was furious, with thinly veiled anti-Semitism predictably prominent. Gyula Gömbös, a future Prime Minister, told Parliament that 'our national team members do not represent Hungarians, the Hungarian nation nor Hungarian sport – they represent international professionalism'. At least eleven of the twenty-three players in the squad were Jews.

The influential president of Ferencváros, Ernő Gschwindt, pronounced it 'unnecessary to pick those players based abroad for the Hungarian team'. There were three foreign-based players. The non-Jews Gábor Obitz and Férénc Hirzer later returned to play for the

national team, but Guttmann had no such luck. His international career was at an end.

• • •

After this shambolic Olympics debacle, Guttmann had been delighted to return to his natural habitat. 'I joyfully took the road back to Vienna,' he recalled in an interview many years later. Not only was he a footballing celebrity there, he also set up a dance school in the centre of town, where he taught private clients who included Hakoah's own dance troupe.

Meanwhile, the Hakoah international footballing juggernaut powered forward. Two months after the Olympics, in a two-match tour of Warsaw in July 1924, fully 10,000 Jews turned out merely to greet the Hakoah team at the city's railway station on their arrival. With Guttmann and his teammates at the front holding the Jewish national flag, the thousands then marched in a parade from the station through the main streets of a city that would be shorn of its multitude of Jews a mere two decades later.

The supporters' zeal was rewarded with a masterclass from their heroes. Winning 1–0 against Polonia Warsaw, the oldest sports club in Poland and at that point the darlings of the city's football supporters, they were denied victory only by a storm that caused the game to be abandoned in the second half.

The game provoked uproar in the Polish press, which fulminated against the Jewish upstarts who had humiliated the local team and their patriotic supporters. Newspapers urged Polonia not to arrange any further matches with Hakoah and labelled the Jewish opponents as 'arrogant and tactless', presumably for their temerity in not lying down and losing to their superiors without any fuss. Others even recommended that owners of sport grounds refuse to host any games against the Jews. The publication *Dwa Grosze* ranted that the

match had dishonoured Polish sport, and warned of the wrath of the people if the following week's game against a Warsaw city select team was not called off.

The police were out in force for the second fixture, preventing a possible riot and clearing the way for a rampant Hakoah to chalk up an emphatic 5–0 victory.

Such intoxicating performances proved too much for some, including Reuven Milejkowski, a Jewish youth from near Vilnius, the now Lithuanian capital then occupied by Poland. The Jewish Telegraphic Agency, a cable service, reported that Milejkowski 'was so overwhelmed by the new Hakoah craze that he lost his mind. With motions imitating the various football moves, he keeps on saying "Hakoah must win".'*

The next notable scalp was Ferencváros, defeated 2–1 on their home ground in October 1924, at the start of Hakoah's championship-winning season. How Guttmann must have enjoyed the victory against his former hometown rivals whose president had called for his removal from the Hungarian international team just four months previously. The two Hakoah goals were scored by the left-sided player József Eisenhoffer, a Hungarian who had converted to Judaism to marry his Jewish bride before signing for Hakoah. He died in Budapest during the war, aged forty-four, after sustaining wounds in a German air raid.

In the January of both 1924 and 1925, Hakoah embarked on long tours to British-controlled Egypt and Palestine, playing matches in Cairo, Alexandria, Port Said, Jerusalem and Tel Aviv. The team's

* It could be that Milejkowski's name lives on only through his passion for Hakoah. According to the victims' database of the Holocaust museum Yad Vashem, a certain Reuven Milejkowski from the Vilnius region, by this time in his thirties, was murdered in the Postavy ghetto in Belarus with his wife Chana and two children in 1942. The Nazis raped Jewish women in front of their parents, husbands and children before burning the ghetto occupants alive. Milejkowski is also the former name of the family of Israeli Prime Minister Binyamin Netanyahu.

first arrival in Tel Aviv created another furore. 'A great crowd of thousands of people gathered this morning at 8 o'clock at the Tel Aviv train station to welcome the members of Hakoah,' reported the Hebrew newspaper *Haaretz*. Their number included the celebrated, veteran mayor of Tel Aviv, Meir Dizengoff.

Being a centre-back, Guttmann was not in the ideal position to score many goals, but the Zionist team's visit to the homeland clearly inspired him. He scored two of his rare goals in Palestine, against an English military selection team in Jerusalem, and in an 11–2 thrashing of Maccabi Tel Aviv, which had just become the first Jewish club to participate in local, British-organised competitions.

Seeing their beloved creation playing in the holy city and in Tel Aviv, founded in the same year as Hakoah itself to become the first Hebrew city for two thousand years, must have been an intensely proud moment for Löhner-Beda and his co-founders. But, tragically, their Zionist view of the Jewish future in Europe was to be proven cruelly prescient.

• • •

The tour of the United States in April and May 1926 was a double-edged sword for Hakoah. It marked the pinnacle of the club's international reputation, while also precipitating the club's decline. At least a couple of the players, meanwhile, would have later looked back on it as a lifesaver. Indeed, the mobility afforded by the international game of football was to rescue a good number of Jewish players and coaches in Europe from almost certain death.

As soon as the Hakoah players arrived in New York, players and officials were treated like celebrity film stars, with American politicians eager to take advantage of the team's hero status among the country's rapidly growing Jewish population.

The Jewish department store magnate and philanthropist Nathan

Straus arranged for Körner and two other club officials to visit the White House to meet President Calvin Coolidge, who thanked them for their significant contribution to the game of soccer. The flamboyant mayor of New York, Jimmy Walker, presented the team with the keys to the city on the steps of City Hall. And one of the great Zionist leaders, Vladimir Jabotinsky, who happened to be on a speaking tour of the United States at the time, thanked them at a gala dinner in their honour for reawakening a sense of pride among Jewish youth, and pronounced: 'Let there be many like you in Israel.'

In total, almost a quarter of a million people, no doubt mostly comprising recent Jewish immigrants from Europe and their children, turned up to watch Hakoah's eleven games. This number included the 46,000 who crammed into Upper Manhattan's Polo Grounds to watch the team promoted as 'The Unbeatable Jews' against a New York All Stars Select XI. This remained an attendance record for a soccer game in the United States for fully half a century, until crowds flocked to see stars such as Pelé, possibly the best-known footballer in the history of the game, play for New York Cosmos.

Such was the demand to see Hakoah in the flesh that even a scion of the famous banking family, Henri de Rothschild, could not secure any tickets on his arrival in New York a few days before a game. Straus duly invited him to share his box at the Polo Grounds. In the pre-match ceremony, as the band played 'The Star-Spangled Banner' and 'Hatikva', the anthem of the Jewish national movement, the two teams paraded around the pitch carrying the American and Jewish national flags. Accompanied by deafening cheers and singing from the stands, the players stopped at Straus's box. The 77-year-old patriarch, who had donated most of his fortune to various Jewish projects in Palestine and after whom the Israeli city of Netanya is named, broke down sobbing.

The games themselves, which took place in Chicago, Providence in Rhode Island, Philadelphia and St Louis as well as New York, cemented Hakoah's footballing stature, with the team winning seven and drawing two.

But liberated from the growing Jew hatred in Europe, and lured by the substantial rewards on offer in the newly formed American Soccer League, Guttmann and nine teammates left Hakoah immediately after the tour to sign for New York-based clubs. Hakoah, denuded of its talent, lodged a protest with the Fédération Internationale de Football Association (FIFA). When the complaint was rebuffed, the club decided not to pursue the matter further. By this stage, it was already planning a return trip the following year to play matches against the very clubs that had poached its players.

Guttmann joined the New York Giants together with Grünwald, the other half of the impressive onfield duo, along with Häusler, Schwarcz and Egon Pollak. Meanwhile, Eisenhoffer, Neufeld, Heinrich Schönfeld, Lajos Fischer and Leo Drucker were recruited by Brooklyn Wanderers.

All of the defectors bar Eisenhoffer survived the war. Schwarcz, who later coached the United States national team before becoming the only former Hakoah player to be admitted to the National Soccer Hall of Fame, eventually settled in New York, as did Drucker. Pollak became the first coach of the Israeli national team upon the country's independence in 1948. He was succeeded in the post by another Hakoah old boy – Lajos Hess, a goalscorer in the 1923 rout of West Ham United.*

Others were denied such fortune. The former coach Arthur Baar, later to write a history of the club after he had escaped to Palestine,

* Uniquely among Hakoah players of Guttmann's era, Lajos Hess was a religious Jew. Such was his quality as a player that Hakoah kept him on despite his refusal to participate in matches that took place on Saturdays, the Jewish Sabbath. Like Pollak, he escaped the Holocaust by emigrating to Palestine in the 1930s.

documented thirty-seven former Hakoah athletes murdered in the Holocaust, including seven footballers. Max Scheuer, who captained the team in the West Ham game, was captured by the Nazis in France en route to neutral Switzerland. He was sent to Drancy internment camp before his deportation and subsequent murder in Auschwitz.

With the ten defections to the United States, the team lost its spine and Hakoah's footballing decline was precipitous. The team was relegated in 1928. Although promoted again three years later, the team languished in the bottom half of the premier league until another sorry relegation in 1937 with just one win in twenty-two games. Footballing ignominy was soon to be followed by expulsion and obliteration, reflecting the annihilation of the great Jewish communities from which their players and many passionate supporters hailed.

Hakoah, a light in the gathering gloom for a few glorious and inspirational years, was no more.

THE BIG APPLE

On 10 December 1930, at the corner of Freeman Street and Southern Boulevard in the South Bronx, an anxious crowd gathered outside a branch of the Bank of the United States, then one of the most prominent financial institutions in New York. As panicky rumours about the bank's finances spread, police were forced to restrain the growing hordes pushing to enter the building. With several thousand depositors withdrawing $2 million from the branch on that single day, confidence in the bank's viability quickly evaporated. The following day, the New York State Superintendent of Banks closed the institution, rendering it the largest bank in American history to have failed.

The collapse of the Bank of the United States, an event that marked the start of a general breakdown of the banking system and America's Great Depression, hit New York's Jewish community with particular force. The bank held the savings of up to 400,000 New York Jews, more than a fifth of the total number in the city. Just over a year after the Wall Street Crash had wrought its own devastation, many more thousands of Jewish families and businesses now faced financial ruin. The writer Irving Howe later recalled the harrowing scenes he had witnessed as a ten-year-old: 'We heard that the Bank of the United States – Jewish-owned! – had failed, and I sat in our apartment listening to my aunt

and grandmother wailing over the loss of the few hundred dollars they had scraped together.'

The psychological impact was, if anything, even more far-reaching than the monetary loss. Since it had been founded in 1913 by Joseph Marcus, a former garment manufacturer and an immigrant from Russia, the bank had acted as a powerful symbol of Jewish success. Even its name indicated that the Jews were now part of the furniture in the land of opportunity, a million miles from the misery and death of their European past.

Its failure therefore undermined the community's self-confidence, and presaged an unsettling hiatus in the hitherto unbroken story of American Jewish optimism and advancement. Not only did Jews have to contend with hardship and shattered dreams, the surrounding economic chaos also fuelled the anti-Semitism that many felt they had long left behind. Jews suffered from discrimination in the jobs market, and from a quota system that restricted their entry to top universities. Extreme anti-Jewish rhetoric, from the likes of Father Charles Coughlin and the auto manufacturer Henry Ford, admiringly labelled as 'an inspiration' by Adolf Hitler in 1931, added to the mounting feeling of unease.

It was only the rapidly deteriorating climate in Europe in subsequent years, rather than any immediate upturn in domestic fortunes, which eventually persuaded American Jews that they were in the right place after all. 'The Jewish future in America may have seemed uncertain and even menacing at times,' writes Beth S. Wenger in her book, New York Jews and the Great Depression, *'but the Jewish situation in Europe was decidedly worse.'*

• • •

When Béla Guttmann made his debut for the New York Giants in September 1926, the surrounding environment was altogether more auspicious, and his own prospects reflected the general mood of optimism. Now aged twenty-seven, he was in his

pomp as a player, and had finally found a way to reap some meaningful financial rewards from his talent. Self-confident, savvy and sociable, and lionised by many New Yorkers as a former Hakoah star, the world was his oyster.

It will come as something of a surprise to many football fans to learn that soccer was all the rage in New York in the 1920s. Those of a certain age will remember the exciting period in the 1970s when world-famous players such as Pelé, Franz Beckenbauer, George Best and Johan Cruyff strutted the American soccer stage. The European media often presented these years as an unprecedented awakening of interest in soccer within the United States. The world's most popular sport has finally arrived in the world's wealthiest economy! But this portrayal carelessly glossed over what had happened half a century previously, when identical hopes had been raised in the period labelled by Colin Jose, the meticulous historian of the era, as the 'golden years of American soccer'.

The American Soccer League, founded in 1921, was the first ever truly professional soccer league in the United States. By 1924, the league had expanded to twelve teams. As crowds grew, clubs pursued an aggressive recruitment drive of mainly Scottish players attracted by the money on offer. Alex McNab, a Scottish international, was playing for Greenock Morton in the Scottish First Division when he was approached by the Boston Wonder Workers in 1924. 'I was offered only four pounds a week (by Greenock Morton) … One day a cable from the other side arrived. In it was an offer of round about 12 pounds a week … I jumped at it. Booked my passage … And here I am.'

Nathan Agar and Maurice Vandeweghe, the respective Jewish owners of Brooklyn Wanderers and the New York Giants, had interpreted the Hakoah Vienna tour as further confirmation of the sport's commercial potential. They also concluded that recruiting Hakoah players would attract a large contingent of Jewish fans who viewed them as heroes.

In this respect, there was certainly a big market to tap. Brooklyn was home to 750,000 Jews. The Bronx, which hosted the Giants' home ground, the New York Metropolitan Oval, had 380,000. At around 1.75 million in total, more than 90 per cent of whom were either immigrants or children of immigrants from eastern Europe, New York's Jewish population had mushroomed, increasing more than twenty-fold in less than half a century. It now dwarfed that of any other city in the world, and was more than five times the size of the Jewish population of Warsaw, itself by far the largest in Europe.

According to Moritz Häusler, who harboured ambitions as a journalist when he wasn't scoring goals for Hakoah, Guttmann was the very first of his teammates to take advantage of the Hakoah cachet, and strike a deal with such eager suitors.

Häusler wrote in the Viennese newspaper *Die Stunde* in June 1926 that Guttmann had been besieged by requests from various clubs straight after a bravura individual performance in the penultimate match of the Hakoah tour, against the New York Giants themselves. Playing one club off against another, he negotiated an upfront signing-on bonus of $500, a monthly salary of $350 and the permission to continue with a second career alongside his football commitments, thus paving the way to set up as a dance teacher and pursue other business interests.

This income will have made him very well off, although of course still a far cry from the riches on offer in modern-day football. His annual salary of $4,200 from the Giants was around three times that of the average private sector worker in the United States at the time, and also appeared to compare well to the pay of his footballing contemporaries. For example, the annual salary that made Alex McNab so overjoyed equated to around $2,750.

It was only after Guttmann signed that Häusler, Ernő Schwarcz, Egon Pollak and Max Grünwald, no doubt influenced by their teammate telling them what was on offer, committed themselves

to the Giants. Guttmann had been the one to strike out on his own without waiting for affirmation from others, having the courage of his convictions to set the terms of the deal from which his colleagues would then benefit. His independence of mind and aura of leadership were already in full view.

• • •

The commercial opportunism of Agar and Vandeweghe paid immediate dividends. Their teams, studded with Hakoah stars, drew large crowds. Major cup games, or matches against foreign touring sides, sometimes held such appeal that they even had to be moved to stadiums with a larger capacity.

General interest in soccer continued to grow, and any lingering condescension towards a foreign sport seemed to dissipate. In June 1927, at the end of the former Hakoah players' first season in the United States, a tongue-in-cheek editorial in the *New York Times* summarised new attitudes: 'A taste for soccer is no longer a social error. The game has "arrived". Tickets are sold openly and spectators at the games often give their right names when questioned. In time, a seat at a soccer game may even represent a certain amount of social distinction.'

Guttmann's Giants team was an amalgam of central European Jews and native-born American and British players. Aside from the four Hakoah players, the other mainstays of the team included the prolific United States forward Davey Brown, the Scottish left-half Billy Herd, and the left-sided player from Liverpool, George Moorhouse, who went on to become the first English-born player to appear in a World Cup Finals tournament when he captained the United States team in Italy in 1934.

The Giants performed solidly in both 1926/27 and the following season, when they were further bolstered by the signings of two more

recruits from Hakoah – the now legendary, title-winning goalkeeper Alexander Fabian and the right-back Max Gold. György Molnár, the Hungarian Jewish winger who had played with Guttmann in the championship-winning MTK Budapest team of 1921, also joined.

But neither the Giants nor Brooklyn Wanderers, with Eisenhoffer, Schönfeld, Drucker, Fischer and Neufeld, could hit the heights, merely achieving mid-table mediocrity in the American Soccer League (ASL) in both seasons. In the United States, they were mere footballing mercenaries among other mercenaries, without the close bonds of team spirit or that sense of 'us against the world' that had served to motivate Hakoah Vienna, just as it has done with so many other great sports teams over the years.

'The difference between mediocrity and greatness is the feeling players have for each other,' the great American football coach Vince Lombardi once said. In the case of the New York Giants, unfortunately, that feeling was often one of intense dislike. The world of the 1920s was much less globalised than today, and the team was riven by rancour between the British players and the Jews, as two very different cultures clashed. Two of the British players even declared at one point that they did not want to play with Guttmann and Häusler.

Hakoah Vienna duly arrived back in the United States for a second tour in April 1927, determined to recreate the excitement and the revenue generated the year before. However, just as its former players found it difficult to shine without Hakoah, the club was but a shadow of its former self without its one-time greats.

Despite the continuing popular interest in soccer as a sport, fewer than half the number of spectators turned up to watch Hakoah's thirteen tour games than had done so the previous year. That total included the one blast from the past, the 40,000 who came to the Polo Grounds to watch a 2–2 draw between the Giants and Hakoah, in which Guttmann played against his former team.

Thereafter, the crowds were so small that the tour organisers

even requested that some of the Hakoah old boys turn out for their former team. Guttmann played for Hakoah Vienna at least four times on the tour, even travelling with them to Philadelphia for one match. The ploy didn't do much to rescue the situation, however, and the tour resulted in a $30,000 loss and Ignaz Hermann Körner's resignation as president of the club.

• • •

The season 1928/29 was marked by bitter civil strife within American soccer, which helped to strangle the potential of the sport in its infancy. But for Guttmann's playing career, these events indirectly led to an upturn, temporarily at least.

The 'Soccer Wars', as they have come to be called, were a battle for overall control between the ASL and the United States Football Association (USFA), the sport's official governing body.

The recent success of the ASL had encouraged some of the owners of the member clubs to flex their muscles and achieve a format and schedule that better suited their commercial aims. One of the chief instigators of this confrontational approach was Charles Stoneham, a controversial figure who had already caused ructions within a different sport as the owner of the New York Giants baseball team (unrelated to Vandeweghe's soccer outfit). Intrigued by soccer's newfound popularity, he had proceeded to buy the ASL franchise Indiana Flooring, changing its name to the New York Nationals and signing one of the few remaining stars left at Hakoah Vienna, the forward Siegfried Wortmann.

The ASL accepted Stoneham's idea to restructure the United States Open Cup competition, which many felt disrupted the rhythm of the league schedule and drained financial resources by obligating professional teams to play against amateur opponents in front of non-paying crowds.

But the USFA refused a request to play the tournament at the end of the season, leading to the ASL announcing a boycott of the competition. Three clubs, however, including Guttmann's New York Giants, defied the league's boycott, earning a fine and a suspension from the ASL until they reversed their decision.

The USFA hit back hard, releasing a statement that read: 'Unless the American League rescinds the action in suspending New York Giants, Newark and Bethlehem within twenty-four hours, drastic action will be taken against the league.' The ASL ignored the ultimatum, and was itself duly suspended by the USFA, continuing only as an outlaw league minus the three teams who had refused to toe their line.

In late 1928, the USFA formed a new league that would cater for the three renegade teams, and other entrants. For its first season, the Eastern League included a newly formed team of Jewish players from Austria and Hungary, most of whom had played for Hakoah Vienna. The team, known as New York Hakoah, for just a few months rekindled some of the intense passion, camaraderie and onfield success of previous years, and marked Guttmann's final triumph as a football player.

• • •

New York Hakoah was the brainchild of Maurice Vandeweghe, who also continued as owner of the Giants until the USFA eventually prohibited individual control of two franchises.

To the fury of his rival owners Agar and Stoneham, who then unsuccessfully sought legal injunctions to stop their players departing mid-season, Vandeweghe recruited Drucker and Eisenhoffer from Brooklyn Wanderers and Wortmann from the New York Nationals. Alexander Neufeld, who had returned homesick to Hakoah Vienna after a season at Brooklyn Wanderers, came back to New

York to join the exciting venture. Rudolph Nickolsburger, a forward originally from Hungary who starred on Hakoah's later 1927 tour, also arrived direct from Europe, as did Pavel Mahrer, the Czechoslovak international left-half. (Mahrer later survived the war in the Theresienstadt concentration camp, earning rations by playing football in matches shown in propaganda films to fool the world about the full horror of the Jewish predicament.)

Meanwhile, Guttmann, Schwarcz, Häusler, Grünwald, Fabian and Fischer (who had recently moved from Brooklyn to the Giants), simply transferred their registration from one Vandeweghe outfit to another. Also joining from the Giants was the full-back László Sternberg, formerly of Újpest, a Jew who went on to captain the Hungarian team in their first World Cup Finals, in 1934.

It was a crack outfit, and one that would inevitably arouse huge interest. Vandeweghe instinctively understood that it was not the individual players from their own tribe who so excited the Jewish masses, but the sight of a Jewish team bearing a Hebrew name and a Star of David on their kit fighting tooth and nail against Gentile opponents.

Writing in the 1970s, one New Yorker, Benjamin Horowitz, described the stir the new Hakoah created: 'The new team's followers flocked everywhere to see their heroes,' he recalled. 'Whether Hakoah was at one end of the Bronx or at an equally inaccessible field in the hinterlands of Brooklyn did not matter to the adherents from the Lower East Side, Harlem, Brownsville, Williamsburg, East New York, Tremont or the South Bronx.'

Despite a fine run of form in the second half of the season 1928/29, New York Hakoah were pipped to the league title by Bethlehem Steel. But it was in the United States Open Cup, the national cup competition open to all senior teams in the country, that Hakoah really set pulses racing.

At this time, the tournament was divided into geographical sections, East and West, with the final played between the winners of

each section. The 'Jewish booters', as they were referred to in the press, beat Newark Portuguese in the Eastern Division semi-final to set up a regional final against the New York Giants, which included four players who were later to be inducted into the National Soccer Hall of Fame. As well as Brown and Moorhouse, the Giants now also boasted the Scottish inside-left Shamus O'Brien and another Liverpudlian, the full-back Teddy Glover.

The match was a tense affair, as one might expect with Guttmann and several others locking horns with former teammates, with little love lost between them. It was settled by a solitary goal, a late effort by Eisenhoffer sending Hakoah into the national final.

The final tie, to be decided by the best of three matches, pitted New York Hakoah against the winners of the Western section, St Louis Madison Kennel. The first match, played in St Louis, was another closely fought match, remaining goalless until Eisenhoffer and Wortmann scored two late goals.

New York Hakoah therefore started the second match, played on Sunday 7 April 1929, knowing that victory would make the planned third game redundant, and bring them the United States Open Cup. The match was played at Dexter Park in Queens, New York, a stadium normally reserved for baseball or American football. The ground was packed to the rafters, but still could not come close to meeting the surge in demand for this crucial game.

'Every seat in the grandstand and bleachers was taken,' reported the *New York Times*:

> and extra benches were placed wherever room was found. Points of vantage were found on housetops and even on the adjacent hill. A large force of police was on hand to keep the onlookers in check, as they constantly threatened to surge onto the field. The reserves were kept busy straightening out the sidelines, where the fans unable to get seats were permitted to stand.

Even the official crowd of more than 21,000 stood as a record for an Open Cup Final for more than eighty years until Seattle Sounders won the trophy in their home city in 2010.

The passionate support was rewarded with a comfortable 3–0 victory. Guttmann, whom Horowitz remembered as 'the team's incomparable centre half-back' and whose natural talents as a leader had by now earned him the captaincy, was mobbed by the Jewish hordes at the end of the game. 'The enthusiastic Hakoah followers crowded onto the field at Dexter Park and carried off the Hakoah players on their shoulders,' the Jewish Telegraphic Agency reported. 'Ernő Schwarcz, Max Grünwald and Moritz Häusler, the scorers in the game, and Béla Guttmann, captain of the team, were the heroes.'

Eight years after the Hungarian championship, and four years after the Austrian equivalent, Guttmann had won his third major club trophy. Meanwhile, as we shall see, his star was shining no less brightly off the pitch as he thrived in New York's Roaring Twenties.

Guttmann was drunk on the joys of life, and flying high. But, in a pattern that was to be repeated throughout his turbulent life, things were to turn sour just a few short months later.

• • •

Great sports coaches often say that the hardest challenge is not reaching the giddy heights, but ensuring that idolised young men maintain their hunger, that they take nothing for granted after initial success has been achieved.

More than three decades later, in 1961, Guttmann's Benfica team had just won their first European Cup, and he wanted to warn his players against the dangers of complacency. To illustrate to them how precarious life can be, Guttmann could have chosen from any number of episodes in his life, not least how he came within a hair's breadth of being murdered in 1944.

But perhaps sensing that his charges would be able to identify most easily with the thirty-year-old Guttmann at the height of his playing career, he gathered his team together before the start of the 1961/62 season and wound the clock back to the autumn of 1929.

Very soon after his arrival in the United States, Guttmann had become a shareholder in a large speakeasy, one of the thousands of illegal drinking clubs that had sprung up in New York during the Prohibition era of the 1920s. His investment offers another revealing insight into Guttmann's character. A foreigner in a strange land, he was sociable enough to generate the contacts to open up the opportunity just a few months after getting off the boat. He was also sufficiently fearless to take the financial risk of an illicit venture, and live with the possibility that he could land himself in trouble with the admittedly overwhelmed authorities entrusted with clamping down on the sale and consumption of alcohol.

Many people would have responded to the upheaval and hostility he experienced in Budapest and Vienna by craving security. Guttmann took the other option. If life was so precarious anyway, why not take a risk?

Indeed, it might be that it was in the United States that his life-long predilection for card games and casinos also took root. His nephew Imre, the only child of Béla's younger brother Ernő, was told that one event in particular triggered this weakness. 'Once, while working as a professional footballer in America, back in the '20s, he won a considerable amount of money during a trip in Las Vegas,' Imre said. 'He sent it all home to my father in Budapest straight away.'

As far as the speakeasy investment was concerned, the risk initially paid off and the money rolled in. In conversation with Jenő Csaknády, the Hungarian football coach and writer who collaborated on his autobiography published in 1964, Guttmann revealed that he had saved up $55,000 by October 1929. Given that his initial

football contract would have given him only around $13,000 before tax by this time, the speakeasy venture had clearly been extremely profitable.

He told his Benfica players that he wasn't shy about enjoying the fruits of his new-found wealth. 'Once upon a time in New York, I was young, elegant and witty – just as long as I had a lot of money,' he said. 'The highlight was the late '20s. My circle of acquaintances raved about me. My mediocre jokes prompted uproarious laughter. The ladies were delighted by my charm. The men admired my brilliant chess moves in business! I was so admired and pampered like a star by everyone.'

But then came the Wall Street Crash, and all Guttmann's money simply disappeared. 'I poked holes in the eyes of Abraham Lincoln on my last five-dollar bill,' he said. 'I thought that then it wouldn't be able to find its way to the door.'

All of a sudden, he was no longer the toast of the town. Thereafter, he said, his acquaintances greeted him 'with undisguised contempt' and his 'wittiest compliments attracted at best a compassionate smile on women's lips'. Those who had 'previously wanted a pleasant chat with me now had no time for me'. He was, he said, 'like a beaten dog, with no friends'.

The message to his Benfica players was clear. Life can go awry very quickly. Trust yourself and your teammates; much else is superficial and uncontrollable. Try to cast aside ephemeral distractions and fly-by-night sycophants. Keep working hard at your football; only following your talent can bring lasting glory and satisfaction.

For Guttmann himself, the economic crisis in the United States marked a watershed. If it hadn't been for the crash, this blip in the story of American Jewry, the chances are that he would have lived his life as one of a long list of successful New York Jewish businessmen, his former football career a mere footnote in the history of the game.

• • •

Footballing success on the pitch had come to an end for Guttmann by 1929, a cruel conjunction with his financial failure. At thirty, if not totally over the hill for a player of that era, he could certainly see the descent right in front of him. All that was left was a couple of years in an ageing team, living on past glories in a collapsing league, in a country in the depths of depression.

At the start of October 1929, just three weeks before the Wall Street Crash, peace was declared between the American Soccer League and the Eastern League. The following month, the Atlantic Coast League was formed through a merger of the two.

That was not the only merger to take place, as clubs desperately sought to remain viable in such straitened economic circumstances. New York Hakoah merged with another Jewish team, the recently formed Brooklyn Hakoah of the ASL, to form the Hakoah All-Stars. Guttmann and the All-Stars continued gamely in front of increasingly sparse audiences. 'It is not irrelevant that a large part of Hakoah's partisans were factory workers in industries which were hit the earliest and the hardest by the financial crisis,' recalled Benjamin Horowitz. 'When these proletarians lost their jobs, a sizeable segment of spectators was cut off from the sport.'

In a highly enterprising bid to raise money, principally masterminded by Guttmann himself, the Hakoah All-Stars embarked on a two-month and fifteen-match tour of Brazil, Argentina and Uruguay in the summer of 1930.

No other American club had showed anything like this level of resourcefulness. Nevertheless, the experiment failed, in almost absurd fashion, to realise its financial objectives. Indeed, if Guttmann was already feeling depressed after losing all his money, the tour will have served only to exacerbate his mood, to cement the feeling that life is a constant uphill battle, and that trust should be sparingly dispensed.

The 1930 tour was initially planned for Brazil only. But the manager of an Argentinian team approached Guttmann after a game in Rio de Janeiro to enquire whether the Hakoah All-Stars would consider continuing on to Argentina. Guttmann, who by now stood head and shoulders above his teammates as the self-described 'player, coach, manager and tour guide', handled the subsequent negotiations.

Guttmann was told that the All-Stars could expect attendances of up to 60,000 for each of their games in Argentina, a not unreasonable expectation given football's now massive popularity in that country. Seeing the potential upside, he didn't demand a fixed fee, but agreed to 40 per cent of the gross gate receipts from their seven matches in Argentina.

It looked like a sure money-spinner and a life-saver for the All-Stars and their players. But Guttmann hadn't reckoned on the fact that a very large proportion of Argentinian football crowds were made up of season-ticket holders who didn't have to pay an entrance fee for any individual match.

Neither had he foreseen the World Cup fever that was to grip the country at precisely the same time that the Hakoah All-Stars were trying to drum up support. Footballing attention was understandably focused on Uruguay, where the first ever World Cup Finals were taking place, inevitably reducing interest in the tour games. Six of the seven All-Stars games were played during Argentina's run to the final, where the team was eventually defeated by the host nation.

On the footballing side, the team was showing its age, managing to win only two of the fifteen games overall. But more importantly, the income from the tour was barely sufficient to cover even the expenses.

Although he could not have anticipated it at the time, the tour's short-term pain was nevertheless to translate into long-term gain

for Guttmann personally. As the sport became increasingly global, the intrepid traveller was in pole position to benefit. Always the consummate networker, the contacts he formed on this tour, and later assiduously maintained, were to stand him in good stead in his future coaching career.

The final match of the All-Stars tour was a goalless draw against Peñarol of Montevideo. More than thirty years later, in 1962, straight after walking out on his twice European champions Benfica, he was to go back there for a brief spell as coach. The All-Stars also played two games against São Paulo, winning one and losing one. In 1957, Guttmann returned, triumphantly, winning the league championship for the club in his first season. As the biblical psalm has it, what he sowed with tears, he later reaped with joy.

• • •

Guttmann came back with the All-Stars to New York in the autumn of 1930, his tail firmly between his legs, and his bank balance utterly depleted. He took an opportunity to sign again for the New York Giants, now renamed in what had become the chaos of American league football as the New York Soccer Club, playing for the first and only time in his long playing career in an almost exclusively non-Jewish team.

But the league's disintegration continued unabated. Within a few months, the New York Soccer Club merged with another club and moved to Massachusetts, leaving Guttmann to return once again to the bosom of his old chums at the Hakoah All-Stars.

The team was by now playing in a stadium with a maximum capacity of 3,000 fans. How the mighty had fallen in just five years since their league triumph in Vienna, victims of both economic decline and of their own sporting mortality. Salaries were now meagre. Guttmann, who later admitted that he had been on the brink of

giving up football before the Wall Street Crash to concentrate on his business interests, relied once again on giving dance lessons to get by.

Only once did the All-Stars draw in the crowds reminiscent of yesteryear. In June 1931, the All-Stars hosted a match against the touring Glasgow Celtic, then as now a huge attraction among Irish Catholics throughout the world. Twenty thousand people flocked to the Polo Grounds to see the fixture.

Relations between Jews and Irish Catholics had deteriorated in New York in recent years, as both ethnic groups fought over increasingly scarce economic opportunities. The match was therefore billed as a healing mechanism, fostering camaraderie between the Irish and the Jews. The Mayor, Jimmy Walker, understanding the game's significance in building community cohesion, invited both teams to City Hall a few days before the encounter, thus displaying the same political nous that had led him to extend similar hospitality to the Hakoah Vienna team a few years before.

But if inter-ethnic harmony was the intention of the match organisers, the players failed to keep their side of the bargain. Just after half-time, Guttmann himself, reviving the fire and aggression of his Vienna days, exchanged blows with Charlie Napier. Both were given their marching orders from the field. Later on, a further player from each side was dismissed, and the game, a 1–1 draw, ended nine-a-side in ill-tempered acrimony.

This was the last game of note in Guttmann's playing career in the United States, with the Hakoah All-Stars going the same way as the rest of American soccer. 'When the hardy cadre who, in the late 1920s, turned out by the thousands for Hakoah's games – even in the worst storms and bitterest cold – dwindled to a few hundred, the most optimistic realized it was time to quit,' wrote Horowitz.

By the autumn of 1932, the Hakoah All-Stars had folded, and the league itself followed suit not long after. With barely more than the

clothes on his back, Guttmann returned to Europe in time to bear first-hand witness to a continent hurtling into an unprecedented frenzy of violence. For a Jew, settling back in Europe a matter of months before Adolf Hitler's rise to power could be considered imprudent. Guttmann's decision to make the exact same move six years later was to verge on the suicidal.

CHAPTER 4

LEARNING THE ROPES

After the Nazi invasion of Austria in March 1938, harrowing reports about the fate of Vienna's Jews started to circulate. The world's conscience was pricked into something resembling action. President Franklin D. Roosevelt called for an international conference to discuss the rapidly deteriorating predicament of the Jews now under Nazi rule. But the frantic Jewish quest for escape routes, exemplified by the long daily queues outside consulates, contrasted with the leisurely preparation for the conference, finally convened in July at the picturesque, luxury French resort of Évian, on Lake Geneva.

With the Nazi leadership at that point open to the possibility of mere deportation, the opportunity to rescue the Jews was there for the taking. 'I can only hope and expect that the other world, which has such deep sympathy for these criminals, will at last be generous enough to convert that sympathy into practical aid,' remarked Adolf Hitler. 'We, on our part, are ready to put all these criminals at the disposal of these countries, for all I care, even on luxury ships.'

The 'other world' turned out to be as weak and indifferent as the Nazi world was barbarous. Speaker after speaker from thirty-two countries, witnessed by a 200-strong international press corps in the lovely

surroundings, rose to offer tortured explanations of why they couldn't do much to alleviate Jewish suffering.

'As we have no real racial problem, we are not desirous of importing one,' said the Australian representative. Ireland, for its part, noted that it 'could make no real contribution'. The Belgian delegate gallantly declared that his country deemed it 'a point of honour not to assume fresh international obligations whose consequences she cannot estimate'. Argentina stroked its chin, resolving to 'collaborate in studying and solving the problem'.

Britain, which had agreed with the United States prior to the conference that the issue of immigration to Palestine (which it controlled) would not be raised, was willing to accept some children but not their parents, fearing that 'a sudden rush of Jewish refugees might arouse anti-Semitic feelings'. Central American states issued a joint statement explaining their reluctance to accept 'traders and intellectuals'. Brazil helpfully proposed that every visa application would have to be accompanied by a certificate of Christian Baptism. The United States refused to tamper with existing immigration restrictions. Switzerland, meanwhile, with 'as little use for these Jews as Germany has', determined that it 'will herself take measures to protect Switzerland from being swamped by the Jews'.

Both worlds seemed content with the outcome. The Nazis, for their part, were given free rein to treat the Jews as they pleased. 'We see that one likes to pity the Jews as long as one can use this pity for a wicked agitation against Germany, but that no State is prepared to fight the cultural disgrace of Central Europe by accepting a few thousand Jews,' argued the Danziger Vorposten *newspaper. 'Thus the Conference serves to justify Germany's policy against Jewry.'*

Meanwhile, London's Evening Standard *thought all the Jewish whining a little uncouth, and praised the conference for not dancing to the tune of the Jewish lobby: 'It is felt by many people that we hear too much about the trouble of the Jews. They shout too loudly. They make too insistent a demand upon the compassion of the world. Compassion they get – and deserve – but annoyance is apt to accompany it.'*

Golda Meir, who was to become the Prime Minister of Israel thirty years later, was at the conference in her capacity as a Jewish observer from Palestine. She told the press: 'There is only one thing I hope to see before I die, and that is that my people should not need expressions of sympathy any more.'

Those with the most developed sense of gallows humour simply remarked that Évian spells naive backwards.

• • •

Where does a desperate man turn when he has lost everything, and needs to rebuild? To the place where he had previously felt most alive, where he has the closest friends and contacts, those who can help him back onto the ladder of life.

So when things went awry in New York, Guttmann returned to the city he always regarded more than any other as home: Vienna. From his Hakoah days onwards, he was drawn there when he had nowhere else in particular to go. He would even go back there more than forty years later when his nomadic coaching career had finally come to an end, and this despite the rather significant fact that the vast majority of his people, including close friends and teammates, had been murdered or had fled in the intervening period.

In his six years in the United States, Austria had slipped menacingly towards dictatorship and political violence. In May 1932, a few months before Guttmann's return, Engelbert Dollfuss of the authoritarian Christian Social Party had taken power. It was not long before rallies and protests were banned, the Communist Party and the Nazi Party dissolved, and press censorship tightened. By April 1934, the Parliament itself had been disbanded.

Despite this suppression of democratic freedoms, the era of so-called Austrofascism, which continued right up until the Anschluss of 1938, was in the main a relatively benign era for the Jewish

community. Although sporadic street attacks continued, Dollfuss
set out to reassure the Jews that Nazi-style anti-Semitism would
not be tolerated by the authorities. 'All fears of the Jews in the land
or abroad concerning the Nazi demands may be dispersed since the
government is determined to adhere to its present attitude towards
the Nazis,' he said. When Dollfuss himself was murdered in the
failed Nazi putsch of July 1934, his successor Kurt Schuschnigg
continued this policy of official protection, albeit with diminishing
success as the pressure from neighbouring Germany intensified.

It was in this ostensibly calm, yet ominous, environment that
the returning Guttmann sought to ply his trade once more. In
what must have been a depressing initial year back in Europe, he
committed to play for another season at Hakoah Vienna, whose
fall from grace as a footballing power had been precipitous. Just
a few years before, he had left the city with the world at his feet,
able to take his pick from various clubs vying for his services.
Now he reappeared as an ageing footballer, with no money, plead-
ing with his fast-fading and financially straitened former club to
re-employ him.

He joined up with fellow returnees Eisenhoffer and Drucker on
Hakoah's tour of France in the autumn of 1932.* But there was to
be no recapturing of former glories. After struggling manfully in
a match against Rapid Vienna at the newly built Prater stadium
after a handful of appearances, Guttmann decided that he simply
couldn't take any more.

Looking back several decades later in conversation with the
Hungarian journalist Tibor Hámori, Guttmann gave a graphic de-
scription of what all great sportsmen must feel when the spirit is
still willing but the flesh becomes weak:

* A player named Guttmann played one game for Metz in the French Ligue 1 in the
 autumn of 1932. It was probably Béla, straight off the boat from the United States,
 but we can't know this for sure.

There were two big clocks by the pitch ... There were 15 minutes left. But just as if I had been given a tiring injection, my legs became like lead and everything got blurry and I felt I was completely helpless. And a voice whispered to me: 'Béla, it's time to finish it!' It was a horrible quarter of an hour. But after that I was relieved ... I called the club officials aside and I made my statement: 'Gentlemen, this was my last game!' 'Right,' they said, 'haven't you got a better joke than this?' They didn't want to believe me. But I didn't change my decision. Next day the papers said I was the best in the field, but I was still adamant. I never again stepped on the pitch as a player. Not even at old boys' games.

He may have been leaving the playing arena, but he had no intention of deserting the game itself. Drawn to leadership, as demonstrated by his de facto management role during the Hakoah All-Stars' tour of South America, and in dire need of a steady income, he persuaded the Hakoah board to give him his first taste of management from early 1933.

The board were in no position to be fussy, with the club once again having fallen victim to an overseas tour. The previous coach, Vinzenz Dittrich, had left to join Olympique de Marseille, where Hakoah had played the previous year. Eisenhoffer had already left for the same destination, and Drucker soon followed Dittrich to the warmth of the south of France. The new coach was suddenly the only star from the glory era now at the club.

He may have already earned recognition as a top player, but Guttmann's inauspicious two seasons as Hakoah coach hardly served to alert the world that a great football manager was in the making.

For his first full campaign in charge, he brought back another of his buddies, Moritz Häusler, who by now had also returned from the United States. From being a club of international renown, Hakoah had become a rest home for rather desperate alumni. With the

quality of football reflecting this decline, the club narrowly escaped relegation, winning just five of their league games. The following season, 1934/35, was no better. The team failed to improve its points total, again holding on to top flight status by the skin of its teeth.

But now with a foothold back in Europe in his chosen career, the tenacious Guttmann sought new opportunities and betterment. Even in the meritocratic world of sport, some coaching appointments in the modern day still look like they owe more to connections than track record. Back in 1935, well before the coach was universally accepted as absolutely key to team success, and an even longer time before the results and performances of teams in distant places became so easy to scrutinise, the right contacts would have been even more important. And Guttmann, the sociable wheeler-dealer, was never short of good contacts.

• • •

The best contacts, of course, are those in high places. Since his time working with Jimmy Hogan with the Austrian national team prior to the First World War, Hugo Meisl had become a hugely influential footballing personality both in Vienna and in the wider world. His younger brother Willy, a former goalkeeper and then celebrated sports writer in Germany who effortlessly and remarkably achieved similar status as a refugee in England, later described him as 'the Pitt, Disraeli, Bismarck and Napoleon of Austrian soccer rolled into one'. Here was yet another Jew who shaped the development of football, and it was he who helped Guttmann get the break he so badly needed.

Hugo Meisl had performed a dual role, governing the Austrian Football Association and managing the national team. Both as an administrator and coach, he was a highly impressive pioneer. He had been the driving force behind the creation of a professional

league in Austria in 1924/25 (won by Hakoah), an idea that soon spread to the two other central European countries which then dominated continental football: Hungary and Czechoslovakia.

Shrewdly anticipating the popular draw of non-domestic football, Meisl had in 1927 lobbied successfully for the introduction of the Mitropa Cup, a precursor to the much broader-based European Cup. The Mitropa Cup, where Guttmann later first flexed his muscles as a coach in cross-border football, was designed as a tournament for leading clubs from the central European powerhouses – Austria, Hungary, Czechoslovakia and Yugoslavia. Meisl also worked tirelessly alongside the Frenchman Jules Rimet to establish the World Cup competition, first competed for in 1930.

If you think the great AC Milan coach Arrigo Sacchi or José Mourinho were the first coaches to excel without having first played football to a reasonable level, then think again. Meisl never played the game, but influenced by Hogan and infatuated by the passing style of football, he built up the so-called 'Wunderteam', the Austrian national side viewed by many as the greatest pre-Second World War European international team.

The team's approach came to be known as 'the whirl', a game of flexibility and interchangeability between all ten outfield players. Even in the modern era, we see the legacy of Meisl's philosophy – in the Total Football system of the great Dutch team of the 1970s, or in the fluid Spanish tiki-taka of still more recent times.

Inspired by captain and goal-scoring centre-forward Matthias Sindelar, known as 'the Mozart of football', Austria's results in the early 1930s were breathtaking. Meisl's team embarked on a fourteen-match unbeaten run, scoring, for example, eleven goals against Germany with no reply in two games in 1931. They also beat Hungary 8–2 and taught Scotland, the originators of the passing game, a thing or two in a 5–0 thrashing as the eager students turned the tables on their teachers. A strong favourite to win the 1934 World

Cup, Austria only succumbed to hosts Italy in a semi-final played on a rain-soaked pitch which hindered their normal passing game.

Like Guttmann, Meisl was both multilingual and a master networker. His passion for football and his stellar reputation as an innovative coach won him many likeminded friends and admirers, including Herbert Chapman, the legendary English coach, and Vittorio Pozzo, the coach of the Italian national team that won both the 1934 and 1938 World Cups.

Meisl had taken Guttmann under his wing during the latter's time playing for Hakoah in Vienna in the 1920s, and had no doubt been impressed by him. Football is no different from any other industry – most people who are excellent at their jobs have little interest in the broader questions of general management or strategy, and Guttmann's obvious footballing intelligence would certainly have stood out.

The distinguished coach got wind of a coaching vacancy at the Dutch team Sportclub (SC) Enschede (now known as FC Twente), and promptly recommended the young Guttmann for the role. Such a recommendation could not be easily ignored, and the club handed Guttmann a short-term contract to see what he could do.

So, in 1935, Béla Guttmann left Vienna and travelled through Nazi Germany to his new post in the east of the Netherlands. Mercifully spared humiliation and probable murder, his mentor Meisl died of a heart attack two years later, at the age of fifty-five, before the Nazis could get their hands on him.

• • •

Guttmann was not the only Jew to arrive in the Netherlands in the 1930s. An estimated 35,000 fled there from Germany and (later) Austria, including the future diarist Anne Frank and her family. The influx increased the total Jewish population of the country by a

third. If any of these refugees had much choice about where to flee to, they chose badly. By 1945, three in four of the country's 140,000 Jewish inhabitants lay dead.

Most of the German-speaking immigrants had settled in the capital Amsterdam, 150 kilometres west of Enschede. The few who arrived in Enschede bolstered the small community to around 1,400. Jewish life in the city revolved around the spanking new and lovingly designed synagogue, built in 1928 and standing now as a symbol of tragically misplaced optimism. During the war, the synagogue even served as the local headquarters of the SS intelligence agency, where the details of the disposal of its former worshippers were hammered out.

At the age of thirty-six, Guttmann was for the first time in his life in a city where Jews were not core to the character and feel of the urban landscape. (There was even a sizeable Jewish community in Újvidék – Novi Sad – during his brief stay there). From Budapest, Vienna and New York, pulsating centres of the Jewish and wider world, he now found himself in something of a provincial backwater. Given the city's very close proximity to the border and intimate trading links with its neighbour, his integration into this foreign culture would at least have been eased by the fact that the vast majority of its inhabitants spoke fluent German.

Job-wise, he had taken on a major challenge. Dutch football was at that time dominated, just as it is now, by three clubs. Between 1928 and 1940, all but two of the national championships were won by Feyenoord of Rotterdam, PSV Eindhoven or Ajax Amsterdam, a giant of European football whose pre-war Jewish roots run so deep that opposing fans are even now likely to break out into a rendition of the chant 'Hamas, Hamas, Joden aan het gas' (Hamas, Hamas, Jews to the gas).

The national championship was then divided into five regional leagues, each with ten teams. The winner from each section qualified

for play-offs, where the five teams would play each other home and away for the national title in another league system.

Emerging as the winner of the national title was therefore a tall order, not least for SC Enschede whose solitary success had come in 1926, and who had finished a mediocre fifth place in the Eastern regional league in the season before Guttmann joined. But Guttmann was nothing if not highly self-confident, and a tough negotiator to boot. Once he had settled in and made a strong initial impression, he secured a new longer-term contract that included a provision for a huge bonus in the highly unlikely event that Enschede won the national championship.

The first hurdle was overcome easily, with Enschede winning all but three of their eighteen games to claim the Eastern regional league division title. The team thus qualified for the play-offs where their opponents would include Feyenoord and Ajax.

The club president later admitted that he spent the play-off stages in a state of blind panic. He had agreed the contract with Guttmann without due attention to the bonus clause because the idea of Enschede winning the national championship had seemed to him a pipe dream, borne out of Guttmann's considerable ego. But should fantasy turn to reality, the scale of the prospective bonus was apparently so large that it would bankrupt the club.

Enschede were to come within a whisker of simultaneous glory and extinction. And if the club president wanted someone to thank for allowing his beloved club to continue unscathed, he would have looked no further than another Jew, Richard Kohn.

Kohn was usually known by his Hungarian nickname Dombi (little eminence), which he acquired while playing for MTK Budapest at the onset of the First World War. He was a former Austrian international midfielder whose later career as a coach eventually took him to Bayern Munich in 1931.

Bayern may be a huge name now, but the club had never won the

German national championship before the arrival of this Viennese Jew, who was himself appointed by the long-serving Jewish president of the club, Kurt Landauer.

Just a few months before Hitler took power, the Jewish double act lifted the elusive title for Germany's now greatest football club in Kohn's first season, launching a trophy-winning machine that is still running smoothly today.* The following year, 1933, Kohn took the helm at FC Barcelona, making the opposite journey from that travelled by the great present-day coach Pep Guardiola. The other small difference is that Guardiola was not fleeing racial persecution.

In 1936, Kohn's destiny collided with Guttmann's. Just as Guttmann became coach at Enschede, Kohn took over at rivals Feyenoord of Rotterdam. Guttmann would have pulled off the miraculous feat of the national league title if it were not for the two play-off matches against the more experienced coach, losing 3–1 at home and 4–1 away. Enschede eventually finished two points behind Feyenoord in the five-team league. The little eminence had taught the upstart a lesson, and became something of a local hero. A street named Richard Dombistraat now stands just around the corner from Feyenoord's De Kuip stadium.

• • •

Enschede's form slipped markedly the following year, and we must assume that Guttmann fell out with his employers. We can make this reasonable assumption firstly because Guttmann, as we shall see repeatedly throughout his career, was always falling out with his employers; and secondly, because he went back to Austria, a country sliding inexorably into Nazism. This was a place where few

* In that same season, 1931/32, another European giant, Real Madrid, also won their first ever domestic league championship. Their coach was also a Jew, Lippo Hertzka, from Budapest. He was just twenty-seven years old.

Jews, even the Viennaphile Guttmann, would choose to live in 1937. It seems that Guttmann had only one offer on the table at this point, and that was from Hakoah.

Reappointed as coach, Guttmann had the fateful distinction of being the last coach before the Nazis rolled in and closed the club down. Indeed, Hakoah, by then in the second division, were even heading for promotion back to the top flight before their season was prematurely terminated, their previous glories nullified, and their stadium handed to the occupying power. Many promotion hopefuls in footballing history have faltered in the final furlong through injuries or loss of nerve, but few can blame their failure on Nazi stormtroopers.

It has been generally assumed that Guttmann was in Vienna at the time of Anschluss on 12 March 1938, and that he stayed there until leaving for Hungary in the summer to take up the job of coach of Újpest. But the truth is quite different, and more remarkable. He would actually have been listening to the terrifying news of the invasion on a radio while 7,000 kilometres away.

No doubt seeing major trouble ahead, he had obtained a United States entry visa at the American consulate in Vienna on 18 January 1938. He sailed from Cherbourg in northern France, arriving in New York on 2 March, ten days before the Nazi troops were to be greeted by an overwhelmingly friendly reception from the Austrian public. 'The people in their worship of anti-Semitism are entirely at one with their brothers in the Reich,' reported the then Viennese resident Sigmund Freud.

The visa Guttmann obtained was for 'lawful permanent residence'. It is difficult to exaggerate how highly prized such a visa was at this time. They were a lifeline to security and survival, and extremely difficult to come by. The United States immigration quota for each country was a complex calculation, based on the number of American citizens whose origin could be traced back to

that particular country. As a result, merely 869 Hungarian citizens were permitted entry to the United States in 1938.

All the more extraordinary, therefore, that he arrived back in Nazi-occupied Vienna on 6 August 1938. Stating both his ordinary and last abode as 'United States' on his registration document, he left for Budapest eight days later.

I searched for statistics on the number of Jews voluntarily moving to continental Europe from the United States in 1938, but without success. Needless to say, this number would have been extremely small. According to the evidence, that is nevertheless exactly what Béla Guttmann decided to do. In fact, he would have set sail for Europe a matter of days after the conference at Évian had effectively consigned the panicked Jews of Europe to their fate. The question is: why on earth did he do it?

It is possible that he travelled to New York with the intention of returning to Europe once he had cemented his residency status, which could then act as an insurance policy for him should the situation in Europe worsen still further.

Indeed, The United States Citizenship and Immigration Services informed me that he would not necessarily have forfeited his right to residency by returning: 'The fact that he returned would not in itself necessarily result in loss of resident status,' I was told:

> The Immigration Service would have used a number of factors to determine whether or not he had forfeited residency. The short length of time he spent in the United States and the length of his absence would have been two factors they considered. In general, though, Lawful Permanent Admission did not 'expire' without action on the part of the migrant which indicated he/she intended to remain abroad permanently.

More likely, he wasn't planning that far ahead. In January 1938, in a dead-end job at Hakoah and sensing huge personal danger, he

joined thousands of other Jews in Vienna in considering the United States to be a highly attractive proposition. But when he arrived there, one suspects, Guttmann would have been at a loss.

While in New York, he was interviewed by the Hungarian newspaper *Pesti Napló*. He revealed that he was attempting to establish a new all-European team to compete in the reborn American Soccer League, boasting that he had a 'business partner' and 'serious capital'. He claimed that he was looking at sports grounds to rent and had made a list of European players to invite over to the United States.

But it was all just hot air. By the time the interview was actually published, on 4 August 1938, Guttmann was almost back in Vienna, in the full knowledge that his plan was dead in the water. There was absolutely nothing going for it. Visas for foreign-based players would have been nigh-on impossible to obtain. Soccer was being watched by tiny crowds, with amateur or semi-professional players earning much of their income from other means.

Nor was the broader environment conducive to the raising of 'serious capital'. The American economy, having recovered from the Great Depression of the early 1930s, had nosedived again in 1937. Unemployment reached a rate of almost 20 per cent, and did not show any sign of improvement until the country entered the war in late 1941.

As the ridiculousness of his hare-brained idea dawned on him, Guttmann would have felt bereft. He knew football, and little else. It is hard to imagine him working in an office or factory, and the timing for an alternative entrepreneurial venture, such as a dance school, would have been equally inopportune.

He most likely got wind of the potential vacancy at Újpest through some of his contacts during the summer. The club's coach László Sternberg, a former captain of the Hungarian national team who played alongside Guttmann when New York Hakoah lifted the

United States Open Cup nine years earlier, had himself decided to leave Budapest for New York. His own visa application was granted in Budapest on 2 June 1938, eventually arriving in September. Either Guttmann was offered the job as Sternberg's replacement while still in the United States, or he finalised the deal after arriving in Europe in August.

Hungary was not at that time occupied by the Nazis. But Sternberg's decision to abandon Újpest, a top club in a major footballing country, to come to the United States, reflects how difficult life had already become for Hungary's Jews. He wasn't the only high-profile Jewish footballing personality to leave the country that year either. Ferenc Sas, who played in the Hungary team beaten in the final of the 1938 World Cup in France, emigrated to Argentina straight after the tournament.[*]

The situation for the Jews had gone further downhill since Guttmann had abandoned his birthplace for Hakoah Vienna sixteen years earlier. To understand why, we need some brief historical background.

After the First World War, the victorious Western powers had imposed harsh treaties on the defeated nations. Under the 1920 Treaty of Trianon, for example, Hungary's territory and population were slashed to a third of their former size. Many of the non-Hungarian ethnic groups of the pre-war kingdom now resided outside its borders.

The largest remaining non-Hungarian minority were now the Jews, the perennial scapegoats during such times of national humiliation. Miklós Horthy, who led the White Terror and had remained as regent of Hungary, was clearly no fan. 'I have considered it intolerable that here in Hungary everything, every factory, bank,

[*] Born Ferenc Sohn, he Magyarised his name to Sas to increase his chances of being chosen for the national team.

large fortune, business, theatre, the press, commerce, etc. should be in Jewish hands, and that the Jew should be the image reflected of Hungary, especially abroad,' he wrote.

In 1932, Horthy appointed Gyula Gömbös as his Prime Minister. Gömbos was the arch anti-Semite who had spoken out in Parliament against 'international professionals' (Jews), such as Guttmann, appearing for the Hungarian national team in the wake of the Paris Olympics debacle of 1924. Now he sought to rebuild Hungary's failing economy by rapidly increasing trading links with Nazi Germany. In return, as Germany acquired territory through its expansionist policies, it restored to Hungary some of the lands it had lost at Trianon, such as parts of Slovakia and Yugoslavia, and northern Transylvania.

These intimate relations inevitably spelt big danger for the Jews. In May 1938, just three months before Guttmann's return, the Hungarian Parliament passed the First Jewish Law. The law imposed a 20 per cent ceiling on the proportion of Jewish lawyers and doctors (constituting, therefore, a considerable reduction), and a similar limit for all businesses and industrial enterprises employing more than ten people. As far as Jews were concerned, the environment in Hungary wasn't yet murderous, but it was certainly poisonous.

So here is my own answer to the question of why Guttmann left the United States to take a job in Hungary, when others, such as Sternberg and Sas, were bursting to get out of there. While others prized survival and security above everything else, I think he loved football so much that he couldn't envisage a life without it; that a life without football was unthinkable to him, whatever the possible consequences. This stark understanding came to him, I believe, as he reflected on the futility of his European soccer team plan while in New York in the summer of 1938. Modern-day football commentators like to tell us that certain highly committed players 'put their life on the line' for their teams. Béla Guttmann, it seems, literally put his life on the line for his love of football.

Risk-takers like Guttmann know that they can lose absolutely everything, but they can also win big. Sternberg lived out a quiet and secure life as a watchmaker in New York, and entered into relative footballing obscurity. Guttmann, meanwhile, was to endure some horrific experiences and come within an ace of being murdered, only to emerge to write his name in bold letters in the annals of the game.

• • •

Újpest was then a town bordering Budapest, and has since been merged into the city. It was founded by the nineteenth-century industrialist Izsák Lőwy who had been denied permission to build a shoe factory in Pest (the eastern section of Budapest) because he was Jewish. As one does, he decided instead to build a new town where he could put his factory.

In footballing terms, the move to Újpest's already well-established football club marked a major step up for Guttmann. The team had won the Hungarian league four times in the 1930s, and the Mitropa Cup in 1929. And the domestic victories were won, let us not forget, in a country at the very forefront of world football.

The Hungarian national team that had come so close to winning the World Cup in 1938, beaten only in the final by Italy, was composed of players from the three dominant clubs – MTK, Ferencváros and Újpest. The goalscoring star of both the national team and Újpest was Gyula Zsengellér. Under Guttmann's guidance in the 1938/39 season, Zsengellér scored a remarkable fifty-six goals in twenty-six appearances, as Újpest came out top in the usual three-horse race, their first title for four years.

Guttmann's risk-taking nature, evident outside of football through his speakeasy venture in the United States and his more recent danger-filled return to Europe, was always reflected in the

teams he managed. As happens with all great and charismatic coaches, the team became an extension of his own personality. That meant Guttmann's teams played on the front foot, fearlessly, with attack deemed the best means of defence. 'I never minded if the opposition scored, because I always thought we could score another,' he once said. That season, Újpest bore his unmistakable signature, scoring 107 goals in the league season at an average of more than four per game.

Újpest thereby qualified for Meisl's brainchild tournament, the Mitropa Cup. With the country now deemed by the Nazis to be part of Germany, Austrian teams were no longer competing. Nevertheless, the footballing strength of the nations represented could not be underestimated. As well as two teams from Hungary (1938 World Cup finalists), there would be two teams each from Italy (winners in both 1934 and 1938) and Czechoslovakia (finalists in 1934), and one each from Romania and Yugoslavia. Make no mistake, the Mitropa Cup was a big deal in 1939.

Újpest first disposed of Ambrosiana Inter, the name temporarily foisted on Inter Milan by Mussolini's fascist government after its forced merger with another club. Beogradski, the Serbian conquerors of the holders Slavia Prague, were the semi-final opponents. Újpest lost the first leg 4–2 in Belgrade, but a few days later Zsengellér produced a masterclass back in Budapest, scoring five second-half goals in a 7–1 demolition, and earning Újpest a two-legged final against local rivals Ferencváros.

Rather than playing cagily in the first leg of the final away from home, Guttmann typically went for the jugular, and his team emerged 4–1 victors. It wasn't all over though. Ferencváros grabbed two first-half goals in the return leg the following week, and were now only one goal behind on the aggregate score. But with Guttmann doing his bit to settle his team's nerves at half-time, Újpest grabbed two goals to claim the title. A quarter of a century later

in his autobiography, Guttmann recalled with pride the delirious scenes of celebration that followed.

That second leg had been played on 30 July 1939, a little more than a month before Europe descended into full-scale war. The Jew Guttmann thus held the most prestigious European football club trophy in his hands throughout the war years, a fitting tribute to the continent's Jews who had played such a pivotal role in the development of the game. Their influence would continue to be seen in the years after 1945, but only the remnants of this extraordinary people would remain to witness it.

The Mitropa Cup was never the same again. It was restarted in the 1950s, but with the establishment of the great European Cup competition in 1955, it was shunted into insignificance. The last time it meant something, in other words, Guttmann won it.

To appreciate what happened to Guttmann next, it is again perhaps best to look beyond the published words, the face-saving and the bluster. Many years later, he claimed that he had met with Lipót Aschner, the Jewish club president and seasoned industrialist, the day after the victory:

> 'My dear Guttmann, when you have a long beard, you can still be our coach here!' 'Thank you, Mr. Director,' I said, 'but I have a request. God has blessed me with a large family, so I would like to ask for a pay rise.' 'No way,' he said ... I didn't sign the contract.

On 1 August, 1939, two days after the final, the newspaper *Sport-hirlap* reported that Guttmann was leaving Újpest, adding that the decision had been made before the final. Interestingly, the news had been deliberately withheld from the players, who 'respected the coach', for fear of disrupting their mental preparations before the big game. The article also mentioned that Guttmann had received 'a very lucrative foreign offer'.

It is difficult to imagine where 'a very lucrative foreign offer' would come from in the summer of 1939. Italy had been a popular destination for Hungarian-born coaches, but recent racial laws in that country had now put paid to the careers of the Jews among them. The other main footballing centres in continental Europe – Austria, Germany and Czechoslovakia – were already Nazi-occupied. English clubs were not interested in foreign coaches. It is feasible that there was an offer from South America, but the fact that Guttmann didn't take up any such position does suggest that the alleged job did not actually exist.

My suspicion, also, is that someone as streetwise as Guttmann would have been instinctively aware that a Jew couldn't push his luck too far in negotiations at this precise juncture in Hungary's history. A more likely explanation is that Aschner was placed under huge pressure to remove his fellow Jew from such a high-profile coaching post, and that no such financial negotiations actually took place.

By now, after all, the screws had been tightened. The Second Jewish Law had been passed in May 1939, with the title 'About the Restriction of Public and Economic Encroachment of the Jews'. It excluded Jews from state and municipal office. It dismissed all Jewish teachers in non-Jewish schools. It limited the Jewish membership in the chambers of lawyers, engineers, doctors and journalists to 6 per cent, and likewise in theatre and film. Jews were altogether prohibited from being editors and publishers, or directors of theatres.

Even if the job of 'sports coach' was not specifically included in a further long list of now barred occupations, a Jewish leader of arguably the best club team in Europe, in such a highly visible and popular pastime as football, would have been a particular affront to the authorities. It would be difficult to think of a much clearer example of the 'public encroachment of the Jews'. The *Sporthirlap* article cites a comment from Guttmann that 'he would love to stay,

but circumstances beyond his control forced him to look for a job abroad'. I think we can guess what those circumstances were, and money didn't have much to do with it.

Less than five years later, on the day of the Nazi invasion of Hungary, 19 March 1944, the 72-year-old Lipót Aschner was dragged from his home in the wealthy Rószadomb district of Budapest, and sent on his way to Mauthausen concentration camp. As he was moved out of the palatial villa, Adolf Eichmann moved in. In the very rooms where Aschner had relaxed with family and friends, and had perhaps informed Béla Guttmann of his fate, the Nazi henchman set about planning the final pieces of his genocidal jigsaw.

CHAPTER 5

DODGING DEATH

When Béla Guttmann and his team won the Mitropa Cup in July 1939, the Megyeri úti stadium in Újpest was full to capacity, with 15,000 fans roaring on their heroes. In early May 1944, around the same number of Újpest Jews were crammed into a small ghetto surrounding that very stadium, in the town that had been founded by a Jew a hundred years earlier. The ghetto comprised just seventy houses, each marked with a yellow star.

Just after the war, the Hungarian Jewish relief organisation, the National Committee for Attending Deportees, recorded the personal stories of Hungarian Holocaust survivors. An unnamed rabbi from Újpest described what happened in the fateful weeks after the ghetto had been established.

At first, the Jews were allowed to leave the yellow-star houses for two hours a day. In the middle of June, even that luxury was forbidden. Two weeks after that, on 2 July, they were marched to the train station, from where almost all of them would depart their hometown for the last time. 'The derision of the inhabitants followed us the whole way,' recalled the rabbi. 'There were two other rabbis with us, handsome, tall men. People shouted the nastiest words at them. They did not throw stones at us only because the gendarmes chased them away from there. We did not see regretful faces at all.'

They were loaded on trains to a deportation centre at Budakalász, less than 10 kilometres away. And there they waited, for several days, in the open air, in the incessant pouring rain.

'My sister's eight-month-old baby was with us and we could not feed it, nor could we wash it,' continued the rabbi:

> *The nights were especially terrible. Crowds of people went mad; they were shouting and yelling, we could not get hold of any water … The Jews of Kispest, Újpest, Rákospalota and Pestszentrerzsébet were there and a great many people from Pest too. About 30,000 people were in that camp. A gendarme shot somebody in front of us, because he had dared to contradict him at the unloading. We wanted to bring a doctor to him, but the gendarme did not let us. He had to die in sight of everybody. The (Hungarian) gendarmes abused us continuously; the SS men, who were ethnic Germans, committed atrocities against us … Masses of people committed suicide together; people poisoned themselves with their medicines.*

Between 6 and 8 July, the Jews of Újpest made up a large number of the 24,128 Jews forced to board eight trains of cattle cars, for their final, long, slow, insufferably hot, 400-kilometre journey north. Eighty to one hundred people crammed into each car, with no air, equipped with one bucket of water and one waste bucket, for two and a half days. Among them were the sick, the dying, the already dead. 'Finally, the train stopped in Auschwitz,' said the rabbi. 'We saw a lot of people in striped clothes, marked with yellow stars … We had heard them speaking in Yiddish, so I asked: "Who are you?" And a man answered: "Jews, just like you."'

• • •

The River Danube splits Budapest into two sections, Buda and Pest. On the Pest side of the river, not far from the Parliament, sit iron models of sixty pairs of shoes, the type locals would have worn in the 1940s. The memorial

recalls the thousands of the city's Jews shot by Hungarian forces on that very bank, known then as 'The Jewish Cemetery', in the winter of 1944–45.

'I heard a series of popping sounds,' wrote the Jewish eyewitness Zsuzsanna Ozsváth:

> *Thinking the Russians had arrived, I slunk to the window. But what I saw was worse than anything I had ever seen before ... Two Arrow Cross* men were standing on the embankment of the river, aiming at and shooting a group of men, women and children into the Danube – one after the other, on their coats the yellow star. I looked at the Danube. It was neither blue nor grey, but red.*

The grisly methods of execution were infamous. In many cases, the Arrow Cross men tied together the hands of two or three Jews, adults or children. They would shoot one, and all three would fall into the river and float away. If the killers noticed that any Jews were still alive in the freezing water, they used them for target practice.

Nearly half of the Jewish population of Budapest, numbering around 250,000 in 1944, were murdered in the Holocaust. But so utterly comprehensive was the annihilation of European Jewry that we can say, almost unbelievably, that the Budapest Jews got off relatively lightly. Even the Jews in the immediate environs of Budapest, such as those in Újpest just 10 kilometres to the immediate north, experienced near complete obliteration.

Those Jews in Budapest who lived to tell the tale (or those like Béla Guttmann, who lived but hardly told any of the tale) owe their rare survival to a number of factors.

First, Hungary was on Germany's side in the Second World War and wasn't therefore occupied by the Nazis and their killing machine until

* The pro-Nazi Arrow Cross party led the Hungarian government from October 1944 to March 1945.

eleven months before the eventual Soviet victory. (That is not to say things had exactly been rosy for the Jews in Hungary since the start of the war. Up to 19,000 Jews, in the main foreign nationals but also including plenty of Hungarian citizens, were deported to Ukraine in 1941, where most were murdered. The anti-Jewish laws, severely restricting Jewish commerce and employment, had resulted in an estimated 220,000 losing their livelihood. Jews were excluded from army service, but many were forced to perform unarmed military labour service instead. Between 25,000 and 40,000 Jewish labour servicemen perished before the German invasion, either during Hungarian military action on the Russian front, in Soviet captivity, or at the hands of brutal Hungarian guards and officers.)

Second, Miklós Horthy, still head of the government even after the invasion, called a halt to the deportations to death camps on 6 July, albeit a fraction too late to save the Jews of Újpest. Horthy, fearing military defeat was now inevitable anyway, had buckled under the pressure of international pleas and threats of Allied retaliation. The Jews of Budapest, who had been left until last, were thus spared deportation.

Third, by the time Horthy was overthrown by the pro-Nazi Arrow Cross party in October 1944, the highly efficient apparatus of mass murder was crumbling as the war reached its conclusion. In November, Heinrich Himmler, the head of the SS, ordered the destruction of all gas chambers at Auschwitz in an attempt to eliminate evidence. The Arrow Cross therefore had to resort to the messy methods favoured by the Einsatzgruppen in Poland and the Soviet Union at the start of the war, shooting Jews rather than gassing them.*

Fourth, tens of thousands of Jewish lives were saved by the intervention of neutral nations such as Switzerland and Sweden, which distributed protective passes and established an international ghetto of safe

* SS death squads

houses in Budapest, and by the heroism of individual diplomats from those countries, such as Carl Lutz and Raoul Wallenberg.

• • •

This background, detailing the experience of the Jews in Újpest and Budapest, is essential if we are to grasp the sheer improbability of Béla Guttmann's survival during this very time and in those very places.

So how exactly did he survive?

If you go on the web and read articles and book excerpts dealing with Guttmann, the war years are always glossed over with a sentence or two. The substance of these couple of sentences hardly varies from article to article. And what's more, the substance is almost always entirely false.

Here are just some examples of many:

The exact details of his experiences were never divulged. What is known is that he somehow made it safely to Switzerland, where he lived out the war in an internment camp. – *World Soccer magazine*, June 2014.

While family members, including a brother, perished in concentration camps, Guttmann escaped to Switzerland where he was held in internment. – CNN.com, May 2013.

It seems probable that contacts from Hakoah helped him escape to Switzerland, where he was interned. It was certainly there that Guttmann met his wife. – Jonathan Wilson in *Inverting the Pyramid* (2008).

Guttmann's older brother died in a concentration camp during the war, but he is reported to have spent the war years in an internment camp in Switzerland. – *New York Times*, May 2013.

There are suspicions that he took refuge with former Hakoah members in Switzerland, although there is no evidence for that. Likewise, little is known about how and where he met his wife Mariann, but the wedding took place in 1942. – Hardy Grüne (alias R. Keifu) in *Die Trainerlegende* (2001).

Family members were certainly murdered, but both his brothers survived. He didn't get married in 1942, but in 1945. Neither Guttmann nor his wife were anywhere near Switzerland.

The detail of the real story is actually rather more extraordinary than the conventional wisdom, and can be summarised as follows:

This great football manager, the José Mourinho of the post-war era, spent months crawling around an Újpest attic as thousands of his fellow Jews across the street and around the corner were being herded like sardines into ghetto houses and trains, and then transported to their gruesome deaths. After surviving the deportation from Újpest, he then spent months in the extremely harsh conditions of forced labour camps in both Budapest and Vác, a small Hungarian town near the capital. Just before he was about to be transported from there to an almost certain death in Nazi Germany in the winter of 1944–45, he somehow escaped together with another great Jewish football manager. Several members of his family, including his father and sister, were gassed at Auschwitz.

Heroic non-Jews who risked their lives to save Jews in Europe during the Holocaust were relatively few in number. Lutz and Wallenberg were two. Guttmann owed his life to a less celebrated hero.

• • •

To piece together what happened to Béla Guttmann during 1944–45, and indeed in the earlier war years when Hungarian Jews were victimised and severely endangered but not yet earmarked for

total extermination, we cannot speak to any direct descendants who might have been privy to the intimate details of the story. Guttmann did not have any children. Instead, we have to rely principally on two written sources, both published in Hungarian.

One is an interview that Guttmann gave to the Hungarian sports journalist Tibor Hámori, published in 1984 (three years after Guttmann's death) in the book *Régi gólok, edzősorsok* (Old goals, the fate of coaches). In this interview, an elderly Guttmann talks at length about his past life.

The other is an interview with Pál Moldoványi, published in 2015.* Moldoványi is the nephew of Guttmann's wife Mariann.

Guttmann had met Mariann Moldován, a non-Jewish daughter of a hairdresser in Újpest, during the glory season of 1938/39. Along with her two sisters, she had apparently been very much in demand among the menfolk of the area, and Guttmann's trademark competitiveness stood him in good stead.

'The Moldován girls were pretty, striking and elegant, always having the latest haircuts,' says their nephew. 'Males circled around the house: footballers, actors, comedians and a coach, of course. In the end, it was Béla who won the cup, but he had to fight for Mariann.'

Pál Moldoványi echoes Grüne's opinion that they got married in 1942. This struck me as highly doubtful, as I was aware that marriages between Jews and Gentiles, and extra-marital sexual relations between a Jewish man and a Gentile woman (but not vice versa), had been banned as part of the Third Jewish Law, which came into

* The interview was included as an appendix to the Hungarian translation of Detlev Claussen's biography of Guttmann, first published in German in 2006. In that original book, despite missing some crucial and already published evidence, Claussen's instinct was sharper than most. He wrote: 'Guttmann disappeared in the years 1939–45. To date, it is unclear where he survived the years of World War 2. He probably remained hidden in Budapest. He supposedly married his wife Mariann in 1942, but where is not known.' Of Guttmann's family, Claussen talks only of an unnamed brother 'in a German concentration camp in 1945'.

force in August 1941, under penalty of five years' imprisonment for both parties. Later on, while researching Guttmann's application for Austrian citizenship in 1956, I discovered that they were married only after the war had ended, in November 1945.

But whatever their marital status, it won't have been easy to stop tongues wagging. It was surely common knowledge that Guttmann was in a relationship with an attractive non-Jewish woman – an illegal activity in itself – and a host of jealous potential informants would have made his predicament yet more precarious when the deportations started in 1944. Not that there weren't already plenty in Újpest who would have been happy to see the back of him. 'Even though Béla didn't have much money back then, people were still envious of him because of his success as a coach, and they started Jew-bashing him,' says Moldoványi.

On the career front, meanwhile, circumstances demanded that he tread water in the early war years. Having left his job as Újpest coach in 1939, Guttmann had once again faced the prospect of penury. (Some biographical sources have stated that Guttmann coached Salgótarján, a second-division team in north-eastern Hungary, for the 1939/40 season. This is incorrect. The coach in question was actually Emil Guttmann, not Béla.)

Some unspecified time later, perhaps taking pity on him and feeling a sense of guilt about the circumstances of his departure as coach, the Újpest president Lipót Aschner had an idea to help Guttmann. This was typical of the benevolent Aschner, who had got round the legal limit on the proportion of the Jewish employees at his industrial enterprises by hiring as many new non-Jews as necessary, whatever the financial cost.

Although he couldn't now have a Jew in the conspicuous position of coach, he could certainly use Guttmann's skills and experience in the background, away from the glare of the authorities. 'Come and be my secret advisor,' Aschner said. With the Hungarian league

continuing as normal until 1944, Guttmann went to watch Újpest's performances up and down the country and reported back to Aschner on their shortcomings. In this way, Guttmann was saved from destitution.

(Our only clue indicating when this informal employment took effect can be found in Guttmann's interview with Hámori. The actual excerpt reads as follows: 'He [Aschner] got [Lajos] Lutz to be the coach for Újpest instead of me immediately. And I was left there without a job. I mean ... one day Aschner caught me: "Listen to me, come and be my secret advisor."'

In actual fact, Lutz did not become Újpest coach until 1943, four years after Guttmann had been forced to vacate the position, with the club hiring two other coaches in between. It is my suspicion that Lutz loomed large in Guttmann's memory because he was the coach in charge when Aschner made his offer of the scouting position. If this is the case, the question of how Guttmann supported himself for four years remains unclear. Given his excommunication from football, and the huge obstacles facing Jews in the employment market, it seems that considerable poverty would have been inescapable. As we shall see later from his nephew Imre's testimony, what we do know is that he lived at some stage during this period with his younger brother Ernő and his wife Margit, and that his relationship with Mariann had continued. Otherwise, this period in Guttmann's life has been blurred by the fog of war.)

Meanwhile, Mariann's only brother, the father of Pál Moldoványi and bearing the same first name, had inherited the family hairdressing business. (Mariann's brother was known as Pál Moldován, while his son later adopted the ancestral version of the surname.) He ran two salons in Újpest, one in the town's theatre and one on the intersection of Árpád Way, Virág Street and Petőfi Street. He, his wife and two-year-old daughter lived in an apartment next to the latter salon. It was above this apartment, on the very outskirts of

the ghetto in which thousands of Újpest Jews were squeezed, that Pál Moldován hid his future brother-in-law Béla Guttmann from those intent on killing him.*

• • •

Pál Moldoványi was born two years after the war, and his testimony will have been based on later conversations with his parents and relatives. Many family histories, no matter how gripping, inevitably lose some of their accuracy through forgetfulness, selective memory, the desultory nature of everyday discourse between family members, or a lack of rigorous questioning on the part of the younger generation. It is no surprise, as we saw with his estimate of when Béla's marriage to Mariann took place, that the chronology of Moldoványi's account is not fully coherent.

For example, he doesn't specify the exact time Guttmann went into hiding. We are left to assume that he did so in the weeks before the Jews of Újpest were rounded up into the ghetto in May 1944.

Guttmann told his interviewer Hámori that he was working in his consulting role for Aschner right until the Nazi invasion two months before the roundup. He even found out about the invasion while working away from home. On Sunday 19 March, the very day the Nazis moved in, he was watching Újpest lose 2–1 in Nagyvárad, a city then part of Hungary, and now known as Oradea in western Romania.

'At half time, Gábor Kompóti Kléber, the journalist, came to me and whispered in my ear: "Béla, we have a big problem,"' Guttmann recalled. '"The Germans have marched into Budapest!" On the way back people were checked, but I got off the train before Pest and escaped it all.' In the immediate aftermath of the invasion, with the

* A small car park can now be found on this site, opposite a confectionery store.

centre of Budapest crawling with recently arrived German soldiers, he instead sought the familiar security of his girlfriend and her family in Újpest.

The hiding place was in the corner of the attic of Pál Moldován's apartment. 'It was a good hiding place,' says Moldoványi:

> There was a ladder leading up to the attic, and a little corner at the back [of the attic] could hardly be noticed. When you looked in through the attic door, you could only see this long room, you couldn't make out the little corner at the back. The Nazis were lazy; they didn't climb the forty to fifty metres on the dusty beams to reach the back. My father walked around there with a plank of wood on purpose, so that dust would stay on the floor, and his footsteps wouldn't be seen. He always put the plank in front of him and he went in and out like that if he had to do so.

The authorities, their suspicions no doubt roused by local gossip, hunted for Guttmann several times. 'The gendarmes turned up at Mariann's on several occasions,' says Moldoványi:

> Once the Gestapo raided my father's shop and the apartment, too. My mother was a Swabian girl, she spoke very good German and convinced them that we were a decent Catholic family. In the meantime, Béla was hiding up in the attic. My mother was so shocked by the event and so afraid that she took my two-year-old sister and moved to Nagykovácsi [a small town a few kilometres from Budapest] to her parents and stayed there until the end of the war.

Moldoványi's mother was extremely angry that her husband had risked the life and security of his young daughter by hiding Guttmann. But the strongly anti-fascist Pál Moldován was nothing if not a man of redoubtable resolve and courage in the face of extreme danger.

At one point, someone informed on Moldován himself to the authorities. 'They probably realised that Mariann was my father's sister and they knew they were hiding Jews,' explains his son. 'My father was caught and taken to a hearing when he was on his way to the shops. First, they just shouted at him, calling him a "dirty Jew-lover", but after my father swore at them, they hanged him by his feet and beat him up.'

Guttmann, meanwhile, was not the most reliable and patient of fugitives. Perhaps it would have been too much to expect a much-travelled and highly successful professional sportsman and coach to stay cooped up for months on end, but Guttmann engaged frequently in impromptu walkabouts. 'Often he got really lucky that he didn't get caught,' says Moldoványi. 'What's more, it was terribly hard to hold him back. He always wanted to go somewhere and he often did get away from home.'

One time, seeking safety during one of the unrelenting Allied air raids, he was stopped and interrogated in the street. But yet again, Guttmann had Lady Luck on his side. 'He was walking in the street without a yellow star or anything. One of the policemen who was also there knew my grandmother, and he vouched for his identity saying that "this is a Christian family, I know them",' says Moldoványi. 'After this event, Béla became more cautious.'

• • •

Guttmann's spell in hiding in 1944 and early 1945 was interrupted by time spent in a labour camp. But we can only estimate when he entered the institution, and how long he was there.

In June 1944, concerned about the shortage of manpower available to perform war-related tasks, Hungarian Minister of Defence Lajos Csatay issued instructions for every Jewish male between the ages of eighteen and forty-eight to report to a labour camp. For

the next four months, this labour service offered a reasonable route to survival.

But after the Arrow Cross coup on 15 October 1944, the government handed over a large number of labour service battalions to the Germans. Conditions rapidly deteriorated. Around 70,000 Jews were transported to Nazi Austria in November and December 1944, through forced marches and rail deportations. Those prisoners who did manage to survive the extreme slave labour conditions building fortifications along the Hungarian–Austrian border were sent on further death marches and trains to various concentration camps in early 1945, where many of the remainder died.

When exactly within this four-month window did Guttmann report for duty? Some call-up notices to forced labour camps were actually handed out in ghettos prior to deportation. Such people would have clearly viewed labour service as the preferable alternative, and had no choice anyway as their whereabouts was known to the authorities. The Újpest rabbi, whose testimony we saw at the start of the chapter, revealed that a number of men from the Újpest ghetto were called into labour service at the start of June when Csatay's order took effect, a month before the liquidation of the ghetto.

But Guttmann would have already been in his hideout in June in order to avoid being placed in the ghetto in the first place. A good bet would be that he stayed there for a matter of weeks or months after Csatay's order, but then, alarmed by the close shaves with the authorities, he decided that the safest option would be to report for labour service. Despite the halt in deportations to the death camps at the beginning of July, rumours were rife that they would start again at any moment. Horthy did indeed approve the resumption under heavy German pressure in August, before the increasingly dire military situation allowed him to renege on his commitment.

We can also speculate that Guttmann would have at least waited until the Újpest Jews had all been deported in early July before

venturing out of his hiding place. Up to that point, would he have risked his intrepid walkabouts around Újpest, or left the attic to report for labour service, when he could have been severely punished for disobeying the earlier order for all Jews to live in the ghetto?

There is no way that anyone would have opted for labour duty once the Arrow Cross had taken power in October and started handing over Jews to the Germans. So, most probably, Guttmann arrived at his labour camp between early July and October 1944.

It might have been preferable to Auschwitz, but this was still a brutal experience, particularly after October. In the most open portrayal on record of his Holocaust experiences, the man with two European Cups to his name told Hámori what life was like there:

> We were ordered around in a gruff manner: up with the [yellow star] arm-band, take the shovel, shut up! I was taken to Vác [a town north of Budapest]. From here, I was taken to Erdőváros then to Timót street [both in Budapest, in the south of the city]. Young people today don't even know what kind of place Timót street was like then. Our sergeant had served in the French Legion: that's where he learned how to torture people. If he was in a good mood, he only made us carry tarred stones to his bunker and we had to keep shouting in the meantime 'we are shit, we are shit!' Was I a footballer from the national team, was I a successful coach? Was I a man? Who cared, you had to forget all about it! And how much more humiliation, my friend!

• • •

In December 1944, with preparations afoot to transport his labour company by train to concentration camps and almost certain death, Guttmann plotted his escape. One of his accomplices in the escape was Ernő Egri Erbstein.

Guttmann will have encountered Erbstein in 1927, when the

latter was a member of the Palestine Maccabees team who toured the United States and played the New York Giants. With their careers following a similar path into coaching, he will have continued to keep tabs on him throughout the 1930s. Erbstein had travelled to Italy, taking charge of several clubs including the illustrious Torino, before being forced out in 1939 by anti-Semitic pressure from the Mussolini government and returning to his home city of Budapest.

Whether Guttmann had befriended Erbstein during the early war years and they had enlisted for the labour camp together, or whether they simply bumped into each other while working there, we don't know. But in a remarkable account, Guttmann describes how these two men conspired to free themselves from the clutches of death:

> Our company was put on a train and taken to Germany. But before that, five of us had jumped out of a window on the first floor and escaped from the settlement. We'd been studying the area for days, watching when the guards changed, we had softened the ground so that we wouldn't break our ankles, then ... Hold on ... Who were those five men? Sanyi Gál, the actor I can see him before me, I wonder if he's still alive. Ernő Egri was also among us ... I cannot remember the other three even if you beat me to death.

The escapees went their separate ways as soon as they were clear of danger. Guttmann doesn't go into any detail about what happened next, merely saying: 'The point is, I was saved. Because there were kind people who took a risk and hid me.'

It stands to reason that Guttmann will have again sought out Mariann and her family, his past saviours. Pál Moldoványi, in his interview, never mentions Guttmann's time in the forced labour camp. But he does describe an incident that could well relate to the aftermath of the escape. 'One night my father was called over from

the other block by one of the neighbours whose phone was still working,' he says:

> The neighbour said someone wanted to talk to him. It was Béla, he had got into trouble. He said he couldn't stay at the place right where he was. My father went to him on his tricycle and hiding him under some sheets, he took him home, but from where I don't know.

Guttmann had then to get through the remaining weeks until the last Germans in Budapest finally surrendered on 13 February 1945. Despite the fact that they were facing inevitable defeat in those last chaotic weeks of fierce fighting, the manic German thirst for Jewish blood remained unquenched. Adolf Eichmann, the Nazi who masterminded the logistics for the mass murder of Hungarian Jewry, even planned a total massacre of the Jewish ghetto in Budapest as late as mid-January 1945. The plan was aborted only after Raoul Wallenberg got wind of it, and managed to convey a message to the German military general in charge of Budapest that he would be held directly responsible for this crime.

As well as the constant shootings into the Danube, there was also the little matter of the Budapest siege to contend with. In December, Soviet troops had encircled the city. Terrible food shortages ensued, with around 25,000 people dying of starvation. Bodies piled up in the streets of the ghetto, or in the courtyard of the city's main synagogue.

At some point around this time, the Arrow Cross sent the fearless and insubordinate Pál Moldován to a labour camp. 'When my father was taken into forced labour, Mariann didn't know what to do with Béla or where to take him,' his son says. 'In the end, she managed to hide him somewhere in the Tunsgram factory for a week.* Then he came back.'

* Tunsgram is a Hungarian manufacturer of electronic equipment.

Even in the weeks following the German surrender, abhorrent acts of cruelty and violence continued under Soviet occupation. 'Rape is causing the greatest suffering to the Hungarian population,' reads a Swiss embassy report from the time. 'Violations are so general – from the age of 10 up to 70 years – that few women in Hungary escape this fate. Acts of incredible brutality have been registered. Many women prefer to commit suicide in order to escape monstrosities.'

Pillaging was also widespread. 'Russian troops looted the city freely,' the report continued. 'They entered practically every habitation, the very poorest as well as the richest. They took away everything they wanted, especially food, clothing and valuables.'

• • •

Béla Guttmann somehow made it to the end of war unscathed, save some hellish memories. The same could not be said for several of his loved ones. Slowly but surely, I have pieced together what happened to them through the help of Jewish researchers in Hungary, through my own investigations, and through my conversations with Béla's nephew Imre Guttmann, a retired textile merchant in his mid-eighties and living near São Paulo in Brazil.

Béla's mother, Eszter, was lucky enough to escape the carnage, dying at the age of sixty-five in December 1941 from complications related to diabetes. Her gravestone, in the Kozma Street Jewish cemetery in Budapest, was apparently erected in 1947, probably by her two sons then living in the city, Béla and Ernő. The inscription reads: 'Our mother, Guttmann Ábrahámné,* 1876–1941. Commemorating Ábrahám Guttmann, Szerén Guttmann, Ervin Guttmann, who died abroad.'

* In formal Hungarian, a woman gives up her first name and adds the suffix -né to her husband's name.

'Died abroad' stretches the meaning of the word 'euphemism' to its very limits, suggesting that Béla Guttmann's family had moved out of choice to some foreign place where they all died peacefully in their beds, surrounded by loved ones. 'Abroad' was in fact Auschwitz, and they most likely 'died' only after being gassed.

Although Eszter died in a Budapest hospital, her death certificate states her permanent residence as 'Debreczeny Street, Miskolc'. Before I had the photo of the gravestone or even knew the names of Béla's siblings, I had trawled the victims' database of the Yad Vashem Holocaust museum in Jerusalem in an attempt to find his parents. The only Ábrahám Guttmann I could find with his birth year of 1866 (his age was on Béla's birth certificate I had in my possession) had lived in Miskolc, an industrial city in north-eastern Hungary, 150 kilometres from Budapest. Although I noted that several murdered Guttmanns were also from Miskolc, I didn't pay this much attention as I had assumed the family had still been living in the capital.

But then Zsolt Gulyás, a Hungarian Guttmann enthusiast who had conducted the interview with Pál Moldoványi, sent me the photo of Eszter's grave. Szerén Guttmann and Ervin Guttmann, the names on the grave, were also on the list of 10,831 names of Holocaust victims from Miskolc and surrounding areas, compiled by the few local survivors after the war. The puzzle was coming together. But who exactly were they?

I commissioned specialist Jewish researchers in Hungary, a company called Etz Hachaim, to find out more. They discovered details about two of Béla's siblings – Szerén, a sister five years his senior, and Ernő, a brother two years younger than Béla.

Szerén married Majer Rosenfeld, a merchant, in 1913. According to the Budapest electoral roll, they were still living with her parents in 1930. For whatever reason, it seems that Szerén, her husband and parents had all moved to Miskolc by 1941. Perhaps Majer was

pursuing a business opportunity there, and Szerén's parents, not getting any younger, decided to join their daughter and son-in-law. Perhaps they all considered it somehow safer to be outside the capital. But by moving to Miskolc, they had all unknowingly reduced their chances of surviving the imminent Holocaust to almost zero.

Soon after the German takeover of Hungary in March 1944, the normal procedure was followed in Miskolc. The Jews were ordered to wear yellow stars and confined to a ghetto, with most housed in a large shed that previously operated as a brick factory. 'The overcrowding was unbearable,' recalled one survivor, Edith Potok. 'In this shed there were no elementary sanitary arrangements or enough living space.'

They stayed there for several weeks, before deportations to Auschwitz began. Edith Potok describes the conditions that Béla Guttmann's family, including his 78-year-old father Abrahám, would have been forced to endure on this journey:

We were brought to the train station. With screaming and beating they forced us into the cattle cars. The one and only window in each cattle car had barbed wire on it. The car was filled completely with people without any room at all. At each stop they would bring in a small container, a little bit of water. The conditions were excruciatingly inhumane. The train sped on for many days till we got to a large gate. On it was written: *Arbeit Macht Frei* (work sets you free). We had arrived at Auschwitz.

Abrahám, if he had not already died on the journey, would have been gassed on arrival due to his advanced age. Majer (56), also on the Yad Vashem victims' database, and Szerén (50), would probably have met the same, immediate fate.

Etz Hachaim did not have any documents on Ervin Guttmann, the remaining name on Eszter's gravestone. Nor did they possess

anything on Ármin Guttmann, the brother who played alongside
Béla at his first club, Törekvés, and escaped with him to Novi Sad
during the White Terror.

A Hungarian contact had informed me that Ármin had died in
Buchenwald in January 1945, which tallied with several references
I had seen to a brother who had died in a concentration camp. I
was sent the relevant web page with the details of the said Ármin
Guttmann. It read: 'Ármin Guttmann – Date of birth: 27.10.1893 in
Budapest. Date of death: 03.01.1945. Place of death: Buchenwald.'

But a closer examination of Szerén's birth certificate revealed
that this Ármin could not be the right one, that this was instead
one of the dozen or so other Ármin Guttmanns murdered in the
Holocaust. Szerén was born on 25 April 1894, only six months after
the alleged birth date of her brother.

So what did happen to the real Ármin? And who was Ervin?
Around this point, someone sent to me an interview with Imre
Guttmann, Béla's nephew, which had appeared in a Hungarian
Jewish community magazine in 2014. In this interview, Imre talks
of his memories of Béla, and his own wartime experiences, but
doesn't go into detail about the fate of the overall family. I managed
to track down the interviewer and author of the article, a Budapest
tour operator named Róbert Vago Wallenstein, and asked him for
Imre's phone number.

Imre seemed to be my only hope of getting to the full story. I sat
at my desk in London, and called the number in Brazil. Imre an-
swered. He spoke in faltering but understandable English. He was
delighted to help. I peppered him with just a few of the countless
questions my brain was generating. By the end of this first ten-
minute conversation with the nephew of a man whose life story had
become something of an obsession for me over the previous two
years, I was shaking and close to tears.

Ármin was the second of the four siblings, born after Szerén.

Imre's father was Ernő, the youngest of the four. Ármin's only child was a son called Ervin, born in the same year as his cousin Imre, 1930. The fourteen-year-old Ervin was murdered at Auschwitz in 1944, alongside his mother, Ármin's wife Irén, aged forty-one. I found her name on another list of former Miskolc residents, also put together by survivors from the town after the war. Before being forced into the ghetto, she and Ervin had lived together with Abráhám, Szerén and Majer, still on Debreczeny Street.

It later emerged that Ármin played as an amateur for Attila Miskolc from 1927 to 1932, and had probably lived there since then. His sister and parents must have followed him there. He himself had been sent to a labour camp before the deportation to Auschwitz, but had survived. He returned to Miskolc after the war, remarried to a non-Jewish woman, and ran a very popular dance school from the same family house on Debreczeny Street, a place full of the ghosts of his tragic past.* According to a knowledgeable contact inside the local Jewish community, he kept quiet about his Jewish identity during these post-war years. Ármin Guttmann died in Miskolc in 1975, thirty years later than previously believed by those writing about the life of his famous brother. (The Miskolc Jewish community later provided me with a photograph of his grave in the city's Jewish cemetery. It reads: Ármin Guttmann, dance teacher, 1896–1975, and his son Ervin Guttmann, 1930–1944, a victim of Hitlerism.)

As for Imre, he attributes his own survival to Béla and Mariann, and to her brother Pál Moldován. 'We survived the Holocaust thanks to the acquaintances he [Moldován] had,' he confirms. (We could say, indeed, that Béla Guttmann's decision to enter into a close relationship with a non-Jewish woman opened up the contacts that ultimately led to his and Imre's survival. This, it appears, was not an uncommon story.)

* Debreczeny Street was renamed Régiposta Street at some point after the war.

Speaking of his relationship with Béla, Imre says that 'the two of us became good friends'. He continues:

> I became his favourite relative from our family maybe because I didn't only accept [his Christian girlfriend], but also loved her very much … It was Mariann who was hiding my uncle in her flat [*sic*] and I was also given a fake certificate of baptism. At the age of fourteen I worked in Pest at a bakery which catered for the army. I felt relatively safe until the bakery was destroyed by bombing. After that, I lived on the streets. I was in hiding. When my papers got stolen I had to go to my [maternal] grandparents, who lived in a house in the city centre.

At that point, Imre's young life sunk to the depths. 'The Arrow Cross took all of us from there to the ghetto on 10 January 1945,' he said. 'On our way there, my grandfather was beaten to death with a rifle butt and I had to bury him, within ten minutes, in a pit dug out by a spoon.' It is an account corroborated by the death certificate of his maternal grandfather Mihály Hegedüs in the Budapest city records.

Imre's parents, Ernő and Margit, 'were deported but, miraculously, both of them returned'. Imre left Hungary after the Communist takeover in 1948, eventually settling in Brazil in 1954. His parents later joined their only child. His father Ernő, Béla's younger brother, died in 1970.

What about the central hero of Béla Guttmann's wartime story? Pál Moldován was rewarded for his awe-inspiring courage by having his hairdressing business expropriated by the post-war Communist government. In 1958, he managed to emigrate with his family to Bad Wimpfen in southern Germany, and died from cancer in nearby Heilbronn in 1975, aged sixty-five.

• • •

Béla Guttmann is one of the greatest figures in post-war world football. So why then is his experience in the Holocaust glossed over, and why are the details fed to us about these years so often incorrect?

Establishing that he was not in a Swiss internment camp is a relatively simple task. One email to the Swiss government department responsible for the records of foreign refugees during this period raised my own suspicions at a very early stage of my research. 'We found quite many [*sic*] files for the name "Guttmann" but not for "Bela",' came the reply. I did some searching myself on the relevant database supplied to me. No sign of Béla Guttmann, or of any Guttmann (or similar spelling) with anything approximating his date of birth. An oversight, perhaps? The Swiss authorities are not known for their bureaucratic sloppiness.

Of course, as some have indeed speculated, he could feasibly have been smuggled into Switzerland towards the start of the war without those authorities knowing. There are certainly accounts of Jews who were saved in this way. But when we establish that he was in Hungary in 1944, this theory loses plausibility. Would Guttmann have risked travelling through Fascist Italy or Nazi Austria back to a country from which he had supposedly already fled, and which had adopted highly repressive laws against Jews? We can say, without much fear of contradiction, that he was in Hungary throughout the war.*

Indeed, the 2014 interview with Imre Guttmann suggests that his uncle Béla was living with him and his parents, Ernő and Margit, in

* Guttmann would have surely contemplated returning to the United States in the early years of the war. As I learned from the United States Citizen and Immigration Services, his return to Europe in 1938 wouldn't necessarily have invalidated his permanent residency visa. More than 10,000 Jews who managed to get to the port of Lisbon in neutral Portugal did indeed sail across the Atlantic until 1942. We can only speculate that the dangers of the trip through war-torn Europe to Lisbon, plus his blossoming relationship with Mariann, persuaded him to stay put and hope that things would eventually improve in Hungary.

Budapest in the early stages of the war, probably in the years before the scouting role with Újpest. 'In many ways he was different from my parents, who didn't approve of his living with us, his not getting married but being in love with a Christian woman,' he said.

The received wisdom about Guttmann's wartime experiences reflects, perhaps, a frightening aspect of the internet era, and we are all at times unwitting victims. If a falsehood is mentioned on the web often enough, we can easily be persuaded to accept it as the truth and repeat it, further cementing the falsehood's credibility.

But Guttmann died long before the internet dominated our lives. It seems reasonable to suspect that the myth about the Swiss internment camp either originated with him, or more probably, was not denied by him when other people at some point conjured up the false rumour. So why did Guttmann behave in this way, at least until his interview with Hámori in the years leading up to his death in 1981?

In 1964, he published *Die Béla Guttmann Story* in partnership with the Hungarian football coach and author Jenö Csaknády. The book was partly written in the first person, as if by Guttmann, and partly in the third person. Its section on the Holocaust years lasted three sentences in a book of more than 80,000 words:

> In the last fifteen years, countless books have been written about the destructive years of struggle for life and death. It would thus be superfluous to trouble our readers with such details. In these years, Guttmann suffered and endured no more or less than many millions of his European contemporaries.

There is no mention of the word 'Jew' in the entire book, and only cursory references to his career at Hakoah Vienna or New York Hakoah (although there are several to the 'All-Stars', without the offending Hakoah prefix). When Guttmann's wife died in 2000,

his personal collection of photos taken during his career was found and sold at auction. Although he included several of these photos in the 1964 publication, he used not one of the many in the collection from his Hakoah days, with that problematic Star of David emblazoned on his shirt.

This book was written in German, less than two decades after Guttmann was crouched in a dark attic desperately hiding from a German regime which had decreed that he should be put to death. He clearly had no wish to broach, even indirectly, this rather delicate issue with the mostly German and Austrian (and male) target readership, many of whom will themselves have either been involved in atrocities against Jews, approved of them, or turned a blind eye to them.

In the very year the book was published, Guttmann was coach of the Austrian national team. As we shall see later, he resigned from this position, citing anti-Semitism within the governing football body in that country. This was hardly a favourable environment in which to launch into an open recounting of Holocaust experiences or a discussion of his unmistakably Jewish upbringing, social network and playing career. Guttmann will have instinctively known this.

Such conversations would have been similarly awkward in most of the countries where Guttmann lived and worked after the war. Hungary was on the Germans' side in the war, and the authorities played an important role in the murder of 600,000 Jews, implementing, often brutally, the Nazi policy of ghettoisation and deportation; the Romanians had participated in the general Jew-killing with much enthusiasm and no small measure of creativity in their favoured methods of slaughter; Italy, too, had been Nazi allies, and thousands of its Jews had been murdered; South American countries, mostly Argentina and Brazil, had welcomed 9,000 Nazi war criminals as citizens after the Holocaust.

Although it is wrong to say that no survivors talked and wrote openly about their experiences in the immediate post-war period, general discussion and cultural representation of the Holocaust mushroomed from the 1970s onwards. This is no coincidence. A new generation had grown up in Europe without blood on its hands. The intense discomfort felt in hearing Holocaust stories had subsided somewhat, albeit far from completely. Few enjoy admitting that their father or grandfather could well have been a murderer, or that their nation had recently been active or complicit in genocide.

It wasn't just sensibilities that were at stake, either. The prevailing post-war ideological framework within Europe ensured that open discussion of the Holocaust was stifled. Many European non-Jews, such as the Hungarians raped and pillaged by the Soviets, had also suffered. Lumping everyone together as victims helped to deflect attention away from their own participation in the Holocaust, while preserving the collective self-esteem necessary for the massive rebuilding process after the war.

This utilitarian history was particularly evident in eastern Europe. Hungary and Romania, where Guttmann spent the immediate post-war years, had both become Soviet satellite states. Distinct national identities were whitewashed. Jewish culture, education and religious observance were all suppressed, and prominent Jews victimised. Jewish-centric narratives about the war years were similarly frowned upon. 'The official line was that what had happened prior to the Russian liberation of Hungary was that the Fascists persecuted the anti-Fascists,' writes the historian Raphael Patai. 'The Communist leadership rejected the idea of special Jewish suffering, saying that "in the old system, the entire working people suffered".'

Further afield, it inevitably took some years for historians and researchers to digest and register the sheer scale and the specific nature of Jewish persecution. The BBC, for example, edited any mention of Jews out of the famous Richard Dimbleby broadcast

from the Bergen-Belsen concentration camp in 1945. According to Dimbleby's son Jonathan, the organisation had feared that 'if you mentioned one group of people and not others, it might seem biased or wrong'. The term 'Holocaust' itself did not become common parlance until the mid-1960s at the earliest in the English-speaking world.

So Guttmann played to the gallery of the time. We all experienced bad times, didn't we, so let's put the war aside and talk about football instead.

For their part, European football journalists of the time seemed content to let Guttmann get away with this reticence. They were remarkably incurious, and not one appeared to deem the mystery of Guttmann's wartime years, or the fate of his family, sufficiently interesting to investigate with any vigour.

Neither of two lengthy profiles of Guttmann in the prestigious *World Soccer* magazine, both written by the experienced football journalist Eric Batty and published in 1961 and 1965 respectively, discuss his playing career in Jewish teams, or say anything whatsoever about his Jewish heritage or his wartime experiences as a Jew.

'Apart from one season with Bucharest club Ciokanal [*sic*], Mr. Guttmann remained in Hungary [*sic*] from 1938 until 1949,' writes Batty in 1961. What is this nonsense? *Remained in Hungary*? This sentence doesn't just involve a minor omission. There is a gaping void here, and it is laughable.

In the 1965 article, Batty characterises Guttmann as a 'Hungarian-born, naturalised Austrian'. No 'J' word to be seen in this article either, nor the 'H' word or anything similar for that matter. To define Guttmann simply as an 'Austrian', whatever was written on his passport, again borders on the farcical.

This sidestepping of the destruction of European Jewry may be partly explained by men being men, often preferring to talk about sport than anything truly serious. And, of course, many of the

journalists of the time will have fought in the war and lost friends and family themselves, and so were more inured to suffering than more recent pampered generations in the West.

But it still seems bizarrely neglectful, to say the least, for seasoned story writers to completely overlook the remarkable human story of a central-European Jew coaching a football team to successive European Cups sixteen years after the Holocaust. Even if they believed the Switzerland fabrication (and Batty's articles suggest that the story hadn't entered English-speaking folklore by the mid-1960s), Guttmann would still have been a refugee fleeing from genocide whose family was murdered.

(Indeed, it seems that some of the truth about Guttmann's Holocaust experiences was already known in some Jewish circles, if Batty and others had really wanted to use a modicum of their journalistic know-how to discover it. A book entitled *Stars of David*, by Arthur Goldman, was published in South Africa in 1963, and contained a chapter on Guttmann. 'With Europe plunged into the holocaust,' writes Goldman, 'he had to do forced labour, but somehow managed to escape a worse fate.')

Embarrassment, shame, a fear of being labelled an anti-Semite just for identifying someone as a Jew, an unwillingness to specify Jewish victimhood – whatever it was, the Jewish question was at that time just too toxic for European journalists. In modern parlance, they just didn't want to go there. The continent had not even started to come to grips with the enormity of what had happened, and the silence was deafening.

Meanwhile, the battered vestiges of European Jewish communities were unsurprisingly reeling from the shock of near-genocide. Many instinctively reacted to the recent memory of being hunted down as Jews by playing down or even (like Ármin Guttmann) hiding their Jewishness, rendering them less likely to be vocal about their specifically Jewish experience during the Holocaust. 'After the

war, some French Jews were reluctant to mark their sons through circumcision, and conversions and name-changing became a noticeable phenomenon,' writes Paula Hyman in her book *The Jews of France*. 'Of the name changes that occurred between 1803 and 1957, for example, a startling 85 per cent took place between 1945 and 1957.'

This was hardly irrational paranoia. Violent Jew hatred was rampant in eastern Europe in particular in the years immediately following the Holocaust, and Guttmann himself was the periodic victim of anti-Semitic innuendo and prejudice, particularly in the wake of the most successful chapter in his career when many will have felt that the Jew had got too big for his boots. It seems that in the post-war years at least, Europe was split into two – either awkwardly silent on the Holocaust, or just gamely plodding on with age-old racism against Jews as if the Holocaust had never happened.

The specifically Jewish impulse to generalise the lessons of the Holocaust partly resulted from the understandable fear of hatred and exclusion, and from the corresponding desire to fit in. In 1952, Anne Frank's father, Otto, wrote to a prospective scriptwriter to warn that her now famous diary 'is not a Jewish book, so do not make a Jewish play of it!'

Both Jews and non-Jews might talk more openly about the Holocaust than in the decades immediately following the war, but the tendency to generalise has remained a constant theme throughout. Even today, Holocaust museums and memorials frequently focus on the general message of intolerance, as if intolerance per se, a regrettable but ubiquitous human failing, resulted in countless children and babies being herded into gas chambers.

This universalist approach to the lessons of the Holocaust skirts around a rather more pressing question, namely: why was much of Europe, after many centuries of a remarkably repetitive and widespread history of murder and expulsion of Jews, content to see

modern technology employed in a bid to wipe them out once and for all? 'Anne was at Bergen-Belsen, as she had been while hiding in that annex in Amsterdam where she wrote her diary, because she was a Jew,' writes Walter Reich, an academic and former director of the United States Holocaust Memorial Museum. 'One can leave the Anne Frank Huis [in Amsterdam] without appreciating this.'

Perhaps those who either create or advise on various Holocaust memorial projects shy away from the salient question for fear of the answer they might find. Perhaps they want to make Holocaust memorials palatable to non-Jews. Perhaps, in Guttmann's case, the assertive Jewishness of the Hakoah years had been bludgeoned by bitter experience, and reshaped by the persistent fashion for Holocaust generalisation, into a more circumspect approach.

Even before the war, we can detect a change in his relationship with Jewishness. On the manifest for the ship on which he arrived in New York in 1926, he and his teammates stated their 'race or people' (as opposed to citizenship) as 'Hebrew'. Returning to the same city on the same ship (RMS *Berengaria*) twelve years later, with Europe's Jews desperately seeking sanctuary, his answer to the same question was 'Magyar'.

Neither should we discount a rather more simple explanation for Guttmann's silence – that he was so traumatised by his experiences that he didn't want to revisit them. 'I understand that Béla didn't talk about this period,' says Pál Moldoványi. 'His family was exterminated. I know a lot of Jews who simply don't like to talk about it.'

When I asked Gunnar Persson, a Swedish journalist who wrote a comprehensive history of Hakoah Vienna, why the remarkable story he documented is now so little known, he replied in a similar vein. Survivors never passed the story down, and hence it was largely forgotten. 'It hurts to talk about things lost, things you have been bereaved of in a brutal manner without any say at all,' says Persson. 'Could be anything. Love, a job or a place. Here it all went at once.'

But it was the desire not to be mired in the horrors of the past, and instead focus on a brighter future, that perhaps represented the most important single factor contributing to the relative Jewish silence in the immediate post-war years. Ferociously ambitious survivors such as Béla Guttmann, still only forty-six at the war's end, had no wish to be defined by victimhood or to wallow in a painful past. His mind, always on the next big job, the next trophy, was successfully diverted from the memories of wailing children and their desperate mothers being marched to their deaths. 'My uncle lived for football only,' says his nephew, Imre. 'He was obsessed with the game.' A point proved, one might add, by the fact that he risked his very life for football in 1938.

In his book, *Against All Odds*, William Helmreich charts the life-affirming stories of many Holocaust survivors who built highly successful careers in a diverse range of fields in the United States after the war. He came to believe that it was the same character traits that helped such people to survive – adaptability, initiative and tenacity – which also explained their later success.

Sheer random chance is perhaps a more convincing explanation. Thousands upon thousands of Jews, possessing in abundance every single one of the traits Helmreich identified, will also have been murdered. But it could certainly be said that one common response to a reprieve from near-certain death is to have no fear, to take risks, to live life to the full, to look forward, not back. We could already see those characteristics in Guttmann before the war, and his Holocaust experiences surely served to consolidate them.

Of course, Guttmann did eventually look back on his labour camp experiences in his interview with Hámori. 'You want to hear the inside story?' he had asked Hámori at the start of the interview. 'Sure, I have no reason to keep things secret any more,' he continued. But despite these words, he still did not give a fully honest account.

In Hámori's record of the interview at least, Guttmann neglected to give any detail about his period in hiding, or to talk about what happened to his family. Questions abound. Was he ashamed? Did he feel that hiding was somehow less manly than time in a forced labour camp? Did he feel guilt that he hid while so many of his fellow Újpest Jews were being deported to their deaths? Did he find the murder of his father, sister and wider family too painful to discuss?

Guttmann also failed to make it plain to Hámori why he was in a labour camp in the first place, and made only an oblique reference to being Jewish when saying that the Hungarian Football Association didn't 'let my kind of people work' during the early war years. When the interview took place, probably around 1980, the Communist system was still very much in control in Hungary. The interviewer, the state publisher, the state censor and Guttmann himself may still have been mindful not to specify Jewish suffering.

The narrative he recounted may have been very incomplete, but why did Guttmann choose this moment to reveal anything at all?

By this stage, at least two of the factors inhibiting the truth about his experiences no longer applied. He was retired. There was no job or trophy to pursue. He could let his mind drift to the past, knowing that such reflection was not time wasted when he could be plotting his next triumph. Just maybe, he also felt that this was his last opportunity to open up so that future generations would have some inkling of what he had to overcome in his life.

Meanwhile, the sensibilities of the Hungarian readership would not now be so delicate. Three decades had passed, and a new generation had grown up. When Guttmann talked of being treated brutally by Hungarian guards in a labour camp, his words now represented history, not a direct accusation.

• • •

Back in 1945, despite his horrific ordeals, the fires of ambition were still burning strongly. In the years since he had last sat in the dugout, in that ecstatic Mitropa Cup victory against Ferencváros in 1939, he had lost several members of his family, and many friends and acquaintances. News of what had happened in Miskolc would have trickled through to him at the end of the war, if not before, most likely through his brother Ármin. But the great survivor dusted himself down, wiped the tears from his eyes, and eventually emerged from the rubble of Budapest to take the helm of a football team once more.

CHAPTER 6

THE SURVIVOR RETURNS

Towards the end of May 1946, more than a year after the Nazis had been defeated, two Jews walked into the Budapest offices of Új Élet, *a Hungarian Jewish newspaper. There they recounted the horrific events they had just witnessed in their home village of Kunmadaras, 130 kilometres east of the capital.*

'The Jews returning from deportation were received by a population irked to see them again,' they reported:

> *They did not wish to return the property stolen from the Jews … The plan for the pogrom was born at a meeting held at the local trade union board. The Protestant school issued a warning to the parents that they should not let their children go into the streets unescorted. On the day of the pogrom, at 8 a.m., many women gathered in the marketplace and shouted: 'When do we begin, it's 8 o clock already?' The mob then attacked all the Jews who could be found in the marketplace … they invaded Jewish homes and started to beat up women, old people and children until they bled.*

'They killed Rosinger, a poor carter,' the witnesses continued:

They killed Kuti, a poor pedlar, and pillaged his home. The third victim, Mailander, died from his injuries … Polonyi [a policeman] asked them what the problem was with the Jews. There came an answer from one of the mob: 'Nothing. They just kill our children.' … During the pogrom, the murderous mob posed a couple of questions to those begging for their lives to be spared: 'Did you have to come back? Why didn't you stay in Germany?'

Two months later, in the city of Miskolc from where Béla Guttmann's family had been deported to their deaths two years before, a Jew by the name of Jungreisz was accused of black-marketeering and lynched. When sixteen people were arrested for the related pogrom, 25,000 marched on the prison holding them, and a crowd beat a Jewish police captain named Farago to death while his armed subordinates stood watching. Only 105 of the pre-war Miskolc Jewish population of more than 10,000 had survived the Holocaust.

During the immediate post-war years, Jewish survivors throughout east central Europe emerged from the dark shadow of the Holocaust to return to a more familiar routine – violence and murder of a more sporadic, less efficient, kind.

In Svinna, a village in north-western Slovakia, fifteen Jews were murdered immediately after the war on their return from a concentration camp. In September 1945, in nearby Topol'čany, a Jewish doctor was accused of injecting Christian children with poison in another variation of the blood libel that had first surfaced in England some eight centuries earlier. A mob attacked the doctor with knives, all Jewish apartments and offices were demolished, and other Jews were beaten with iron bars. The police did not intervene, except to arrest fleeing Jews. The anti-Jewish riots continued to spread like contagion.

The worst was reserved for Poland, where the Jewish death toll from pogroms in the two years following the war exceeded 1,500. The most gruesome massacre took place in Kielce, in southern Poland, where the

pre-war Jewish community had numbered some 24,000, a third of the total population. In July 1946, a Christian boy accused Jews of imprisoning him in a cellar, where he also claimed to have seen the bodies of other boys. Of the 200 Jewish survivors from the Holocaust, at least forty-two were murdered in the ensuing pogrom, and fifty wounded. Some were shot, while others were knifed, stoned or clubbed to death.

In such circumstances, many Jews were understandably eager to wave their final goodbyes to the continent of their birth. They had made a simple calculation – Europe equals death. Tens of thousands refused to return to their former homes after the Holocaust, and instead sought sanctuary in displaced persons camps.

In May 1946, even before the Kielce pogrom, the United Nations agency responsible for the camps conducted a poll of their Jewish inmates. 'By far the largest number of Polish and Ukrainian Jews express a desire to go to Palestine,' the agency reported. '...Hundreds of ballots showed just one word as an explanation for not returning home: "Palestine".'

One respondent had commented simply: 'All my relatives were killed in Auschwitz. I can't live among the murderers of my parents.'

In the six years after the Holocaust, close to half a million Jews left Europe to start a new life in the reborn Jewish state of Israel, founded in 1948 to end a blood-spattered exile that had lasted for two millennia.

For the Jewish nation, as for Béla Guttmann, a new day was dawning.

• • •

If Guttmann's pre-war coaching career was marked by turbulence, what followed afterwards was even more so, and over a longer period. And this time, we can't ascribe the constant upheaval to Nazism and the breakdown of European civilisation. At least not directly, anyway.

'During the first season, the coach gets to work quietly, the second is more difficult, and the third one is fatal,' Guttmann once said.

The truth was even more striking. He managed a third season only once, at Benfica in 1961/62, before leaving the club immediately after winning two European Cups in succession. Between 1945 and 1967, he changed clubs no fewer than seventeen times, while also fitting in three short-term national team coaching roles for good measure. To trace Guttmann's movements during these years is to engage in a mind-spinning activity.

At the risk of over-simplification, the great modern-day football coaches can be divided into two groups. There are those who build clubs over a long period, developing young players and instilling an esprit de corps and a winning mentality that breed self-perpetuating success. Alex Ferguson of Manchester United and Arsène Wenger of Arsenal clearly fall into that category. Ferguson's predecessor Matt Busby, and the great Liverpool duo of Bill Shankly and Bob Paisley are other obvious examples in a category that has been more common in Britain than among the giant clubs of Italy and Spain.

At the other extreme are the 'shock and awe' managers, the change agents, those who come into a club, and by their sheer force of character, reconfigure the team in their image, sometimes with lightning-fast results. Their tenure tends to last a maximum of two or three seasons, before either they seek the next big challenge and pay cheque somewhere else in Europe, or their uncompromising personality leads to an irreversible breakdown in their relationship with the club authorities, or even with the players.

The Portuguese coach José Mourinho, who has won titles with major clubs in England, Italy, Spain and Portugal, stands now as the classic example of this latter grouping, a growing phenomenon in a football world demanding instant success.

But it was Béla Guttmann who first set this trend, albeit with three main differences from Mourinho himself. First, his horizons stretched to South America as well as Europe. Second, unlike

Mourinho, who has built his teams around highly disciplined defensive organisation, Guttmann was a man for unbridled attack. Third, whereas Mourinho is cautious about introducing young players with no experience, Guttmann felt no such constraint.

We can attribute the whirlwind nature of Guttmann's career to several factors, for the most part a complex combination of coaching style, fickle bosses and a deep-seated personal and financial insecurity, borne out of an intimate knowledge of penury and fear.

On the footballing side, Guttmann's approach was characterised by activity so intense that it would have been difficult to sustain at any one club. Again, we can see echoes of this workaholism in many modern-day coaches. He trusted his instincts, acting decisively as soon as he took charge, with sweeping changes to tactics and training regimes. This resolve was most infamously demonstrated at Benfica in 1959, when he overhauled his squad, triggering immediate success. You could argue, too, that in his prime, he didn't need as much time as less perceptive coaches. He made the necessary changes, won trophies, then moved on, job done.

'A new trainer can capture the imagination of his players,' Guttmann told *World Soccer* magazine in 1961. 'New training ideas can give a team a renewed enthusiasm. If the ability is there as well, this can carry them to the top. Next season, it will be different. Nothing will be new and it is difficult, often impossible, for a trainer to maintain their new found impetus.'

The intensity was not just psychologically unsustainable, for both him and his players; it could be physically so, too. Particularly during his years in Italy, he had a tendency to overtrain the players, leading to clear signs of physical exhaustion. This was a mistake he would learn from and rectify, with great results, later on in his career, but again, the similarities with his foremost modern-day heir are striking. 'Mourinho burns out his players after a year and a half, at most two years,' said the Italian Fabio Capello of his fellow coach.

Another integral feature of Guttmann's approach was his insistence on total control over anything related to the footballing activity of the club. He believed that if that control was openly and effectively challenged, his authority would then be irrevocably undermined with the players, rendering him ineffectual. In such a scenario, there was no point hanging around. 'A coach is like a lion tamer,' he said. 'He dominates the animals as long as he shows self-confidence and has no fear. But when the first hint of fear appears in his eyes, he is lost.' He later declared himself to be 'proud of the fact that players could never control me'.

Dictatorial and undemocratic it may seem, but many great football coaches appear to have sworn by the same philosophy. It could well indeed have been Béla Guttmann who first articulated it so clearly, with others since following suit. 'If the coach has no control, he will not last,' Alex Ferguson has said. 'You have to achieve a position of comprehensive control.'

Ferguson's authority at Manchester United was boosted by long-term success at the club. He also desperately wanted to continue as the successful manager of Manchester United. If players did challenge him, he would fight to get rid of them, so maintaining his position. Guttmann never had the advantage of longevity, and didn't feel similar affinity to any club he coached. If his grip was loosened, he would just shrug his shoulders and seek another employer in the big, wide world out there.

Alternatively, his bullishness would run into conflict with club officials whose considerable egos stemmed from successful business careers, and he would be sacked. 'I always got offended easily and my stubbornness didn't allow me to give in,' Guttmann said in retirement:

If someone raised his voice or made an unfair remark, that was enough for me and I left the scene. It sounds strange now, as if I had been over-sensitive and should have been given special treatment,

but believe me it was not like that. I had all the responsibility. Why then should I have let others control me?

Guttmann could be charming and sociable, building up many friends and contacts, principally Jews, who helped him with his career over the years. But he was not interested in ingratiating himself with authority. If some people are natural insiders, who instinctively play politics and form alliances purely to preserve their livelihood and social position, Guttmann was the natural outsider. 'I always had two burdens to carry,' he was quoted as saying in an article in the international football magazine *Libero International*, published well after his death. 'One is due to the fact that I am everywhere a foreigner, and the other is because I am a Jew.'

Given that he spent several years as a coach in his native Hungary, his claim that he was 'everywhere a foreigner' speaks volumes. When results on the pitch turned sour, he never had a pool of chummy good will to draw on.

Indeed, his lack of any real attachment to any particular country was another factor in his itinerant career. Guttmann may have enjoyed his retirement in the coffee shops of Vienna (although it was his wife Mariann who is said to have been particularly keen on living there), but he must surely have found it difficult to feel truly at home in a country from which he had once fled for his life, and where he was later forced out of a job for exactly the same reason. One German-language writer, Hardy Grüne, described him as 'a restless wanderer without peace who's at home nowhere and jumps from one challenge to another'. Another, W. Ludwig Tegelbeckers, made a similar observation, calling him a 'wanderer of the world who showed no compromise'.

Joseph Stalin's Soviet regime sought to build up popular resentment against Jews by labelling them as 'rootless cosmopolitans', the implication being that they weren't fully committed to the mother

country. In Guttmann's case, the label rings true. He embodied the age-old Jewish experience of spiritual homelessness, constantly upping sticks and leaving places that offered neither security nor deep emotional connection. It seems fitting and inevitable that a Jew should become the first recognisable symbol of the globalisation of the world's most popular sport.

Guttmann's life experience – the rapid decline in the treatment of Hungarian Jews during his adolescence, the fleeing from Budapest in both 1920 and 1922 and from Vienna in 1938, the extreme hostility he and his Hakoah colleagues experienced, the hiding and imprisonment in 1944 – was hardly likely to forge a trusting nature or engender loyalty to any club or country. The world was not going to do him any favours. He would look after himself, thank you very much.

His fierce independence was certainly very much to the fore when it came to handling his finances. He had been poor throughout his childhood, lost every cent in the Wall Street Crash, suffered forced unemployment during the early war years, and had lived through the Budapest siege in which thousands died of starvation. After the war, he experienced the sack on several occasions. It isn't the greatest surprise that he fought hard to maximise his earnings and safeguard his future when his bargaining power was at its strongest.

For any modern-day football manager, or for any ambitious person for that matter, this would now be regarded as completely reasonable behaviour. Who wouldn't want to better themselves? But Guttmann was a footballing pioneer, hawking his coaching wares far and wide in a manner commonplace today, but unheard of then. Unaccustomed to such bargaining, clubs of his era tended to rebuff his demands, fracturing their relationship with him. Anti-Semitic innuendo about his alleged money-grabbing followed him throughout, an accusation that clearly grated on him, undermining any developing attachment to a particular place. 'The press was always picking on him, calling him a demanding, greedy coach,' says Imre Guttmann.

Another factor in Guttmann's constant quest for financial advancement could have been his weakness for card games and casinos. As we shall explore in more depth later on, his nephew Imre Guttmann believes that his gambling was no innocent pastime, but amounted to a self-destructive addiction, most likely developed during his years in the Roaring Twenties in the United States.

Guttmann liked to live well too. Rumour has it, for example, that he insisted on wearing silk shirts while playing for Hakoah Vienna. Any inclination for spendthrift short-termism later in life may well have been heightened by childlessness. With no descendants to pass his fortune on to, he would have felt few constraints. And after his wartime experiences, a carpe diem philosophy can hardly be considered remarkable.

• • •

With his coaching reputation still high after bringing the Mitropa Cup to Hungary, it didn't take long for Guttmann to get back in the saddle after the war. His first match back was on 7 July 1945, ending an enforced six-year break from his chosen career. His new team was Vasas, a club based in the neighbouring district to Újpest in the north of Budapest. They weren't one of Hungary's big three (MTK, Ferencváros and Újpest), but needs must when scarce food has to be put on the table.

In the immediate post-war years in Hungary, shortages were rife and inflation was mind-boggling, even reaching the highest recorded level for any country in history in 1946. Always on the lookout for the best deal, Guttmann capitalised on the fact that some leading bigwigs in the capital's still privately owned food industry were well-known supporters of the club.

He negotiated a contract that paid 50 per cent in cash, and the other 50 per cent in kind – baskets full of eggs, potatoes, flour and

sugar, the sort of essentials for which many desperate people in Budapest were giving up their most valued possessions

Such goodies would have come in handy for any wedding cele-brations. With Jews now free to marry Gentiles, it must have been a mammoth relief for Béla and Mariann to finally come out in the open and tie the knot, in November 1945. For the era, and partly as a result of forced circumstance, they were both married relatively late. Béla was forty-six, Mariann thirty-three. They were virtually inseparable until Béla's death thirty-six years later.

Back at Vasas, demonstrating his uncanny eye for footballing potential, Guttmann secured the inspired signing of striker Gyula Szilágyi, who went on to score almost 300 goals in fifteen years at the club. That was to be Guttmann's sole major achievement for Vasas. Guttmann stormed out in hallmark fashion after just eight months.

Two powerful patrons of the club had asked him to divulge team formations and line-ups before games, just so they could boast to their friends about their inside knowledge. When he refused, the slighted grandees ran to a newspaper and told them that the manager had left the club. Guttmann duly obliged by handing in his resignation, saying that he couldn't stay at an institution where such machinations were possible. 'I would rather go hungry than abandon my principles,' he later said.

He moved straight into another role, becoming coach of Cio-canul Bucharest in February 1946. His year-long stint in Romania marked Guttmann's last involvement with a Jewish football club, a personal association that had stretched back a quarter of a century.

• • •

Ciocanul had been known before the war as Maccabi Bucharest, a Zionist club in the mould of Hakoah and their less-renowned

variants throughout central and eastern Europe. The club was based in the heavily Jewish district of Dudești.

Although not as dominant as in Hungary and Austria, Jewish footballers had certainly been prominent in Romania. Maccabi's goalkeeper Samuel Zauber was the first representative of a Jewish club to go to a World Cup when he was selected for the Romania squad at the first such tournament in 1930. That Romanian team was captained by another Jew, the prolific goalscorer Rudolf Wetzer. The man who led the national team on to the world stage on this proud occasion for his country was later to be accused by the post-war Communist regime of 'revisionism and bourgeois ideology'. He emigrated to Israel.

Maccabi Bucharest were expelled from all competitions in 1940, at the onset of a brutal two-year war against the Jews conducted by the government of Ion Antonescu, a close ally of Nazi Germany. Between 280,000 and 380,000 Jews from the Romanian regions of Bessarabia, Bukovina and Dorohoi County, and from Transnistria, the part of Ukraine under Romanian administration, were exterminated.

The Wiesel Commission published its research into the Romanian holocaust in 2004, finally revealing to the Romanian people the magnitude of a shameful history long suppressed by the Communist authorities. The report conveys the unvarnished truth in simple terms. 'The Commission concludes, together with the large majority of bona fide researchers in this field, that the Romanian authorities were the main perpetrators of this Holocaust, in both its planning and implementation.' The renowned Holocaust historian Raul Hilberg wrote that 'no country, besides Germany, was involved in massacres of Jews on such a scale'.

The events at Iași in eastern Romania in June 1941 came to symbolise the broader barbarity. At least 8,000 Jews were beaten to death or shot by Romanian police, soldiers and crowds of civilians

in the initial pogrom. A further 4,500 Jews were crammed into two trains that went back and forth in the Romanian countryside, one for fully seven days, with most dying of thirst and starvation before the torture was eventually terminated. Hans Frank, the Nazi Governor-General of Poland, was apparently none too impressed with what he considered thoroughly un-German methods of slaughter: 'We use surgery, not butchery. Has anyone ever seen a massacre of Jews in the streets of a German town?'

In comparison to much of European Jewry, the 100,000 Jews of Bucharest must have counted themselves as very fortunate. Antonescu, arguably for similar reasons as Hungary's Horthy, suspended deportations before they reached the capital.

Bucharest Jews were therefore subjected only to mass expropriation and job dismissals, forced labour, crippling taxation and isolated deportations. The lucky Jews of the capital suffered just one pogrom worth its name, in January 1941. Synagogues and homes were looted and set on fire, many women raped while their husbands were taken away and tortured, and 125 were murdered. Five among them, including a five-year-old girl, were taken to the kosher abattoir and hung on hooks, still alive. Once dead, the inscription 'kosher' was carved into their bodies.

When the Soviets had taken over the city in 1944, Maccabi combined with another club to form the short-lived Ciocanul (meaning 'the hammer') Bucharest. After Guttmann's time, a second merger in 1948 created Dinamo Bucharest, one more European club with Jewish origins that has dominated its country's domestic football for long periods.

Pista Kaufmann, the club president and textile industrialist, attracted Guttmann to Ciocanul with the offer of a higher salary and free accommodation. He wasn't to be disappointed with his investment. 'Before Guttmann came here, the Ciocanul players knew only that the ball was round,' he told the Romanian press. 'But this

great magician from Budapest has taught them to play modern and beautiful football.'

The impact was characteristically powerful, the stay predictably brief. Although he arrived in February 1946, the first full official season in Romanian football didn't start until August of that year. Ciocanul began promisingly, and looked to be in contention for the championship before Guttmann walked out in early 1947, returning to the scene of his former glories, Újpest. He later claimed that he had 'longed to be in Pest', and it is undoubtedly true that, compared to Hungary at that time, Bucharest was a footballing backwater.

But, with Guttmann, exits were seldom so mild-mannered. The sport historian Hardy Grüne believes that Guttmann had actually fallen out in a major way with the Romanian football authorities. The reason was never explicit, but Grüne speculates that Guttmann would have had no truck with the corruption that was common in the Romanian league at that time.

• • •

The Újpest team that Guttmann returned to mid-way through the 1946/47 season was flying high. Nine of the national team that took the field against Italy in May 1947 were Újpest players, including the captain Gyula Zsengellér, who had scored so many goals under Guttmann in the Mitropa Cup-winning season before the war, and Ferenc Szusza, another top striker. It wasn't difficult for a coach of Guttmann's quality to guide such talent to a second successive Hungarian championship by a comfortable margin. So easy, perhaps, that he took the opportunity that year to supplement his scant income by opening a textile wholesale shop in Budapest.

In between all the winning, however, Guttmann had been busy falling out with people again. When some of the team had gone away on international duty towards the end of the title run-in, he

relaxed his customarily tough training schedule for a few days and told the remaining squad members to have some much-needed rest. A club official disapproved, urging Guttmann to keep the players sharp. 'If you are so confident about your technical skills, you can be the coach from now on,' snapped Guttmann. 'I wouldn't want to stand in the way of your coaching career.'

The relationship was broken and Guttmann left at the end of the season, again lasting less than a year at one club. He waited a few months for his next opportunity, taking over at Kispest in early 1948, his fifth and last club in the environs of Budapest as a player and coach.

At Kispest, who had finished runners-up to Újpest the previous season, Guttmann would manage two young starlets who were set to grace the Hungarian and international game for many years. There was the 22-year-old József Bozsik, a half-back who would play more than 100 times for his country; and Bozsik's closest childhood friend, the twenty-year-old forward Ferenc Puskás, whose glittering playing career would involve eighty-four goals for the national team and three European Cups with Real Madrid.

By the time he assumed the reins at Kispest, Guttmann was already acquainted with the two blossoming maestros. In the time between jobs at Újpest and Kispest, he had been asked to train the Hungarian national team for at least one game under the overall stewardship of Tibor Gallowich, who remained in control of team selection.

In what may have struck him as something of a turnaround, Guttmann thus took on a role of national responsibility less than three years after being hunted down and imprisoned by the national authorities, spending his days shouting 'we are shit, we are shit' at the top of his voice. It may also have crossed his mind that the Hungarian national team had been deprived of an entire generation of Jewish footballing potential, extinguished at Auschwitz in a matter of weeks.

In October 1947, he helped guide the team to a 3–0 victory over Romania back in Bucharest in the Balkan and Central European Championship, with Puskás bagging two of the goals. It is likely that he trained the team for other games too, but as he was not head coach, there is no available evidence. We can certainly say that Guttmann played some part in laying the foundation for the next coach Gusztáv Sebes, who built the infamous Golden Team that remained unbeaten for thirty-one matches in the early 1950s.

Guttmann took over at Kispest with fifteen games remaining in the 1947/48 season. The team lost just two of them as the season finished on a high. Giving some indication of his ability, Ferenc Puskás scored twenty-eight goals in that period. Short and unusually rotund for a top athlete, he possessed a left foot that mesmerised defences with elusive dribbling and a powerful shot. He also played the game with supreme intelligence. 'Of all of us, he was the best,' his international teammate Nándor Hidegkuti once said. 'He had a seventh sense for football. If there were 1,000 solutions, he would pick the 1001st.' Puskás is a permanent feature on lists of the top ten all-time greats in world football.

But Béla Guttmann laid down before no man, however great he may have been. Eight games into the following season, during an away match in Győr in November 1948, all hell broke loose.

The previous coach, Ferenc Puskás Senior, had indulged the young protégé, allowing his powerful personality to dominate the dressing room. Under the new regime, however, the absolute authority of the coach was non-negotiable. 'Guttmann refused to tolerate the sort of thing that Puskás's father had let his son get away with,' recalled the veteran Hungarian sports journalist Kálmán Vándor. 'He [Guttmann] was a very serious guy, a good man at heart and a real expert in his field. The problem was – and it was well known – young Puskás was virtually running the Kispest team from around this time.'

At the game in question, Guttmann was angered by the aggressive antics of one of his defenders, Mihály Patyi, who was kicking and hitting opponents behind the referee's back. The coach's admonishments from the touchline fell on deaf ears, with Patyi carrying on as before. Despite there being no substitutes in football at that time, an exasperated Guttmann called for Patyi to come off the pitch.

Puskás had other ideas. He ordered his teammate to stay where he was, and Patyi obeyed. Guttmann's reaction was immediate. 'I stood up from the bench and went up to the stands without a word, thus indicating to the club officials that I'd ceased to be the coach of Kispest,' he later said.

After the match ended in a 4–0 defeat to a much weaker team, Guttmann marched into the dressing room to make a statement:

> I told them I didn't belong to the team any more as I had just lost face before my players! My words were accompanied by silence. They were sad about the incident and asked me to forget about it, but I couldn't change my character on this occasion either. I didn't even travel home in the same train compartment as the team.

Guttmann would get the last laugh over Puskás fourteen years later, in Amsterdam. But back in 1948, the Association of Hungarian Coaches barred Guttmann from his trade for a month for having the courage to stand up to the young darling of Hungarian football, claiming that he had shown disloyalty in leaving a club in the lurch with such a sudden resignation.

It is worth at least noting that this accusation of disloyalty was hardly out of kilter with the time and the place. The new Communist regime, seeking to stymie the widespread yearning for emigration to Israel, was busy accusing other Jews of exactly the same thing. The following year, in the first Stalinist show trial in

post-war eastern Europe, the Jews Tibor Szőnyi and András Szalai were forced to confess that they had been members of 'Zionist spy rings' and were hanged.

THE ITALIAN JOBS

On the Piazza San Marco in Venice, on the waterfront, stand two columns. On top of one is a statue of a winged lion, the symbol of the patron saint of the city, San Marco. On top of the other stands a statue of San Teodoro, the previous patron saint. It was between these two columns, on 6 July 1480, that three Jews were impaled and burned alive before the thronged masses, having been convicted of murdering a six-year-old Christian boy and then draining his blood for ritual use.

The allegations will be wearingly familiar to anyone with a cursory knowledge of European Jewish history. All the elements are there, the actors being the sly, clannish, conspiratorial Jews alongside the pure, innocent victim of a gruesome murder. According to the charges, two of the Jews had abducted the boy, a beggar, from the marketplace at Treviso, north of Venice. They took him to nearby Portobuffolé, a small village where, as in Treviso and throughout the Republic of Venice at that time, a small Jewish community resided.

There the kidnappers, Mose da Treviso and Giacobbe da Colonia, went to the house of their supposed co-conspirator, the moneylender Servadio da Colonia. Like Giacobbe, Servadio's name suggests that their families had been refugees from Cologne, from where Jews had been expelled half a century before.

In Servadio's house, the child was said to have been murdered in the presence, and with the active participation, of other local and foreign Jews. It was claimed that they took the body to the house of Mose da Treviso, himself a moneylender, where the body was alleged to have been burned in an oven. The anonymous boy was immediately rebaptised after death with the name of Sebastiano Novello, after the early Christian saint and martyr.

Denunciations flooded in to the prosecutor, most notably from Donato, Servadio's servant, a Jew who had converted to Christianity. Despite the best lawyers that money could buy, the three Jews were condemned to death before the Portobuffolé court, a sentence confirmed after a futile appeal. The three later confessed under torture.

Chronicles of the execution reported that at least one of the defendants, Servadio, faced death in prayer. 'In the Piazza di San Marco, packed with innumerable people, they watched that maddened lunatic being burnt alive in his Jewish error, scorning the offer of baptism,' one writer recorded. 'They were tied up and wood was piled up all around them,' wrote another. 'The wood was set alight, which they saw, and they looked all around them while the wood roasted and burnt them, with their laments and screams. The oldest one of them, tougher than his associates in martyrdom, exhorted them by reciting Jewish law.'

As he faced death, Servadio is said to have pointed out the informer Donato to his fellow Jews in the crowd. As they will have been wearing the distinctive yellow circle that all Venetian Jews were obliged to sew onto their clothing, they would have been easy to identify.

• • •

What did Guttmann and Ernő Egri Erbstein talk about at night in their labour camp barracks in the autumn of 1944? Exhausted, humiliated, their shared love of football must have offered them a mental and emotional escape in the months before they engineered a physical one.

They will have dwelt on the good times. For Erbstein, these will have involved his years before the war coaching various teams in Italy, by the beaches of Cagliari, in the mountains surrounding Nocera, by the port in Bari, in the bustling metropolis of Turin. How Erbstein must have dreamed of returning, how Guttmann must have let his mind wander to the hope of a future in such seemingly magical places.

By 1946, Erbstein was back in Italy. Three years later, Guttmann had resolved to join him. Wary of the tightening Stalinist grip in Hungary under the dictatorial regime of Mátyás Rákosi, and with so many bad memories of the war years, he was keen to test his coaching mettle in the country that had won the last two World Cups before the war. He was never to live in Hungary again.

In making the trip from Hungary to Italy, the two men were following an established pattern. During the 1920s and 1930s, Italian clubs of all levels had hired more than fifty coaches from Hungary, which together with Austria represented the Silicon Valley of global football at the time, brimming with innovative ideas.

Many of these coaches were Jews, such as Gyula Feldmann and Árpád Weisz, who played with Guttmann as a young man at Törekvés, and went on to win the Italian league as coach with the great Inter Milan in 1930, at the young age of thirty-four. Twelve years later, Weisz's wife Elena, his twelve-year-old son Roberto and his eight-year-old daughter Clara were separated from him on their arrival at Auschwitz, and sent straight to the gas chambers. By 1944, with that terrible knowledge lodged inside his head, Weisz had himself met the same fate.

Guttmann first had to use all his wiles and contacts to obtain an exit visa from Hungary, not an easy task in 1949. Indeed, by the following year, the emigration door had slammed completed shut. His life may well have looked very different if he hadn't intuitively grasped that time was fast running out for anyone who cherished freedom.

He went with Mariann to Vienna, using it as a base for some months to canvas for jobs in Italy. He will have seen a very different city. When Guttmann had left Vienna for the United States in 1938, the Jewish population of the city had been around 185,000, or just shy of 10 per cent of the population. On his return a little over a decade later, it had shrunk to 9,000, or 0.6 per cent.

He eventually arrived in Italy, armed with a document purportedly containing an invitation from AS Roma to be their coach. But with the pledge soon proving to be worth less than the paper it was written on, Béla and Mariann found themselves all dressed up in Rome with nowhere to go.

Erbstein came to the rescue, recommending Guttmann's talents to the president of Padova in the Venetian city of Padua, from whose cobbled medieval streets eighty-five members of its tiny but centuries-old Jewish community had been dragged to their deaths just five years before.

Guttmann did not yet have his late friend's pulling power among the country's footballing fraternity. Unproven in Italian football, and desperate not to return to Hungary, Guttmann was in a weak negotiating position vis-à-vis the Padova hierarchy. As at Enschede before the war, he accepted a negligible salary with bonuses dependent of performance, and set about establishing his reputation once more.

After all they had been through, this favour was to be Erbstein's final farewell to his friend. Less than five years after his dramatic escape with Guttmann, Ernő Egri Erbstein was the victim of an unspeakably cruel twist of fate. On 4 May 1949, he was returning home with his Torino team from Lisbon after a friendly match against Benfica. Their plane crashed into the Superga hill on the outskirts of Turin, killing Erbstein, eighteen players, many of them Italy internationals, and twelve other club officials and journalists. Erbstein's team was on the verge of picking up its second successive Italian championship under his guidance.

• • •

Padova had been promoted to Serie A (the Italian premier league) in 1948, and had spent the following season consolidating their position in the top league, finishing mid-table. But Guttmann flew into his coaching role in the summer of 1949, dedicating himself to mastering the Italian language, and introducing his rigorous training regime, tactical knowhow and attacking philosophy.

The effects were typically immediate. With a third of the season gone, spurred on by goals from Giancarlo Vitali and the Argentinian midfielder José Curti, Padova lay in second place. Fit and well-organised, they had successfully competed with the aristocrats of Italian football, beating Roma in the capital, drawing with Inter Milan in their famous San Siro stadium, hammering the traumatised champions Torino 4–1 at home in Padua, and recording their still highest ever victory in Serie A, 8–0 away to local rivals Venezia in the region's capital.

Juventus, the league leaders, arrived in Padua in December for a much-heralded clash. But the 2–0 victory for the visitors propelled the teams in opposite directions. Juventus went on to win the league, whereas Padova plummeted. By early April they had lost eight consecutive games. A 4–0 defeat in the return match at Juventus at the end of the month, consigning Padova to fifteenth in the table (out of twenty), was to be Guttmann's last game before he was unceremoniously dismissed.

On the face of it anyway, his departure was not simply an outcome of dashed hopes, of a failure to fulfil early promise. A murkier explanation also emerged. Much of the poor run coincided with the introduction into the team of the Yugoslav goalkeeper Zvonko Monsider, half way through the season. He played seven times, and his woeful performances were roundly criticised. The Padua hierarchy accused Guttmann of bringing Monsider on loan from Lazio

only because he benefited from some kickback as a result of the deal, and terminated his contract after what they claimed was a full and proper internal investigation.

Guttmann was indignant, insisting that he had nothing to do with the recruitment of Monsider, and claiming that the directors were looking to find an easy pretext to replace him anyway so they could rehire Pietro Serantoni, a friend of the club's vice-president. Serantoni, a member of Italy's 1938 World Cup-winning team and a national hero, had walked out on Padova the year before to pursue business interests in Rome, but had returned with his tail between his legs asking for his old job back.

The Italian football association initially suspended Guttmann's coaching licence pending its own investigation. He launched an appeal, while also unsuccessfully suing Padova for defamation in the courts. The costs, both emotional and financial, of trying to clear his name in repeated hearings took their toll. Mariann sunk into depression, escaping to Vienna for a holiday to get away from the stress of it all, while her husband was left alone to contemplate how he could pick himself up once more.

• • •

He need not have worried. Despite the negative headlines and the ostensible suspension, Guttmann's tremendous start at Padova, coupled with his previous exploits in other countries, was starting to build up a considerable reservoir of esteem. With the football association now determining that he should be allowed to continue working while its investigation dragged on, he took up the position of coach for the 1950/51 season at Unione Triestina, in the city of Trieste in the north-east of Italy, bordering what is now Slovenia.

Trieste is often said to lie at the intersection between different cultures – Latin, Slavic, Balkan and Germanic – each bearing an

influence on the city's mixed ambience. But this characterisation, based on geography alone, omits the hugely significant Jewish contribution to the commercial and artistic life of the city before the Holocaust.

It was here that James Joyce befriended the Jewish businessman and writer Italo Svevo, who allegedly inspired the character of Leopold Bloom in *Ulysses*. It was here, in 1831, that the Jew Giuseppe Lazzaro Morpurgo had founded the global insurance giant Assicurazioni Generali, from which eighty-six Jewish directors and top-ranking employees were either dismissed or forced to resign a little over a century later. And it was from here, in 1943, that 620 Jews were sent to be murdered at La Risiera di San Sabba, a concentration camp on the outskirts of their home city.

The cosmopolitan feel of the city must have appealed to football's eternal nomad. So too Triestina's insistence that they firmly believed his side of the story in the Padova affair, calling it a 'baseless slander', and that they would work alongside him to clear his name once and for all.

The new coach will have been less enamoured with the board's decision to sell most of the first team shortly before the season started, in a bid to raise much-needed funds. 'Mr Guttmann,' said the club president, 'If we don't get relegated with this team, we will have your statue put up in front of the stadium.'

It wasn't long before the press was talking of the 'miracle of Trieste'. In the second game of the season, Triestina were winning 2–0 away at Juventus after an hour before getting pegged back to a draw. This feat was followed by two home victories against Torino and Roma.

But as in the previous season at Padova, the early highs eventually gave way to a slump. A ten-game sequence without a win in the latter stages of the season put Triestina in danger of relegation before the final game, a home match against mid-table Novara.

Three second-half goals secured the necessary win, and the stadium resounded with chants of 'Viva Guttmann!', in honour of the man who had guided such an unproven team to safety.

Things were looking up again for Guttmann, particularly as the Italian football association had by now completed its report, acquitting him of all charges. He signed an improved contract, and prepared for his second season at Triestina.

It wasn't long, however, before he was reminded of the extreme capriciousness of Italian football culture. By the end of the 1–0 home defeat against Torino in November 1951, leaving the team second from bottom of the league, the crowd's mood had soured. Five months after 'Viva Guttmann', it was now 'Vai Via Guttmann' pouring down from the terraces – 'Go away, Guttmann'.

The Jewish president Leo Brunner treated Guttmann to a tortured explanation of why he had to sack him. 'We are all ministers of the club, but one of the ministers must leave now in order to calm the people. The difference between the directors and you is that we provide the money, so we have to stay. You are the foreign minister, so you have to go.'

'The promised statue never did get put up,' an elderly Guttmann reflected with bitter irony. '…This was the second time I got the sack in Italy. Have you got that? Don't worry, there will still be two more.'

• • •

After his sorry exit from Triestina, Guttmann was down in the dumps again. His first two jobs in his Italy adventure had started promisingly, but ended badly. Exhaustion had also set in. Even for someone who lived life at breakneck speed, the last decade must have been an utterly draining experience. Hiding, labour camp, escape from labour camp, more hiding, the murder of his family, straining to rebuild a career interrupted by genocide and war, coping with

Béla (left) with father Abráhám and brother Ármin, his team-mate at Törekvés. COURTESY OF AGON SPORTSWORLD

Guttmann (with cross on shorts) in the MTK Budapest championship-winning side of 1920/21. COURTESY OF AGON SPORTSWORLD

Hakoah Vienna players get ready for action. Guttmann is tying his shoelaces, second from left. COURTESY OF JEWISH MUSEUM VIENNA

The Hungarian national team before the 1924 Olympics. Guttmann is sixth from left, standing. COURTESY OF HUNGARY OLYMPIC AND SPORT MUSEUM

Hakoah as champions of Austria, 1924/25. Guttmann stands next to coach Arthur Baar, who holds the trophy. COURTESY OF JEWISH MUSEUM VIENNA

Béla Guttmann, the centre-half and fulcrum of the championship-winning Hakoah side. COURTESY OF JEWISH MUSEUM VIENNA

The debonair dance teacher. COURTESY OF AGON SPORTSWORLD

Hakoah on tour: this time victorious in Antwerp in 1925. COURTESY OF JOSEPH YEKUTIELI MACCABI SPORTS ARCHIVE

LEFT Captain of the touring Hakoah All-Stars in Montevideo in 1930. Guttmann was to return to coach Peñarol more than thirty years later. COURTESY AGON SPORTSWORLD

RIGHT Adolf Eichmann's residence in 1944 in Budapest. The house belonged to Lipót Aschner, Béla Guttmann's boss. PHOTO: LÁSZLÓ HARRI NÉMETH

The site in Újpest, now a car park, where Béla Guttmann hid from the Nazis in 1944.
PHOTO: LÁSZLÓ HARRI NÉMETH

The grave of Béla's mother, Eszter, in Budapest. The inscription also remembers Béla's father, sister and nephew, all murdered at Auschwitz in 1944.
PHOTO: ZSOLT GULYÁS

The grave of Béla's brother, Ármin, in Miskolc. The inscription also remembers Ármin's fourteen-year-old son, Ervin, murdered at Auschwitz in 1944.
PHOTO: MISKOLC JEWISH COMMUNITY

Pál Moldován, the man who saved Béla Guttmann's life. COURTESY OF PÁL MOLDOVÁNYI

Guttmann (left) walking in the Piazza San Marco on the day of Padova's 8–0 victory over Venezia, 20 November 1949. COURTESY OF CALCIO PADOVA

Guttmann celebrates with his Padova players.
FROM *DIE BÉLA GUTTMANN STORY*

A tender moment together with Mariann in Venice. FROM *DIE BÉLA GUTTMANN STORY*

Leading a training session as coach of AC Milan. COURTESY OF AC MILAN

In the dugout at San Siro. COURTESY OF AC MILAN

On tour with Honvéd in 1956, together with Sándor Kocsis (centre) and the great Ferenc Puskás.
COURTESY OF AGON SPORTSWORLD

Guttmann (left) with Gusztáv Sebes, coach of Hungary's Golden Team. COURTESY OF HUNGARY OLYMPIC AND SPORT MUSEUM

Winner of the 1957 Campeonato Paulista as coach of São Paulo. COURTESY OF SÃO PAULO FUTEBOL CLUBE

ABOVE Celebrating another title win, this time with his FC Porto players in 1959. FROM *DIE BÉLA GUTTMANN STORY*

LEFT Béla and Mariann in their prime. COURTESY OF PÁL MOLDOVÁNYI

With Mário Coluna, preparing on
a snow-bound pitch for Benfica's
1962 European Cup quarter-final in
Nuremberg. COURTESY OF PA IMAGES

With the great Eusébio. '*O menino é ouro!*', Guttmann said of his
signing ('The boy is gold!') COURTESY OF AGON SPORTSWORLD

The victorious
Benfica side, twice
European champions
under Guttmann.
COURTESY OF
DOCUMENTATION
AND INFORMATION
CENTRE, SPORT LISBOA
E BENFICA

BICAMPEÕES EUROPEUS 1960-61 1961-62

1.º plano: Cavém, Humberto, Serra, Santana, Ângelo, Mário João, Germano, Simões, Cruz e Neto — 2.º plano: Hamilton Pena (massagista),
Artur, Eusébio, Dr. Sousa Pinho (médico), Costa Pereira, Béla Guttmann (treinador), Águas (capitão), José Augusto, Coluna e Saraiva

The innovative coach
puts his Benfica team
through their paces.
PHOTO: ROLAND
OLIVEIRA, COURTESY
OF DOCUMENTATION
AND INFORMATION
CENTRE, SPORT LISBOA
E BENFICA

LEFT Béla Guttmann, who survived Europe's Holocaust, proudly holds his two European Cups.
COURTESY OF AGON SPORTSWORLD

BELOW Training with the Austrian national team in 1964. Guttmann was to resign within months, citing an intolerable atmosphere of anti-Semitism.
COURTESY OF PA IMAGES

Past his best: an ageing Guttmann as coach of Panathinaikos in Athens in 1967.
COURTESY OF PANATHINAIKOS FC

Béla Guttmann's grave in Vienna, where Eusébio is said to have prayed. PHOTO: AUTHOR

intra-club showdowns and conflict, adapting to a foreign country, accusations of corruption, sacking, another sacking.

And let's spare a thought for Mariann. She might have bargained on an exciting and glamorous life when she got together with Béla, but not on the extreme anxiety and stress that she nevertheless had to experience. In Padua, the cumulative strains had finally got the better of her, and she had to get away. A couple of years later, both she and her husband were driven by the same impulse.

Guttmann needed to generate a second wind from somewhere, a fresh start, a new perspective. After Hugo Meisl and Ernő Erbstein, it was to be three other central European Jews who offered a helping hand this time – Imre Hirschl, József Künsztler and Lajos Czeizler.

Imre Hirschl, whom Guttmann affectionately referred to as a 'big con man', was a man for whom the Hebrew word *chutzpah* could have been invented.* His story defies belief.

He was born in 1900 in Apostag, a small town 70 kilometres south of Budapest. It is commonly believed that he played for the great Ferencváros, and was part of their touring squad to South America in 1929. But there is no record of him as a player in that squad, or indeed of him ever playing for Ferencváros, or for any team of any stature for that matter. Guttmann maintained that Hirschl had actually been a (presumably, kosher) butcher in Budapest. He was also an adventurer who, according to his daughter, was once wounded as an underage soldier in a Zionist unit of the British army in Palestine towards the end of the First World War. He eventually found his way to South America around the time of the Ferencváros tour.

He met Guttmann in São Paulo in 1930 during the Hakoah All-Stars visit, persuading him that he was a top masseur who would

* *Chutzpah* is usually translated as audacity, cheek or nerve. The author Leo Rosten defined it as 'that quality enshrined in a man who, having killed his mother and father, throws himself on the mercy of the court because he is an orphan.'

be invaluable for the upcoming Argentinian leg of their trip. When Hakoah ran out of money to pay him, Hirschl told all and sundry in Argentina that he had actually been the coach of the New York team, and managed to talk his way into a similar role with a premier league club, Gimnasia.

He may have lied to land himself the role, but once in situ, he demonstrated talent. When the team fared well, he was taken on by River Plate in Buenos Aires, one of the most famous clubs in world football. Earning the nickname *El Mago* (the wizard), the Jewish butcher from Hungary not only escaped the Holocaust, but won the Argentinian league twice as coach in the 1930s, before performing the same feat in Uruguay with Peñarol after the war.

Hirschl, now sporting the Latinised first name Emérico, never forgot Guttmann's favour in hiring him for the All-Stars tour. A few months after leaving Triestina, Guttmann received a telegram. Hirschl, now coach at San Lorenzo in Buenos Aires, was suffering from ill health and wanted Guttmann to take over.

By the time Béla and Mariann arrived there after their long journey by sea, San Lorenzo had already found another coach. But the adventure was nevertheless worthwhile. Already relaxed after the trip on the luxury liner, Guttmann spent months educating himself, observing the different training methods at various Argentinean clubs and imbibing the passionate footballing culture. He was successfully putting some of the recent stresses behind him and rediscovering his zest for football.

He held talks with Boca Juniors, the main local rivals of River Plate, but the club were performing poorly on the pitch and financially, and the two parties couldn't strike a deal. Instead, in order to make some money, he had to make do with a coaching job at Quilmes, a brewery-sponsored Buenos Aires team in the second tier of Argentinean football.

With their batteries recharged, and the job at Quilmes offering

little in terms of career advancement, Béla and Mariann sought a return to Europe. Another timely telegram arrived, this time from József Künsztler, a Budapest Jew who had enjoyed many triumphs as coach of Panathinaikos in Greece, and of Apoel in Cyprus, where he still holds the coaching record for the number of championships won.

Künsztler had resigned from Apoel the previous year, and persuaded Guttmann to take over at his beloved club. Guttmann was to stay in Nicosia for only three months of the 1953/54 season, before he got his biggest break yet. The *Rossoneri* of AC Milan, one of the giants of Italian and European football, had come calling.

• • •

AC Milan had started the 1953/54 season in mediocre fashion. A dismal 3–0 defeat against local rivals Inter in their shared San Siro stadium precipitated a search for a new coach, a very regular pastime for the always impatient club hierarchy.

Although Guttmann had now been sacked in his two previous Italian roles, his energy and imagination had continued to make an impression on the country's footballing elite. Antonio Busini, a native of Padua who had played many times for Padova, was now the long-standing technical director at AC Milan. He had admired Guttmann's efforts in his home town, and approached the highly respected Lajos Czeizler for a supporting reference.

Czeizler was a Hungarian Jew* who at that point was coach of

* Czeizler never played for a specifically Jewish team (although he did play for the youth team of the heavily Jewish MTK), and as he spent the war in neutral Sweden, was not affected by the Holocaust. Perhaps because of these factors, I could find no direct reference to his Jewishness. However, judging by the pages of references to Jews by the surname of Czeizler from his region of Hungary who were murdered in the Holocaust, it seems to me that his move to Sweden was a wise one. 'I am 99 per cent sure that Czeizler was Jewish,' says Tamás Kárpáti, whose knowledge of pre-war Hungarian football is second to none.

the Italian national team. He would take them to the World Cup
in Switzerland at the end of that season. After a playing career
that started as a youth team player at MTK Budapest, he had
achieved great success as a coach, winning the Swedish champion-
ship five times with IFK Norrköping, and then leading AC Milan
to their first Serie A title in more than forty years, in 1951.

He gave the nod to Busini, and the club resolved to get their
man. 'They phoned me four times in two days, they even told me
when the flight from Cyprus to Rome would leave, then the train
to Milan,' remembered Guttmann. 'I figured they were in trouble
and desperately needed the work of a new coach. But Italy again?
Weren't Padua and Trieste enough? Everything would be different
in Milan, I thought.'

So, in November 1953, a mildly hesitant but nevertheless optimis-
tic Guttmann alighted from his train at the central Milan station,
underneath which more than 850 Jews had been transported from a
secret platform to their deaths in Auschwitz just a few years before.

Not only was this the biggest job he had ever taken on in football
terms, it was also by far the most lucrative and the most pressurised.
Media and public scrutiny were intense and often savage. Support-
ers would flock to see public training sessions, and the players and
coach lived in a goldfish bowl, accosted wherever they went.

As could be expected with a club of this size, Guttmann had an
abundance of talent to work with, not least a Scandinavian triumvi-
rate: the Swedish striker Gunnar Nordahl, the top scorer in Serie A
in five separate seasons, still a record; his compatriot, Nils Liedholm,
who captained his country when it hosted the World Cup tourna-
ment in 1958, scoring in the losing final against Brazil; and Jørgen
Sørensen, a Danish international and another prolific goalscorer.

Guttmann didn't waste any time in introducing his ideas. He re-
jected the highly defensive tactical system of *catenaccio*, which was
just starting to take root in Italy at the time. 'Since I had outstanding

players, I gave them my orders: Attack!' he said. With similar fearlessness, he instigated his tough twice-a-day training regime, confronting what he saw as an excessively relaxed dressing room culture. 'The duration and severity of the training had been defined by the top stars … nobody should cross the boundaries of comfort,' he recalled drily.

With Guttmann in charge for three-quarters of the season, the team finished the season a creditable third, behind champions Inter and Juventus. There were some notable wins, too, including a 2–0 victory against Inter in the return match in March 1954. Guttmann will also have particularly enjoyed a 6–0 thrashing of Triestina on his former employers' home turf.

He was offered a new contract by the club's new president, the publishing tycoon Andrea Rizzoli, and got ready for the new season, bolstered by two major signings. The creative playmaker Juan Alberto Schiaffino, often regarded as the greatest Uruguayan footballer ever, joined from his native Peñarol for a world-record transfer fee; and the Argentinean winger Eduardo Ricagni was recruited from Juventus, also for a large sum. Meanwhile, the young centre-half Cesare Maldini, father of the great AC Milan and Italy player Paolo Maldini, joined from Triestina.

Guttmann girded himself, determined that this year he would get his hands on the infamous *scudetto*, the Italian league championship. By early January, everything was going to plan. After winning 4–3 at Juventus, Milan had won ten of their first twelve fixtures, and had sailed into a comfortable lead.

But the restless Guttmann was never entirely satisfied. To win this highly competitive league over thirty-four games, the players and the coach would need to be on exactly the same wavelength, working in unison throughout. With the addition of two megastars to an already pampered squad, Guttmann suspected that he still had some work to do to impose his ideas.

As was his wont, he waited for an ideal moment for a showdown

to assert his authority. His preferred strategy was always to take on a leading player. If he could prove a point against a supposedly indispensable star man, the lesser players would know to fall into line. This time, his target was Ricagni.

Schooled in a central European tradition that believed in the value of tactics, rather than just relying on the players' attributes, Guttmann would give detailed and repeated lectures to his team about how he wanted them to play. Such a meticulous approach, rare in most of the world, did not necessarily go down well. Some players would become restless, others piqued or apprehensive that they were being asked to perform an unfamiliar function.

'I gave them lectures,' Guttmann said:

I drew it all up on a blackboard telling them I would show them how it would work on the pitch in reality … I told them I had an idea according to which Sørensen and Ricagni should swap places during the game. Ricagni jumped up. 'I can't do that!' 'And why not?' 'Because I can't,' he said tersely. 'All right,' I said, 'we'll see!'

The slighted coach marched to Rizzoli's office, persuading him to write a letter confirming that Ricagni was available for transfer at the same price paid by Milan to secure his services in the first place. He showed the player the letter. 'The boy turned so pale as if I had sprinkled flour all over his face,' Guttmann said. 'Nothing like that had ever happened to him before. Well, he was bought at a big price. He was the emperor.'

Guttmann claimed that Ricagni backed down, and followed his advice from that point on. But such a confrontational strategy could work both ways. When things are going well, he was the maes-tro coach. When the results on the pitch deteriorated, the players sought to deflect blame away from themselves towards an allegedly dictatorial coach.

It seems likely that, on this occasion, Guttmann's policy back-fired. He was soon to pay the penalty.

• • •

Three successive draws followed the Juventus victory. With Schiaffino ruled out injured for several weeks, worse was to follow with a 4–3 defeat at struggling Triestina. The intense pressure of life as Milan coach was telling on Guttmann, as demonstrated by an extraordinary incident in a Milan bar in early February.

After a disappointing World Cup with Italy, Czeizler had been dismissed from his national role and became coach of Sampdoria in Genoa. On a visit to Milan prior to Sampdoria's fixture against Guttmann's team, Czeizler invited his friend for a night out with their respective wives.

They didn't finish the night as friends. The newspaper *La Stampa* reported: 'In a Milan bar, there was an altercation between the two Hungarians. The two wives intervened, one of whom [Czeizler's] threw a bottle towards the other.' Punching and screaming were also witnessed.

The following Sunday, there wasn't much love lost in the dugout area as the men's teams locked horns in the San Siro. The result was a hammer blow for Guttmann, as well as a personal humiliation in his duel with Czeizler. Sampdoria, in the lower reaches of the league, emerged as 3–1 victors.

Although the team was still top, the Milan board had gone into panic mode. Two days later, on Tuesday 15 February 1955, the president Rizzoli tapped Guttmann on the shoulder. 'Nothing to worry about,' he said, 'but just take your training session, and come back here for the board meeting tonight.'

The board deliberated for five hours, and called in the waiting Guttmann at 2 a.m. He was told that his contract was to be terminated.

The spokesman cited 'misunderstandings between Guttmann and the team, a situation that had been dragging on for weeks and which had recently deteriorated, resulting in a reciprocal feeling of distrust'.

According to *La Stampa*, the directors could well have been concerned that Padova and Triestina had also deteriorated in the second half of the season under Guttmann. Perhaps, it was felt, his fitness regime was too rigorous, draining the players' energy as the season wore on.

Guttmann himself was furious, suspecting that his assistant Ettore Puricelli was plotting with Czeizler to unseat him. With a memorable line, he greeted the assembled journalists who had gathered for the impending execution: '*Sono stato licenziato anche se non sono né un criminale né un omosessuale. Addio.*' ('I have been fired, even though I am neither a criminal nor a homosexual. Goodbye.') From that day on, he claimed, he was to insist on a contract clause stipulating he could not be sacked if his team were top of the league.

Perhaps feeling guilty for their role in his departure, the players penned a warm letter to him a few days later to say goodbye. Despite the friction, they knew Guttmann's worth and what he had done for them.

By June, the team was crowned champions. At the end of that month, Milan hosted the great Honvéd team from Budapest, including Ferenc Puskás, for a friendly game. The Hungarians invited Guttmann to come along to the celebratory banquet for the two teams after the match. The Milan players got wind that he was coming, and presented him with a gold plaque, on which was engraved: 'Bela Guttmann, coach of AC Milan, champions of Italy 1954/5.'

• • •

The next major incident in Guttmann's life is as absent from biographical sources as his Holocaust experiences. It is a sorry and

unsavoury tale that casts a dark shadow over his life and his many achievements.

At around lunchtime on Saturday 2 April 1955, six weeks after being sacked, Béla Guttmann was driving his friend's large American car at great speed in central Milan. He did not have a driving licence. He lost control, and crashed into two students standing by their scooters on the pavement, at the intersection between Via Pellizza da Volpedo and Via Mosè Bianchi. One, Giuliano Brene, aged seventeen, was killed instantly. His friend, Graziella Brianzoli, aged eighteen, sustained serious injuries and spent a month in hospital after the incident.

The owner of the car, and sitting in the passenger seat that day, was Desző Solti, a man whose name will be familiar to those with an intimate knowledge of the history of post-war European football. As with several people whose stories I have come across in the course of my research, it would be entirely possible to write a book just about him.

After arriving in Italy in the late 1940s, he had first set himself up as a theatre impresario. Perhaps initially using Guttmann's contacts, he became involved in football. His eventual specialism was not, however, coaching or scouting or anything conventional like that. His job was to bribe referees.

In the 1960s and '70s, Solti was the main actor in the most significant match-fixing scandal yet uncovered in football history anywhere in the world. On behalf of Inter Milan and Juventus, he would entice referees with large amounts of cash and lavish gifts prior to major European Cup ties. A 1974 investigation by the journalist Brian Glanville for the *Sunday Times* eventually revealed his crimes, including his corrupt role in Inter Milan's European Cup triumphs of 1964 and 1965. An indefinite suspension from football ensued.

In that strange language of theirs, modern-day journalists writing about the Solti corruption story usually refer to him as a 'Hungarian refugee' or 'Hungarian expatriate' and, bizarrely, just leave it at that.

But scratch the surface, and a remarkable human story is revealed. Solti was actually born Desző Steinberger in Balmazújváros, a small town in eastern Hungary, in 1911. To be yet more precise, Solti was a Jew who survived the unspeakable depravity of Auschwitz. The Jews of Balmazújváros, several hundred strong, were almost all, to a man, woman and child, obliterated from the face of the earth.

Solti was not just a crook. He was also a man who escaped death against all probabilities. What's more, he was something of a hero. A fellow survivor from Balmazújváros, Sándor Schwarcz, recounted in old age how he put himself forward to play for one of a handful of football teams in Auschwitz, set up to entertain Nazis bored with the everyday nine-to-five of murdering people. He did so because the footballers were given extra rations, increasing their otherwise meagre chances of survival.

When putting his hand up to volunteer, Schwarcz falsely claimed that he had played for Bocskai, the team from the town of Debrecen (near to Balmazújváros), which had been playing in the Hungarian First Division throughout the 1930s. At precisely that point, Schwarcz caught a glimpse of Solti, who was performing a role as a general servant to the football team, out of the corner of his eye. Knowing that Solti had been a major local personality with close connections to Bocskai, Schwarcz immediately feared that his lie would be exposed. 'I thought I was done, and the guards would cut me to pieces right there,' said Schwarcz. 'It is to Steinberger's credit that he didn't bat an eyelid although he knew exactly who I was and he knew that Bocskai would never have considered signing me up.'

There is more. In a documentary made for Hungarian television in 1990, an elderly Solti recalled how Josef Mengele, the infamous doctor of Auschwitz and so-called 'Angel of Death', had selected him as a personal runner and general assistant, due to his linguistic abilities. Solti used this privileged position to save a niece, but could do nothing for the other forty-nine members of his extended

family, who were all murdered. I have found supporting evidence for these claims. Immediately after the war, Solti was interviewed by the American authorities as a witness to Mengele's crimes.

'He looked very good,' Solti reported. 'He looked exceedingly well groomed – in this sad environment, I noticed that immediately. His hair was very thick and dark. I remember his eyes; they were uncommonly bright. He really didn't look like a murderer.'

But back to 1955, half way between Auschwitz and Solti's later footballing corruption. Here are the bare facts of what happened after the accident: the immediate instinct of the two men, hardwired into these survivors through their life experiences, was to escape. They abandoned the car and fled from the scene. An arrest warrant was issued against them both. Solti was arrested a week later by police in the Austrian Alps, around 300 kilometres from Milan, and sent back to Italy. He wrote a letter to the Chief Prosecutor, declaring that he alone was responsible for the crash. Guttmann was officially absolved from suspicion.

However, several witnesses contradicted this statement during the investigation, insisting that it was Guttmann who was at the wheel. Back in Italy, at that point as coach of Vicenza, he was charged with manslaughter in November 1955, together with Solti.

The pace of Italian justice was slow. The next time we hear of the case is the opening day of the trial in March 1957. With Guttmann now safely in South America, Solti sat in the dock alone. In an emotional statement, *La Stampa* reported, he 'sensationally retracted the confession'. He declared to the court that his original admission was designed to save Guttmann, who, fearing the consequences of his actions, had threatened to kill himself. With Guttmann telling his friend that he would supply the funds for full compensation to the families, Solti had agreed to shoulder the responsibility. But, he now claimed, the accident was absolutely nothing to do with him.

With this bombshell, the court adjourned once more for 'further

verification'. It was fully three years before it convened again, on 17 March 1960. Guttmann was now in Portugal, and Solti was also nowhere to be seen. Both were 'untraceable', a little surprising as Solti had by this stage set himself up in Milan as a luxury travel agent for foreign teams visiting the country.

The court nevertheless reached verdicts in their absence. Solti was now also accused of knowingly allowing an unlicensed driver to take control of his car, but was acquitted of all charges for lack of evidence. Guttmann was sentenced to six months in prison for manslaughter and causing injury through negligence, but immediately pardoned for all six months, on the condition that he pay the sum of four million lire in damages to the affected families.*

To get off so lightly with this crime, Guttmann couldn't have chosen a better partner than Solti, the arch fixer, the ultimate survivor.

We can certainly suppose that the two would have been thinking as one, that their perspectives on the accident would have been similar. If we are to understand how this story unfolded, we should not view it purely through our own eyes. These were men whose families were brutally murdered, who had witnessed horrific scenes of death and destruction. Ambitious and fearless, they were not going to have their lives ruined by what they would have seen as an accident, pure and simple.

We can only speculate about how the two conspired to evade justice. They no doubt came to an agreement as they fled from the crash. Solti would admit everything and Guttmann would pay the damages, possibly with a little on top for Solti, who would have fancied his chances of manipulating the Italian justice system. After all, for a man who got the better of Auschwitz, this comparatively piddling objective would have held few fears for him. 'Leave it to me,' we can imagine him saying.

* Guttmann was earning 400,000 escudos per year (plus bonuses) at Benfica in 1960, equivalent to around 8.7 million lire. Therefore, the penalty amounted to less than half a year's gross income at that time.

But then witnesses threw a spanner in the works. Another plan was necessary. This time, Guttmann was to go abroad, leaving Solti to concoct his story about Guttmann's threatened suicide, and his noble decision to save his friend. We can speculate that generous bribes delayed the process throughout. The final sentence, we may suspect, was the result of a settlement between the judges and the accused. It is interesting to note, too, that neither man was tried for perverting the course of justice, or its Italian legal equivalent.

Guttmann, his conscience partially assuaged by paying substantial damages, was free to continue his career as before. What's more, as the story was reported on only sporadically and superficially, his reputation was unblemished. A major football coach killing someone now would be massive news. That was seemingly not the case in Italy in the late 1950s. Even the news of the trial verdict was tucked away on page 9 of *La Stampa*.

Among the remaining family and friends of Giuliano Brene, however, the name of Béla Guttmann will still, it is fair to assume, evoke the most terrible of memories.

• • •

A few months after the accident, with Guttmann not under suspicion, he returned to management at newly promoted Vicenza. After Padua, it was his second job in the Veneto region, 60 kilometres west of Venice. It was also the fourth and last job in his ill-fated, anxiety-ridden, but nonetheless invaluable, Italian experience.

He took over a young and hungry team, including the young midfielder Azeglio Vicini, who was to manage the Italian national team at the 1990 World Cup played on their home turf. But the 1955/56 season turned out to be Groundhog Day for Guttmann.

By the end of 1955, having played more than a third of the season, Vicenza lay in second place behind eventual champions Fiorentina.

Their away form was particularly impressive. Highlights included 3–1 victories at Sampdoria and Lazio, and a 0–0 draw at Milan, outfoxing his former assistant, and Czeizler's alleged co-conspirator, Ettore Puricelli, who had replaced him at the San Siro.

In the New Year, things deteriorated again. It was now becoming apparent that Guttmann's intensive training regime was at least partly to blame, making the players sharp early on, but increasingly weary as the season progressed. In addition, perhaps, Guttmann's indictment in November was playing on his mind, distracting him from matters at hand.

After four successive defeats, concluding with a 3–1 home defeat in the return fixture against Milan, the team was third from bottom by early April 1956. Relegation was now a distinct possibility. Guttmann left the club a few days later, but it is unclear who initiated the exit. The club released a statement, saying that 'the passionate Hungarian coach has revealed his need for a rest'. By this stage, it was probable that he had agreed with Solti that he should leave the country and find work elsewhere.

Guttmann himself, who never talked publicly about the crash, had a different take, claiming that he was sacked after yet another bust-up with a club hierarchy. A vice-president had allegedly come in to the dressing room at half-time in his last game, only to be told in no uncertain terms by Guttmann that he was not wanted and he shouldn't come back. He maintained that he was sacked following this incident.

What we can say is that the departure suited both parties. The club could bring in fresh blood to rescue their rapidly degenerating season, while Guttmann could make himself scarce before the law caught up with him. After abandoning Hungary for good in 1949, he now left Italy for the last time in 1956, never to return as coach.

New pastures awaited the restless wanderer once more.

CHAPTER 8

LATIN LESSONS

Stefan Zweig and Gustav Wagner were both born and brought up in Vienna, both fled Europe in fear of their lives, and both committed suicide in Brazil in their sixties. And that is where the obvious similarities end.

Born in 1881 as the son of a wealthy industrialist, Zweig became one of the most popular literary figures in the world in the 1920s and 1930s. A prolific writer of plays, novellas and essays, he became best known for biographies, where he often grouped three people together in attempt to find common themes. His book Drei Meister *(Three Masters), for example, isa study of Honoré de Balzac, Charles Dickens and Fyodor Dostoyevsky.*

Zweig also contributed the libretto for Richard Strauss's 1934 opera Die schweigsame Frau *(The Silent Woman). He never got to see it. After three performances in Germany, the Nazi regime banned it, angered by Strauss's insistence that his Jewish librettist should be credited in the programme.*

He left Vienna that same year, moving to England, the United States and finally Brazil, where 17,500 other Jews had fled despite the strict immigration controls. In his autobiography Die Welt von Gestern *(The World of Yesterday), submitted to his publisher the day before his*

death, Zweig lamented the destruction of the civilisation he loved. He noted that 'nine tenths of what the world celebrated as Viennese culture in the nineteenth century was promoted, nourished, and created by Jews'.

His suicide note reflected that 'the world of my own language sank and was lost to me, and my spiritual homeland, Europe, destroyed itself'. He ended by writing 'I send greetings to all of my friends: May they live to see the dawn after this long night.' On 22 February 1942, he and his wife Lotte were found dead, holding hands, at their home in Petrópolis in the hills outside Rio de Janeiro.

The month after Zweig's death, Gustav Wagner was assigned to help establish the Sobibór death camp in eastern Poland. Born in 1911, the Austrian Nazi had joined the SS in the late 1930s before finding work in the regime's euthanasia programme, killing the mentally and physically disabled.

It was at Sobibór, however, where Wagner found his true métier. In an eighteen-month period starting in the spring of 1942, up to one quarter of a million people, virtually all Jews, were gassed on arrival at the camp. One of the reasons Sobibór is not nearly as well-known as Auschwitz is the fact that there were only fifty-eight known survivors, some of whom had miraculously escaped in a prisoner revolt in October 1943. Probability of survival at Sobibór: approximately 0.02 per cent.

Those few survivors had plenty to say about Gustav Wagner. 'He didn't shoot, he tortured,' said Thomas Blatt, who escaped from Sobibór at the age of sixteen. 'He used an axe, a shovel, whip, even his bare hands. I saw him pick up a shovel and simply split a man's head in two. He didn't need a reason for doing it. Perhaps the man was moving too slow. But when he killed, he smiled.' 'He had to kill somebody, even two or three – whoever came in front of him,' said Esther Raab, one of nine female survivors. 'He'd go around and pick his people. Like a drunk that needs drink, he had to have blood.' 'He was a handsome man, tall and

blond – a pure Aryan,' recalled Moshe Bahir. 'In civilian life he was, no doubt, a well-mannered man; at Sobibór he was a wild beast ... He would snatch babies from their mothers' arms and tear them to pieces in his hands.'

Fearing justice after the war, Wagner secured the help of Bishop Alois Hudal, a Nazi sympathiser and rector of a seminary for German priests in Rome. Hudal facilitated his escape to Syria, and then to Brazil in 1950. Here Wagner lived freely and openly in the idyllic woods surrounding São Paulo for almost thirty years, under the pseudonym Günther Mendel, marrying a Brazilian woman. He was one of an estimated 9,000 Nazi war criminals who took refuge in South America after the war, joining those Jews who had fled from them, in terror, some years before.

Although the Nazi hunter Simon Wiesenthal had tracked him down by 1978, the Brazilian authorities refused extradition requests from four countries. Gustav Wagner was left free to end his own life in his own home at the time of his own choosing, 3 October 1980.

• • •

Béla and Mariann were on the move soon after the sacking in Vicenza. By the end of May 1956, they had registered as residents with the authorities in Vienna. Once again, the couple took a breather, and reflected on their life situation. Guttmann was to look back on his time in Italy as 'the most excruciating and leanest years', but a period that was nonetheless 'basically necessary in life if you are to achieve more success'. He had reached another of the many crossroads he encountered in his career, a time for learning and new decisions.

Before even considering his next move in football, Guttmann had to shore up his personal status. He was under criminal investigation in

Italy, and had not lived in Hungary since 1949. Exit visas from Communist countries did not tend to last for seven years. Having stayed abroad without due permission, he was in citizenship limbo, exposed to extradition with no protection from any state he could call his own.

He will have quickly dismissed the idea of approaching the Hungarian authorities for a reaffirmation of citizenship, and returning to Budapest. Not only did he have precious little family left to return to, the political situation was also coming to a head. And as in February 1938, when he had the good sense to leave Vienna less than a month before the Anschluss, Guttmann foresaw no happy ending.

Joseph Stalin's death in 1953 had sparked hopes throughout the Soviet bloc for a more liberal, tolerant form of Communism. Events in June 1956, however, suggested such optimism was misplaced. The Polish government brutally suppressed a strike by the industrial workers of Poznań, who were seeking better living and working conditions. Several dozen protesters were killed.

Neither did the summer of 1956 augur well for Hungary. The recent years had been marked by political turbulence, with a bitter, seesawing power struggle between hardliners and would-be reformers taking hold. Within four months of Stalin's death, the reformist Imre Nagy became Prime Minister, replacing Mátyás Rákosi, who had executed and imprisoned thousands of his political opponents. But while Nagy set about releasing these political prisoners and relaxing state control of the media, the tenacious Rákosi clung on to the position of General Secretary of the Communist Party, using it as a platform to attack the new leadership.

By April 1955, Nagy had himself fallen out of favour with the Soviet politburo. The hardliners, in the persons of Rákosi and Nagy's successor András Hegedüs, were in charge once more. Although Soviet leader Nikita Khrushchev's bombshell speech in February 1956, denouncing Stalin's crimes, did make Rákosi's own personal position untenable,

any hopes of radical change were again soon dashed. Rákosi was able to designate his fellow hardliner Ernő Gerő as his replacement.[*]

'Same old, same old,' Béla Guttmann must have thought, as he viewed the situation from his Viennese apartment. On 20 July 1956, two days after Gerő's appointment, he submitted his application for Austrian citizenship. To the question on the form about his current citizenship, his response was 'stateless'.

When the authorities queried this claim of statelessness, Guttmann replied: 'I was until recently a Hungarian citizen, and fled from Hungary in 1949. I presume that, because of my escape, I have lost my Hungarian citizenship. Whether I have been formally deprived of citizenship, I do not know.'

On 28 September 1956, supported by a letter of recommendation from the Austrian Football Association, he was formally granted Austrian citizenship. As usual, Guttmann was ahead of the game.

Less than a month later, after a period of popular demonstrations against the Communist regime, Nagy assumed the position of Prime Minister once more, and set about instituting far-reaching democratic reforms in the so-called Hungarian Revolution. Khrushchev even agreed to pull his troops out of Budapest.

[*] Like Rákosi, whose surname at birth was Rosencrantz, Gerő was a Hungarian Jewish Communist who had spent the war years in the safety of Moscow. When Rákosi assumed total power in 1949, Gerő was his right-hand man. They both tried to hide their Jewish heritage, and used the powerful popular waves of anti-Jewish sentiment for their own political purposes. Their regime initiated a whole series of trials against different groups of Jews – community leaders, Communists, Orthodox Jews – for the crime of 'Zionism', and expelled thousands of members of the 'opposition' from the cities, with up to 25,000 Jews, mostly from Budapest, forcibly deported on cattle trucks to the countryside in 1951 and 1952. Despite his rejection of his Jewish roots and his obvious anti-Semitism, the Soviets still regarded Rákosi's Jewish blood as a threat to the stability of their puppet regime. 'We know that in Hungary there have been, apart from its own rulers, Turkish sultans, Austrian emperors, Tartar khans and Polish princes,' the Soviet secret police chief Lavrentiy Beria reportedly said to him. 'But as far as we know, Hungary has never had a Jewish king. Apparently, this is what you have become. Well, you can be sure that we won't allow it.'

But the whiff of freedom was to be extremely short-lived. The Soviet regime lost its nerve at the beginning of November, possibly due to Nagy's statement that Hungary intended to leave the Warsaw Pact. Soviet tanks crushed the revolution, with around 3,000 insurgents either killed in the fighting or executed, and thousands more imprisoned. More than 200,000 Hungarians (including around 10,000 Jews), out of a population of just 10 million, fled across the border to Austria.

As these desperate Hungarians poured in, stretching the Austrian immigration authorities to the limit, Béla Guttmann was already off on his travels once more, his shiny new passport tucked neatly in his pocket.

• • •

In 1949, Gusztáv Sebes, the head coach of the Hungarian national team and Deputy Minister of Sport, had come up with a new idea. In order to build a close togetherness and understanding in the national team, he wanted to draw most of his players from one team, where they could be trained in his preferred style of play.

The nationalisation of top Hungarian football clubs gave him the scope to do just that. He looked for a Budapest club to take over. MTK, the so-called Jewish club, had already been claimed by the hated secret police, and its Jewish leader, Gábor Péter.* Due to its nationalist image in the pre-war era, Ferencváros was deemed inappropriate as the breeding ground for players who were to represent the Communist regime.

* Gábor Péter, born Benjamin Eisenberger, led an institution responsible for much brutality, torture and murder. He was later to be a victim of one of the regime's anti-Jewish crackdowns. He was accused of being a Zionist spy for allegedly helping Jews to flee Hungary, and eventually sentenced to life imprisonment in 1954.

Sebes settled on Kispest, the club Béla Guttmann had walked out on the previous year, and which conveniently included the great Ferenc Puskás and József Bozsik. With its new name Honvéd, meaning 'defender of the homeland', the club was duly taken over by the Ministry of Defence and now represented the Hungarian army.

Conveniently, Sebes could use army conscription to supplement the skills of Puskás and Bozsik with young recruits from other clubs, such as the striker Sándor Kocsis and winger Zoltán Czibor. Honvéd contributed seven of the starting eleven that thrashed England 6–3 at Wembley stadium in 1953, and six of the team that should have won the World Cup in Switzerland in 1954, but were narrowly beaten in the final by underdogs West Germany.

A couple of years later, in October 1956, champions Honvéd were yet again top of the Hungarian league when the revolution brought football to a standstill. The club managed to get permission from UEFA, the administrative body for European football, to switch the first leg of their forthcoming European Cup tie against Athletic Bilbao from Budapest to Spain, with the home leg planned, optimistically, for a few weeks later.

Without any domestic league, the players needed to stay sharp for the Bilbao match, to be played on 22 November. The club received the official green light for friendly games in Austria, Germany and France, before travelling on to Spain.

They were also on the lookout for a suitable coach to prepare them for the European tie. Who better than the free agent Béla Guttmann, who had managed the club in its previous guise, was well-acquainted with its star players, and had since broadened his horizons in the high-quality Italian league?

After their fall-out at Kispest, Guttmann and Puskás had buried the hatchet at AC Milan's celebratory banquet the previous year. The influential captain was now all in favour of Guttmann's recruitment

as temporary coach, and the appointment was confirmed once the team had crossed the border to Vienna. Puskás would later describe Guttmann as 'very experienced and talented', and contact him for advice when starting his own coaching career.

Guttmann took up his position in the Honvéd dug out for the match in the San Mamés stadium in Bilbao. It was his first game in the new European Cup competition, which had started the previous season, and in which he was later to establish his legendary reputation. It was also his first competitive international club game since the victorious Mitropa Cup run seventeen years before. Unlike the Mitropa Cup, which was restricted to representatives of certain selected nations, the European Cup was open to the champions of all the nations on the continent, and has continued to this day as the premier international club competition in world football.

Before the passionate crowd of 40,000 Basques, the Spanish champions emerged as 3–2 victors, making the tie neatly poised for the second leg. With the situation still chaotic in Hungary, the team stayed abroad for the time being to remain match-fit, while raising much-needed finance from friendly matches.

The next game was against a combined team selected from both Atlético Madrid and European Cup holders Real Madrid, with Puskás on opposite sides to the great Alfredo Di Stéfano, subsequently his teammate at Real. A thrilling 5–5 draw was played out at the Santiago Bernabéu stadium, where a minute's silence was observed for the victims of the Hungarian revolution.

The tour continued with a 4–3 victory against Barcelona, before the travelling party moved on to Italy for three more games. The European media followed their movements with intense interest, speculating when or if some or all of the players would return to Hungary. Arriving in Milan for what turned out to be a 2–1 victory against his former employers, the coach tried to protect his players from the hungry pack of journalists. La Stampa reported:

'Guttmann gathered around him the many people present and said in his somewhat limited but comprehensible Italian: "During our European tour we have been questioned relentlessly and insistently. Please don't expect impossible answers that could aggravate an already difficult situation."'

The authorities now gave their blessing for a neutral venue, Brussels, to host the second leg of the Bilbao tie, to be played on 20 December. The preparation for the game was hardly conducive to top performance, with players distracted by anxieties about family back home and individual decisions about the future. Emil Östreicher, the Jewish financial secretary of the club, described the strange life they were all leading on this seemingly interminable tour. 'We were carrying money around in paper bags,' he said. 'We had no idea what was going to happen in Hungary, but news wasn't good and we didn't know how long we'd have to survive on the road.' Östreicher used some of that money to smuggle several of the players' wives out of Hungary.*

Invitations continued to arrive from clubs far and wide, all eager to play a game against such renowned Hungarian players. One came from Brazil. 'While we were in Belgium, we got an offer from the chairman of the Flamengo club: US$10,000 a match, plus air tickets, to come on tour,' recalled Östreicher. 'This was a great opportunity for the team, many of whom had longed to play in South America, but no one was overjoyed about it because we didn't have permission from the Hungarian FA.'

Meanwhile, Gusztáv Sebes, a Communist who remained loyal to the Soviet-backed regime, was sent by the Hungarian government

* Östreicher was born in Győr in north-west Hungary in 1914. During the Holocaust years, he was a slave labourer in Ukraine, but managed to escape. He then hid in a church in Budapest. On New Year's Eve 1944, the Arrow Cross raided the church to look for Jewish fugitives. Östreicher jumped out of a window into the freezing street wearing nothing but his underpants.

on a dual mission. His first stop was Zurich, where he managed to secure a pledge from FIFA, the governing body of world football, that no Honvéd tour would henceforth receive official sanction. He then moved on to Brussels in an attempt to persuade the team to return home after the match against Bilbao.

As he arrived, the team was beset by conflict over whether to accept the Brazilian offer. 'The team split into three factions,' said Lajos Tichy, the team's young and prolific striker. 'The first, including Puskás and Czibor, were openly with Östreicher on this [going on tour]; the second were against, including myself, [László] Budai and others. The third was wavering between the two. The three groups constantly argued about what to do.'

The Belgian public flocked to the Heysel stadium on a cold and foggy night, aware that this could be the last time that this great team would play together. The game was turned by an injury to Honvéd goalkeeper Lajos Faragó just after half-time, with the score at 1–1. As no substitutes could be used, Czibor volunteered to go in goal and the team was reduced to ten men.

Bilbao took advantage, scoring two quick goals. Although Honvéd rallied with two goals of their own, they couldn't force the game into a third match by levelling the aggregate score, and the game finished 3–3.*

Puskás felt cheated by events beyond his control. 'If the game had been played in Budapest, we would surely have won the tie,' he said. Sebes had another explanation for the surprise defeat. 'I got the impression that the players didn't really want to win it and go through, because that would have meant a serious rethink of the South American tour,' he said. 'I knew then that I would never

* The current away goals rule in European Cup, where the team that has scored more goals away from home in a two-leg tie will win if scores are otherwise equal, was introduced only in the mid-1960s. In the event of a level aggregate score, the tie would go to a third game, played in a neutral country.

again see those great players of the Golden Squad combined in one team.'

He was right. But before those players went their separate ways, there was to be one last wonderful treat for the football fans of Brazil, a vivid expression of the sport's beauty and innocence in its golden era. All of the top stars bar Tichy refused the Hungarian government's request to return to Budapest, while some other leading players joined the party from MTK, who had been on tour in Europe for similar reasons. Guttmann also drafted in Ferenc Szusza, the Újpest striker who had played under him in 1947.

While in the Spanish capital for the 5–5 draw, Guttmann had been offered the job of coach at Atlético Madrid. He turned down what would have been his only experience in La Liga at one of the great clubs of European football, unable to resist the alternative of taking great players to a nation rapidly emerging as the world's prime hotbed of talent. Always with an eye for an opportunity, for broadening his footballing experience, could he perhaps also find a suitable coaching position in this exhilarating environment?

• • •

Béla Guttmann's Hungarians were greeted by a large, enthusiastic crowd when they arrived in Rio de Janeiro for their 'illegal' tour in early January 1957.

The Brazilian public knew these players only too well. In 1954, their national team had been defeated 4–2 by Hungary in the so-called 'Battle of Bern', a World Cup quarter-final in which József Bozsik and two Brazilian players were sent off. Fighting had later continued in the dressing rooms, with Sebes requiring four stitches to a facial wound after what he described as a 'brutal, savage match'.

Due to this bad blood, the Hungarians had then thought it prudent to abandon their existing plans for a tour of Brazil. By

1957, however, enough time had now passed for all to concentrate on the spellbinding flair on show. Much pride was at stake in the games between teams representing such great footballing nations. In the days before international competition became so prevalent, so-called friendly games were seldom played only for fun, and this tour was no exception.

The first match against the Rio club Flamengo, watched in intense heat by a mammoth crowd of more than 113,000 in the Maracanã stadium, finished 6–4 to the Brazilians. Incredibly, the score was exactly reversed the following week in São Paulo. Three more games followed between the two teams, one back in the Maracanã and two in Caracas, Venezuela. Two of the five matches went to Flamengo, two to Honvéd, and one was drawn. The aggregate score in the five contests was Flamengo 18: Honvéd 17, with Puskás scoring eight.

The farewell game, played in front of 60,000 at the Maracanã, suggested strongly that the tide of world football was changing. Against a combined team of Flamengo and Botafogo players, Honvéd were thrashed 6–2, outclassed by a team inspired by Garrincha, a future star of the Brazilian World Cup-winning sides of 1958 and 1962.

The players arrived back in Vienna towards the end of February. FIFA, shamefully, sided with the totalitarian dictatorship, and banned Puskás for eighteen months from all competitive football. He eventually signed for Real Madrid, while Sándor Kocsis and Zoltán Czibor ended up at Barcelona. Emil Östreicher became technical director at Real – some advancement from slave labour in the Ukraine – and was to be instrumental in the recruitment of Puskás.

As he no doubt always intended, Guttmann stayed in Brazil, far away from the Italian court process. On 1 March, three days before Solti was to stand alone in a Milan dock and contrive his new story,

Guttmann signed a contract as coach of São Paulo, a club he had last visited while on the Hakoah All-Stars tour of 1930. Despite not speaking a word of Portuguese, his talents had apparently made an impression on the club's director of football, Manoel Raymundo Paes de Almeida.

Guttmann thus replaced the long-standing coach, Vicente Feola, who became his assistant. It was to be a relationship that left a clear imprint on the future direction of world football.

• • •

'In the course of my long career I have been to a lot of countries and have also worked in some of them,' Guttmann once said. 'If I saw anything good in football, I stole it immediately and kept it for myself. After a while, I mixed myself a cocktail from these stolen delicacies.'

Given the incredible success Béla Guttmann was to achieve with three teams in the five years from taking over at São Paulo in 1957 to leaving Benfica in 1962 (two European Cups, four national championships and one domestic cup), we can make the case that his experiences in Italy and with Honvéd had rounded off his international footballing education, and that his coaching methods had now reached something like full maturity. With anti-Semitism and then the Holocaust taking six pivotal years out of his career in his forties, Guttmann thus reached his peak later than most coaches, in his late fifties and early sixties.

A few essential elements characterised his approach. We have already seen how he would brook no assault on his control and authority, whether from within the team or from the club authorities. Another chapter in the Guttmann coaching manual could be devoted to the concept of open fairness, and its impact on the psychological contract between player and coach.

Through his actions, he would go out of his way to make the players aware of a simple principle that goes something like this: We are a team, all on the same side. I will always treat everyone fairly. I will show no favouritism, even to the greatest players, in the discharge of discipline. If you show the total commitment I demand of you, I will support you and make you a better player. But if you baulk at this commitment, you will do so knowing the consequences.

In this way, clarity and trust were established. The player knew where he stood. All he had to do was work hard, and then he could rest assured that Guttmann was on his side, working together with the player to achieve the same goal.

'Guttmann is the greatest coach I ever met,' said the Benfica and Portugal goalkeeper Alberto da Costa Pereira in 1963. 'Besides being a student of football and able to transfer his knowledge to the players, he was also their friend. He understood their problems, and was a tireless middleman between them and the Benfica directors.'

Two examples from his earlier coaching career illustrate how Guttmann implemented his principle of open fairness on a daily basis. At Újpest before the war, he instituted a fines system for anyone who was late for training or a team meeting. 'I proclaimed that if someone was late, he would pay a certain amount of money into the money-box and we would spend it together at the end of the year,' he said. 'I, as the coach, would pay double the amount of the fine. But some of them were smiling scornfully as if they doubted my words.'

Keen to reinforce his principle, Guttmann had a plan. 'One day, I went to the pitch half an hour earlier and hid under the stand,' he said:

When I saw that it was ten minutes past the agreed time I came forward and walked to them as if I had just arrived. Zsengellér [the

star player] and his mates welcomed me with a massive ovation thinking, 'We've caught you in the act, old man' and started to shake the money-box right in front of my face. And I put the fine in. Now they were moaning that 'if the Boss pays without a word we will also have to!'

Some years later, at Kispest, he again made the point that absolutely no one could get away with infringing team discipline. This time, it was the great József Bozsik who was to pay the penalty. 'The training session would start, and I would look into the players' eyes...' Guttmann said:

I would watch their first moves, their reflexes, to see whether I could notice any difference in their performance compared to that of the previous session. Well, one day Cucu Bozsik came to the training and his eyes looked slightly dodgy. I called him to the side. 'Cucu, there's something wrong with you!' 'Uncle Béla,'* he said, 'I owe you a confession. I stayed out a little late last night ... but I swear it won't happen again!' We shook hands and I told him to get changed, go home and get some sleep. This is how I 'punished' him. Never again did anything like that happen to him! Not only did he set an example on the pitch but in his private life also.

This was classic Guttmann. Just like Jimmy Hogan before him and José Mourinho after him, he was always racking his brains to think up ways to squeeze that little bit more out of his players, or gain a marginal advantage for the team. When asked in retirement where

* *Básci*, the Hungarian for uncle, is a traditional polite form for addressing older people. Guttmann boasted that 'back home I was called Béla básci even when I was only thirty-five, even by those who were twenty years older than me', indicating his natura; charisma and disposition for leadership.

the secret of his success lay, Guttmann replied simply: 'I could handle the players. I feel I was a good psychologist.'

Few of his charges would quibble with this explanation. 'He was a strict disciplinarian,' remarked Costa Pereira, 'but because of his strong personality and his obvious sincerity we all accepted his rulings without question.'

'He was a very practical man, very clear in his psychology, his mental preparation,' says António Simões, the youngest player ever to win the European Cup when he triumphed with Benfica in 1962. 'He was ahead of his time. Mourinho says the same things today that Béla Guttmann did fifty years ago.' Indeed, as we shall see, Guttmann's preparation for big games might involve influencing the referee's mindset, or intentionally drawing the limelight to himself in order to take the pressure off the players. Modern-day football fans will instantly recognise these Mourinho-like antics. Brought up in Portugal at a time when Guttmann stories would have been notorious among the footballing public in that country, it seems that he was heavily influenced by his great predecessor.

Building up players' confidence was another hallmark of Guttmann's armoury. Well before management theorists formally expounded the Pygmalion effect – the proven theory that people tend to perform according to the expectations of powerful others – Guttmann was instinctively putting it into practice. The combination of talent and application, contrary to popular wisdom, is seldom sufficient to realise full human potential. Younger people, in particular, respond positively to affirmation, to a teacher or boss constantly telling them how good they can be. In this way, the vital ingredient of self-belief is added to the mix.

The shame, perhaps, is that there was an inherent conflict between this approach and Guttmann's brief incumbency in any job. Before his constant encouragement could exert its full, cumulative effect, he was usually on his way out.

The exception was his time at Benfica, where his stint encompassed three full seasons. 'What a great improvement for this team since they won its first European Cup Final against Barcelona a year ago!' wrote Hans Blickensdörfer, the German sports journalist, after Benfica had claimed their second successive European Cup triumph. Guttmann explained the steep progress to him. 'At that time [the Barcelona final] ... the boys had just started to realise what they have in them. For three years, I have been preaching to them that they shouldn't develop any complexes about any other team and that they are actually able to recover from any setbacks.' Certainly, the team's unswerving self-belief, painstakingly constructed by Guttmann and further enhanced by his inspiring half-time team talk, was a key factor in this second final against the mighty Real Madrid. 'I am 5 foot 8,' António Simões told me. 'But after he spoke to us during that final, I felt 6 foot 4.'

His people-management philosophy dealt with the mind; an unusually rigorous training schedule looked after the body. The two were nevertheless connected. Only by establishing total control and implanting the psychological contract would the players willingly submit to his punishing demands with regard to fitness and clean living. 'It was a decisive factor that my players believed in me, and they made an effort to realise my ideas in their private lives and through their lifestyles,' he said. 'It's not easy to get a team in shape, but it's even harder to keep them in shape.'

In Italy, he was to learn the dangers of going too far the other way, of over-training the players. At Padova, Triestina and Vicenza, his teams deteriorated in the second half of the season, possibly resulting from a combination of physical over-exertion and Guttmann's inability to maintain his initial level of intensity. The Milan directors feared their team's slip in form at the start of 1955 presaged a similar collapse, and opted to sack him. His success in the next years, even when burdened with the additional demands

of European Cup campaigns with Benfica, suggests that he subsequently hit upon a more balanced and effective modus operandi. The victory against Real, after a performance characterised by speed, energy and aggression, came in May 1962 near the end of a long season in which Benfica would also go on to win the domestic knock-out cup competition.

In his focus on physical conditioning and lifestyles – a priority passed down from the revolutionary Hogan – Guttmann seems to have been in the vanguard of a global change in attitudes to fitness in football that only began to seep into the British game several decades later.

Even as far back as 1947, in his second spell at Újpest, he talked of two tough sessions a day. The following year, he admonished Bozsik for his suspected hangover. At Benfica, the players stayed together in club accommodation for two or three days before a game to keep them from mischief, and the resident cook was given specific instructions about the required diet. 'For professional players that have to work through sixty to seventy games a season, nightlife is nothing more than poison,' he said. 'It is not possible to maintain good form at the same level for nine or ten months without a strictly regulated lifestyle.'

Simões recalls that Guttmann drummed home his message about excessive drinking to his players every single day:

> When you went to a bar, it is in your head. Somebody would go to get another drink but a teammate would say, 'Hey, don't you remember what Guttmann said? We should stop at one.' He taught us that football is not just a matter of running hard and crossing the ball. You need to have discipline. I am seventy-two years old. More than fifty years later, I am still telling you what he said. It has stayed in my head for ever.

In an amusing aside, Simões also disclosed that Guttmann constantly warned the team against exhausting themselves by staying

up all night having sex. '*Fare l'amore una volta*', would be his con-
stant Italian refrain to his Portuguese players. Make love only once.

At Milan, one of Italy's top clubs, Guttmann believed his players
had never previously been trained so hard. Determining after the
Italy years that he was pushing players too far, he then tweaked his
regime to achieve a delicate equilibrium, still to this day recognised
throughout professional football as the ideal state.

'You have to have great demands, but you have also to know the
limits,' he later reflected. 'The muscles of a player are like stretched
rubber, you can stretch them a bit but at a certain point they get
torn. I was fortunate to have had only a few injured players.'

His sophisticated perspective would not look out of place if ut-
tered by a top coach in the modern era. But contrast, for example,
Guttmann's attitude to that of Bill Shankly, the Liverpool manager,
whose views more accurately reflected the norm, at least among
British coaches, until relatively recently. Shankly would see injury
as an indication of a lack of commitment. Ray Clemence, a goal-
keeper at Liverpool long after Guttmann's peak years as coach, re-
called that Shankly would simply refuse to speak to injured players.
'His philosophy was that if he made injured players feel like lepers,
they'd be back quicker.'

Or compare Guttmann's attitude to late-night drinking with that
of Brian Clough. 'The night before the League Cup Final against
Southampton in 1979, we were blotto,' said the then Nottingham
Forest striker Garry Birtles about a match played two years before
Guttmann's death:

> We had everything we could possibly have wanted to drink. Bitter,
> lager, mild, champagne. There were people who could hardly stand by
> the time we went to bed. But Clough insisted on it. Archie Gemmill
> wanted to go to bed. He wouldn't let him. We were 1–0 down at half-
> time the next day, but once we sobered up we were OK. We won 3–2.

Neither of these stories is meant to question the managerial prowess of either Shankly or Clough, but merely to emphasise Guttmann's pioneering mentality. Since all professional coaches now profess the importance of supreme fitness and clean living, we can certainly make the case that the phenomenal success of Shankly and Clough came despite, not because of, their respective attitudes to injuries and drinking.

Even with his great emphasis on training, Guttmann understood the vital importance of seizing big moments in the heat of the battle. When he said 'a match is not won on Saturday or Sunday, it must be won on weekdays during training sessions,' he was under-estimating his own ability to inspire his players at crucial moments. His record in finals, and in title-deciding matches on the last day of the season, was excellent. When he had five minutes to get his message across to his players, he knew exactly which buttons to press, a true sign of a great football manager. You can have all the coaching expertise in the world, but unless you can get your team over the line when it matters, the trophy cabinet will always be bare.

Guttmann invested considerable time and effort in tactics, displaying the insight, innovation and flexibility common to the greatest Hungarian-born coaches of that era. 'Every team needs to have its own system, adapted to the characteristics of the players,' he told the Portuguese newspaper *A Bola* in 1962, before giving his theory a characteristically colourful twist. 'Just as a tailor does not make the same suit for a hunchback as he does for a normal man, so a coach cannot give all teams the same system.' He astutely moved players around the chosen system – like all great managers in sport or business, he detected previously unidentified strengths in indi-viduals. At Benfica, for example, he switched Domiciano Cavém from left-wing to a very different role on the right side of midfield in order to fit António Simões into the team.

Whichever formation Guttmann chose, the outcome was

high-tempo, direct football played on the front foot. 'I was always for attacking,' he said. '0–0 for me was fine as the latest score. I could never accept it as the final score.'

• • •

Béla Guttmann's spell at São Paulo was very typical – brief (less than eighteen months), feisty and full of energy and new ideas. This time, it was also highly successful.

At that point, given the huge size of the country and limited domestic air travel, there was no national league in Brazil. São Paulo competed in the regional Campeonato Paulista against other giants of Brazilian football, such as Corinthians, Palmeiras and Santos. Pelé, widely believed to be the greatest footballer of all time, played his first full season for Santos in 1957, coinciding with Guttmann's only one in Brazilian football. Despite starting the season at the age of sixteen, Pelé emerged as top scorer in the league, a feat he would repeat for the following eight campaigns.

São Paulo had won the Campeonato Paulista several times in the 1940s, but had been knocked off their perch by Santos and Corinthians in the following decade, with one sole triumph in 1953. Having assumed the reins in March 1957, Guttmann had a long period of pre-season training at his disposal before the task of regaining the title got underway in July.

He had observed that Brazilian players too often prioritised ostentatious displays of crowd-pleasing acrobatics over effective football. What use a breathtaking feat of ball juggling or an overhead kick if no goal resulted from them? Speaking no Portuguese, his constant mantra to his players was 'Pá, pá, pá, pum!', meaning they should take only a couple of touches, and then shoot to score.

He maintained his regime of two sessions a day despite the 30-degree heat. Time after time, he instructed his players to practise

shooting, himself demonstrating to them how exactly to hit a ball hard and low with clinical accuracy. He requested that a specially measured wooden screen be built, placed in front of the goalposts, and divided into eight sections. Relentlessly, he asked his players to aim for each of the eight sections in turn. 'Under Guttmann, the players are learning to shoot, run with the ball, head the ball, and many more things which the players thought that, being Brazilian, they were born already knowing,' reported the *Folha de São Paulo* newspaper in late March.

It is certainly possible to make the case that the focus of those few months of pre-season training in São Paulo in 1957, harnessing Brazilian talent with pragmatism, had a profound effect on football's subsequent course.

Many have claimed that Guttmann introduced the 4-2-4 tactical system to Brazil during this season, and that this innovation contributed heavily to Brazil's dominance on the international stage for more than a decade. Jonathan Wilson, in his history of football tactics, *Inverting the Pyramid*, agrees that Guttmann was highly influential in Brazilian football history, but not in the way commonly suggested.

The 4-2-4 formation, closely associated with the Hungarian Golden Team of the early 1950s and its demolition of England on the hallowed Wembley turf, was meant to add more flexibility to the previously popular W-M. It was the first formation to be described using numbers, and the first with four assigned defenders. The formation was ideal for a Guttmann team, as it exploited the increasing fitness of professional players. The aim of the 4-2-4 team was to attack with six, and defend with six, with highly energetic midfielders performing both roles. As the midfield had fewer players than past formations, defenders needed to be comfortable on the ball, equipped with the skill and confidence to bring it out of defence with a run or astute pass. It was thus an ideal system for the

naturally gifted footballers of Brazil, as it would have been, by all accounts, for the elegant centre-back Guttmann in his playing days.

In truth, says Wilson, the formation had already started to be employed by one or two other Brazilian sides, independently of Hungarian influence, in the early 1950s. 'Guttmann's impact was less to do with system than with style,' he wrote:

> Geoffrey Green [a football writer for *The Times*] perhaps flattered England when he spoke of the Hungary of 1953 as having hit a midpoint between British directness and continental elaboration, but the general point was sound ... so often in that game at Wembley, Hungary transformed defence into attack with a counter of two or three passes. It was not 4-2-4 itself that Guttmann brought to Brazil, but that sense of purpose.

Vicente Feola, Guttmann's assistant at São Paulo, became the Brazil coach for the World Cup of 1958 in Sweden, and introduced Guttmann's tactical system, augmented by his favoured directness and energy. György Orth, Guttmann's close friend from his MTK playing days, witnessed a speech by Feola in Peru after Brazil's triumph in the tournament. 'This victory is 50 per cent down to Guttmann, since I copied his method,' he reportedly said.

São Paulo's 1957 season had started inauspiciously. The league format was divided into two phases. In the first phase, each of the twenty teams played each other, either home or away. The top ten teams would then qualify for the so-called blue series. The slate would be wiped clean, and the title race would begin in earnest, with these ten playing each other home and away.

The first phase saw São Paulo qualifying, but only in fifth place with Corinthians several points in front. A ferocious media rounded on the embattled European coach, who recalled all too well the fate of Izidor Kürschner, a Hungarian Jew whose innovative and ultimately

influential methods at Flamengo were lambasted by the Brazilian newspapers before the war, resulting in his eventual sacking.

Guttmann planned his customary defiance. 'Someone told me that coaches here pay journalists to write good news reports about their teams,' he said:

> One fine day, I invited the most popular sports reporters to dinner, opened a bottle of champagne in their honour and ceremoniously proclaimed that they shouldn't expect me to pay them, not even as little as a penny! They had a good laugh, but later they discussed it and from then on they blew up every one of the smallest mistakes, they were revelling in malice, they didn't hide it that they wanted to slaughter me, to have someone replace me, someone they can rob. There were at least twenty-five sports papers in the town, so you can imagine the scope of the attack I experienced. Everybody knew the gentlemen conspired against me, or to put it nicely, they showed solidarity in this.

There weren't too many sneers from the press in the second half of the season. In stark contrast to Guttmann's teams in Italy, São Paulo just got stronger and stronger, despite a heavy schedule of thirty-seven league games in five months.

After his inspired late-season signing of the 36-year-old Zizinho, a veteran Brazilian international and still then the biggest football star in the country, the title bid gained yet further momentum. Guttmann ordered Zizinho to occupy the more attacking and creative position within his midfield two, and the effect was immediately electric. São Paulo won the first four of Zizinho's games, scoring twenty-one goals in the process, including a 6–2 thrashing of Pelé's Santos away from home in mid-November. 'Zizinho gave a masterclass,' remembered Pelé. 'He was astonishing. His passes, his shots, his positioning – it was all very beautiful.'

Everything was set up for the final game, against Corinthians, with the two teams level on points, and one behind Santos. A victory would clinch the title for either team, and a draw would lead to a play-off series.

This particular *Clássico Majestoso* (majestic derby) between the two teams from the city of São Paulo was to be played on 29 December 1957 at the Pacaembu stadium, shared at that point by both clubs. In customary style, Guttmann sought any tiny advantage before the big showdown. Fearing that Corinthians were close to the hearts of many local referees, he worked hard to secure a Rio-based referee and two English linesmen working in Argentina.

After a tense and goalless first half, São Paulo ran out 3–1 winners to take the title. The final, conclusive goal was scored, according to reports, in a clearly offside position, an offence missed by the English linesman, Ronald Lynch. Another goal was scored by Canhoteiro, a fast left-winger and brilliant dribbler, whose prodigious talent was to be marred by alcoholism. Pelé was later to name Canhoteiro and Zizinho as his greatest footballing idols.

The fans of Corinthians reacted with fury to the defeat, rioting and throwing missiles on to the pitch in what became known as *A tarde das garrafadas* (the afternoon of bottles). A vindicated Guttmann rounded on the assembled media: 'Thank you very much for the unforgettable propaganda with which you have been supporting my work throughout the whole year. Look at this champion's ribbon and don't ask any questions. This can speak better than I could.'

Imre Guttmann, who had by this time settled in São Paulo, was in the crowd that day. He had acted as his uncle's interpreter for the Honvéd tour, but was now just a jubilant fan. 'There will never be a team closer to my heart than São Paulo at the 1957 championship. How could I forget Béla Guttmann's starting eleven from the 3–1 against Corinthians? Poy, De Sordi, Mauro, Sarará, Vítor, Riberto, Maurinho, Amaury, Gino Orlando, Zizinho and Canhoteiro…'

But a couple of weeks after Brazil's triumph in the World Cup six months later, Guttmann was already on his way back to Europe. Results were not the issue. The team had played only two games in the new season, with one victory and one draw. Nor did he have another job to go to. Guttmann later attributed his departure to two causes. He felt the stress of battling the media was taking its toll on him, while the São Paulo climate was similarly sapping Mariann, who had already gone back to Europe to recuperate.

The São Paulo director of football, Paes de Almeida, had another, more convincing explanation, later telling a journalist that the club could no longer afford Guttmann's fixed dollar salary, as the dollar had soared in value against the Brazilian cruzeiro.

Whatever the reason, his departure sparked a mutual love fest, a highly unusual end to a Guttmann reign. 'Unfortunately, I cannot stay away from my wife,' he said in a statement. 'She is not well, and I should leave to take care of what I cherish most. I have no grievance against São Paulo. Rather, I take away an undying memory of the biggest club I've seen in all my life in sport.' 'You leave with a champion title at the end of your extraordinary coaching work,' the club responded. 'You came to São Paulo as a foreign trainer and leave as our best friend.' Mauro Ramos, the club's centre-back who later captained Brazil to victory at the 1962 World Cup, continued to correspond with Guttmann for some time, with at least one letter addressing him as *o Grande Campeao* (the great champion).

On 19 July 1958, the world champion Feola and most of Guttmann's players turned up at Congonhas Airport to see him off. They weren't to know that São Paulo would have to wait until 1970 to win another Campeonato Paulista, by which time their former coach was in retirement, having soared to the very heights.

CHAPTER 9

CONQUERING EUROPE

By the end of July 1492, just four months after an expulsion order had been issued, the last Jew refusing to convert to Christianity had left Spain. Most of those leaving, up to 100,000 in number, opted to go to neighbouring Portugal. It was not long before they came to regret their decision. Such has been the lottery of Jewish wandering.

King Manuel I of Portugal soon decreed that all Jews should be removed from the country by November 1497. But appreciating the economic value of the Jewish community, who were especially active in commerce, he then had second thoughts, resolving to convert as many as possible. On 19 March 1497, Jews were ordered to take any children between four and fourteen years of age to Lisbon. Most were forcibly torn from their parents, who were promptly informed that their offspring would be baptised and brought up by Christians. Some of the Jews managed to kill themselves and their children rather than succumb to the authorities' wishes.

All synagogues, religious schools and Jewish communal buildings were seized by the state. In October of the same year, some 20,000 refusing to convert were lured to Lisbon, under the impression that they would be free to sail to a new life from the port. Instead they were crammed into the courtyard of the Estaus Palace, where they were deprived of food and drink and dragged to a nearby church to be baptised. Many succumbed

to conversion, some were able to commit suicide, others were burnt at the stake for their obduracy.

Many of the converted Jews, the 'New Christians', continued to prac-tise their Jewish faith in private. It didn't really matter either way, as the local population still regarded them all as Jews to be despised. On 19 April 1506, the popular revulsion at the hidden enemy in their midst finally erupted into a savage massacre.

At the Church of São Domingos, next to Rossio Square, someone claimed to have seen the illuminated face of Jesus Christ on the altar, sparking reli-gious fervour. One of the New Christians present was naive enough to voice his scepticism about the alleged miracle. Women beat him to unconsciousness, men finished off the job, and his body was torn apart in the square.

Enraged by such casual blasphemy, thousands of people roamed the streets of Lisbon looking for Jews to murder. Solomon ibn Verga, a Jew who man-aged to escape the mass slaughter and flee to Turkey, gives us his eye-witness account: 'We then saw a mass of people armed with swords, and in three days they massacred three thousand souls, forcing them into the streets and burning them. They threw pregnant women out of windows, receiving them below with swords so their embryos were expelled soon after.'

'They dragged them into the streets with their sons, women and daughters, throwing the mixture of the living and the dead upon the fires, without any pity,' confirmed the Portuguese chronicler, Damião de Góis. 'Such was the cruelty that even infants in their cribs were executed, being taken by the legs and cut into pieces, and thrown against walls.'

• • •

The plane from Vienna arrived at around eight o'clock on a Sat-urday evening at Lisbon's Portela airport. Down the steps de-scended a man who would weave a spell of magic over Portuguese and European football over the next three and a half years. The date was 1 November 1958.

Béla Guttmann had arrived in Vienna back in July with no fixed plans, and waited patiently for the suitors to come calling. Representatives from the Austrian Football Association, looking for a new national team coach after their poor showing in the recent World Cup Finals in Sweden, assured him that the job was as good as his.

Guttmann later claimed that the appointment was delayed and then abandoned by 'frictions' in the organisation. Given that he himself alleged that his eventual tenure as coach of the Austrian national team six years later was undermined by anti-Jewish sentiment, we can certainly speculate what these 'frictions' may have been. Neither can we discount the possibility that Guttmann's salary demands were deemed excessive by some, nor the possibility that both explanations could be valid, and closely linked.

Guttmann said that he received several offers from clubs as well, but settled on FC Porto in Portugal's second city, perhaps influenced by the many Brazilian footballers and coaches who had recently gone to try their luck in the Primeira Divisão. Now speaking a smattering of Portuguese, and with such recent success at São Paulo, he would certainly have been considered a major catch for a club that had fallen behind the other two clubs among the Os Três Grandes of Portuguese football. In the previous two seasons, Porto had narrowly missed out in the league to arch rivals Benfica and Sporting Lisbon respectively.

He joined for the ninth match of the season, with his team already three points off the top in what was always a very tight race. His first match in charge was the O Clássico against leaders Benfica at home, ending in a goalless draw, a very unGuttmann-like result. Alarm bells started ringing after the next match, away at Belenenses on a rain-soaked pitch in Lisbon, with the team again failing to score and this time losing 1–0. The gap was now a very substantial five points.*

* The award of three points for a win was not widely introduced in world football until the 1990s.

But by this stage, Guttmann was right in his prime, ruthlessly decisive and infectiously self-confident. It didn't matter what group of players he had at his disposal. His expertise was entirely portable – potent with any team anywhere in the world.

'I went into the dressing room smiling, and I saw that the president was shocked by that,' he remembered. "What are you so happy about?" "Look," I said to him, "I know who to drop from the team."' The unlucky player was José Maria Pedroto, a Portuguese international and local hero. 'Nobody liked this move, of course, but I had a purpose with it,' he said. Wanting more dynamic midfielders with an ambition to get forward and score, he brought in the young Brazilian Luís Roberto to replace the ageing Pedroto.

The strikers, meanwhile, were detained for extra sessions. As at São Paulo, he drummed home his message that football matches were won by goals, not by displays of outlandish technical skill, telling them plainly that 'as long as I am here, strikers who don't shoot won't be selected'.

Amazing what a couple of tweaks, clear instructions and managerial enthusiasm can do. As if a tap had been turned on, Porto's attacking game immediately started to yield rewards. In their next two games, against FC Barreirense and União Torreense, the team scored twelve goals without reply. The all-Portuguese forward line of António Teixeira, Noé, Carlos Duarte and Hernâni all got in on the act. None of them looked back, scoring sixty-seven goals between them in the 26-game league season.

The defeat against Belenenses in Guttmann's second game turned out to be the team's last reverse of the entire league season. In the return fixture towards the end of the season, with Belenenses realistic title challengers, Porto turned the tables in comprehensive fashion, thrashing them 7–0 at their home in the Estádio das Antas.

All of these goals were to prove invaluable. The last game of the league season was played on 22 March 1959, with Porto and Benfica

dead level on thirty-nine points, but with Guttmann's team ahead by four on the goal difference tally. Both their matches would kick off at the same time.

On paper, Porto looked like a shoe-in to take the title. Although their final game was away from home, they were up against already relegated União Torreense, whom they had thrashed earlier in the season. But with a few minutes to go, the goal difference had been bridged. While Porto had mustered only one goal, Benfica were up 6–1 at home against CUF Barreiro, helped by the award of four penalties by the referee Inocêncio Calabote, who also sent off three CUF players. 'Benfica's match was actually refereed by a man called Innocence,' was Guttmann's subsequent cynical jibe.

Two late goals by Teixeira and Noé eased the Porto nerves. But Calabote had started the Benfica game eight minutes later than stipulated, and added on several minutes of injury time at the end. With their game finished in Torres Vedras, 50 kilometres north of the capital, the Porto players waited for an excruciating twelve minutes before Mr Innocence blew up. Benfica had scored once more, but it wasn't enough. Guttmann had won the title in his first season for the second time in succession, again on the last day, this time by one goal.

As one would expect, he was showered with adoration. He had brought to Porto the title they had won just once in the previous twenty years, upsetting their hated rivals in the process.

The two teams faced each other again in the July final of the national knock-out cup competition, the Taça de Portugal, a match played after the league season had ended. The game turned out to be an ugly, ill-tempered affair, decided by a goal scored after just thirteen seconds by Benfica's Domiciano Cavém, without Porto having even touched the ball.

Unbeknown to the Porto faithful at the game, however, Guttmann already had a secret commitment to become the coach of

Benfica after the final. Benfica (or, to give them their official name, Sport Lisboa e Benfica) were arguably the bigger club, with more trophies under their belt, a larger stadium and a wider fan base. Guttmann also revealed that he was offered a salary of 400,000 escudos per season, almost doubling his Porto salary.

Of course, individuals leave for better-paid jobs and more alluring prospects every day. But this is football, where tribal loyalties are passionately felt. Imagine a manager leaving Manchester United for Liverpool, or Real Madrid for Barcelona. To say that Guttmann was not a popular man in Porto is something of an understatement. When he travelled back to the Estádio das Antas with his Benfica team in future years, he did so only with a personal police guard close by. Not that any of this seemed to bother him unduly. After the hostility he faced on a football ground while playing for Hakoah, this would all have seemed rather tame by comparison.

Referring to his departure from Porto in his autobiography five years later, he gave his most detailed explanation of how he viewed his role as coach, and why he saw no issue with upping sticks. 'I am an international expert with no fanaticism for a particular club,' he said:

> I sell my expertise to a club for a limited time. If I were saddled by a fanatical attachment to any club, I couldn't work for another with total commitment … a proper expert cannot allow such a thing. I left Porto with a clear conscience, like a father who dies leaving his sons well cared for. With the championship title and entry into the European Cup, I left my players in the best situation.

He was not so honest in the immediate wake of his departure, saying that he had to move because Mariann couldn't bear the wet climate. Given that this was the second time in twelve months he had used his wife's aversion to the weather as an excuse for leaving,

we can suspect that this had become his stock public pronounce-
ment, when the real reason was money. At any rate, this line just
wound up the Porto faithful even more.

The sight of Guttmann lifting every trophy in the book with
Benfica over the next three years may well have dispatched a few of
Porto's more ardent followers to an early grave. His place at Porto
was taken by Ettore Puricelli, the man Guttmann believed had
stolen the Milan championship from him back in 1955. Guttmann
must have enjoyed a healthy dose of schadenfreude when he saw
how his second-time successor fared this time – six defeats in nine
games at Porto, including elimination in the European Cup pre-
liminary round to Inter Bratislava, before Puricelli was put out of
his misery in early November. Such a spectacular failure with the
same group of players who lifted the league earlier the same year
served only to augment Guttmann's reputation as a miracle worker.

Porto would in fact have to wait another nineteen years for their
next Primeira Divisão title. Their coach at the end of the drought
in 1978 was José Maria Pedroto, the man whom Guttmann had
unceremoniously dropped from the first team. Such is life in a top-
sy-turvy world, a world with which Guttmann himself was all too
familiar.

• • •

Back in the mid-1930s, Béla Guttmann had surprised the club
president at SC Enschede by asking for an enormous bonus if his
team won the national championship. The president thought the
idea was so preposterous that he agreed, and very nearly came to
regret it.

In 1959, Guttmann is said to have asked for a bonus of 200,000
escudos (half his annual salary) if Benfica were to win the hallowed
European Cup. The president, Maurício Vieira de Brito, having

seen that Real Madrid had won the first four European Cups and that Benfica had not even won the Portuguese league for the previous two seasons, clearly thought the demand as much of a joke as his Enschede counterpart. 'Make it 300,000, my friend,' he replied. His casual underestimation of Guttmann, a great football manager at his absolute peak, was to prove expensive.

Guttmann rolled up his sleeves, clear-headed and purposeful as ever. 'The first thing I did when I took over at Benfica was to sack twenty players and gradually rebuild the staff,' he said:

> I was handicapped by two things – players who were not good enough, and the club rule which stipulated that Benfica would never sign players from outside Portugal or her colonies.* I started to push the best young players through from the youth team to the first team.

His decision to dispense with so many fringe players from the squad stemmed from a desire to work closely with a cohesive group of first-team players. 'Why would we need to keep thirty-five paid professionals when I only get to use sixteen or eighteen of them?' he asked. 'Too many fringe players only create an extra cost for the club, and disturbance for the team. Since nobody is satisfied when they are not in the first team, all those reserve players were a source of unrest.'

The first player he promoted from the first team was Fernando Cruz, a nineteen-year-old left wing-back. He also signed José Augusto from relegated Barreirense. With typical perceptiveness and imagination, Guttmann exploited Augusto's lightning pace and deceptive body feint by immediately switching the 22-year-old

* The no-foreigner rule, which put Benfica at a major disadvantage not just against foreign opponents, but against local rivals Sporting and Porto, was abandoned only in 1979. Players from Angola and Mozambique were classified as Portuguese citizens, however, and were eligible to play for Portugal.

from his previous role of centre-forward to right wing, a position in which he excelled. Two European Cups and a glittering international career later, Augusto had a lot to thank his insightful coach for.

As far as tactics were concerned, Guttmann showed that he was not wedded to one particular system by alternating the 4-2-4 system, which the team had been using in previous seasons, with the more attacking W-M. 'I know 4-2-4 is not suitable for us,' he said. 'I disciplined the Brazilians to play it at São Paulo. Vicente Feola, my assistant, adopted my methods with the national team, and they won the World Cup. But our great strength is in attack, and we must use a system which envisages five forwards.'

His training sessions focused on making best use of these attacking resources, and were to prove devastatingly effective in conveying simple but vital messages. 'My coaching was based on two simple things: passing and shooting,' he said. 'I spent hours working on the quick return ball, what some called the one-two or wall-pass, because I discovered in Brazil that it was the best way of opening up any defence on the edge of the opponent's penalty area.'

Those few changes were all that were needed. Benfica chalked up victory after victory, scoring goals galore, in what became a two-horse race against Sporting Lisbon. Unbeaten Benfica were one point ahead when the teams met in April at the Estádio da Luz (Stadium of Light), three games from the end of the season.

The pre-match media build-up touted this particular Derby de Lisboa as the 'clash of the century'. Emotions ran high among the 70,000 spectators in the huge open-air arena, with many reports of spectators fainting as they watched an archetypal exhibition of pulsating, attacking football à la Béla Guttmann.

The coach had tried to teach his players the footballing version of the 'blitzkrieg', unsettling opponents with bursts of sustained attack in the opening minutes of each half. By the time the other

team had got the measure of the game, they were invariably already recovering from a deficit.

On this occasion, Benfica were two up in just ten minutes. Early in the second half, José Augusto scored his second goal for a 4–1 lead, this time from the penalty spot. Such were the intense passions that the former Benfica goalkeeper Pedro da Conceição, watching in the stands, collapsed and died when the penalty went in.

The league title was now a formality. It was duly sealed in the next game at Leixões, making it three in three for Guttmann.* All this championship winning was fast becoming a habit.

The 1959/60 season was also marked by Guttmann's second stint as coach of a national team, this time Portugal, under the overall stewardship of José Maria Antunes. To place Guttmann's subsequent achievements with Benfica within their historical context, Portugal was at that point a minor footballing nation. They had never previously qualified for a World Cup tournament, and losing out to little Northern Ireland in the qualification for the 1958 finals had come as scant surprise.

Guttmann coached the team that eliminated East Germany in a two-legged match in the European Championship. In April 1960, as preparation for the forthcoming quarter-final against Yugoslavia, Portugal played a friendly against West Germany in front of a 70,000 crowd in Ludwigshafen. Guttmann angrily criticised the match referee at the press conference that followed a 2–1 defeat. FIFA decided that these remarks were unacceptable, and sent the Portuguese Football Association a bill for a fine of US$200.

The officials passed the fine on to Guttmann and asked him to pay up. Guttmann, on a high after the victory against Sporting a

* Guttmann was not the first Jewish coach to win the Portuguese league championship with Benfica. In 1936, the club won its first Portuguese championship. Their coach was Lippo Hertzka, another Budapest Jew, who had also presided over Real Madrid's first league triumph in Spain, in 1932. Hertzka died in Portugal in 1951, aged forty-six.

couple of weeks before, was in no mood to play ball, particularly as he was performing the national role on an entirely voluntary basis. He told the national association in no uncertain terms that they were ungrateful, and duly resigned. With no Guttmann in the dugout a few weeks later, the Portuguese team were routed 5–1 in Belgrade.

The position of national coach was just an extra-curricular activity for Guttmann. Throughout the summer of 1960, he plotted how he was going to scale the footballing heights by bringing the European Cup to Lisbon. He laid the psychological groundwork with his players for the challenge ahead, a characteristically eccentric combination of incentive and threat:

> In professional football there is no success without sacrifice! Without iron discipline no army will ever win a battle, let alone the whole war! And the European Cup can be compared with a war. If any of my players are not willing to make the necessary sacrifice, they can go to work in the sardine factory. It's not necessary for them to earn their bread in football … Of course, if they perform well in football, I will make sure that they will earn a much bigger piece of bread – what's more, butter to go with it – and here rather than in the stinky sardine factory. But for that to happen they must cooperate in everything, otherwise they will get seriously punished.

● ● ●

Guttmann had already inherited several quality players when he had taken over from the Brazilian coach Otto Glória the previous season. He just believed that they needed to be organised in the right way, and supplemented with one or two judicious acquisitions and promotions from the youth team. 'The team started to take shape, to mature like fermenting grape juice,' he said.

José Águas, the captain and focal point of the attack, was one of several players discovered in the Portuguese colonies by a Benfica scouting system that was constantly under pressure to discover gems as a counterweight to the no-foreigner rule. In 1950, he had been a professional hunter in Angola when Benfica arrived to play a representative side. Águas had never played football, but known for his athleticism, was called into the local team when several Angolans dropped out. He was such a revelation that Benfica signed him up and took him back to Lisbon, where he was to score almost 300 goals.

His fellow Angolan, the diminutive Joaquim Santana, played alongside him as the inside-right. Only fully establishing himself in the first team after Guttmann's arrival, Santana possessed great ball control and a deadly right foot. Mário Coluna, from Mozambique, could play either as inside-left or in central midfield, depending on the formation used. Coluna mixed a phenomenal work-rate with power and skill – the complete player.

Guttmann's team could venture into their customary all-out attack knowing that they had a formidable goalkeeper behind them. Alberto da Costa Pereira, also from Mozambique, was a commanding presence, dominating his penalty area with his height and confident handling.

The only signing for the 1960/61 season was surprising, but inspired. Guttmann recruited the 27-year-old centre-half, Germano de Figueiredo, from struggling Atlético, a smaller Lisbon club. Tall, balding and mustachioed, Germano combined resolute defending with the ability to spark a Benfica counter-attack with astute passing and skilful dribbling.

Germano's arrival spelt the end for Artur Santos, who had made nearly 300 appearances for the club over the past decade. 'At age thirty, at the height of my abilities, I was forced to leave the club,' Santos remembers. Sentimentality, or loyalty to popular club stalwarts, was not in Section A of the Guttmann coaching manual.

When asked more than half a century later what he thought of his former coach's statue outside the Estádio da Luz, Santos replied with some sadness that he sees 'a great man, but a great villain for me as he eliminated part of my life'.

Soon after the new season started, Guttmann and his team were off to Edinburgh to face the Scottish champions Heart of Midlothian in the European Cup preliminary round. Benfica ran out comfortable winners over the two legs, with Águas and Augusto getting all the goals. 'We were absolutely outclassed by Benfica in both matches,' recalled the veteran Hearts player Gordon Smith. 'They were streets ahead of us in style, technique and set play. We were running about hoping. They beat us 2–1 here and 3–0 in Lisbon, but frankly the score should have been much bigger.'

The draw for the first round proper took place at a Geneva hotel. The inevitable happened. Benfica came out of the hat with the Hungarian champions, from Újpest.

• • •

After the Communist takeover, MTK Budapest had been claimed by the secret police, and Kispest taken over by the army. Újpest, meanwhile, became the official club of the police force, and were renamed Újpesti Dózsa.

The club had just won their first Hungarian championship since Guttmann had walked out on them in 1947. In the preliminary round of the European Cup, they had comfortably dispatched the highly rated Red Star Belgrade, winning both legs.

But absolutely nothing could have prepared them for what awaited them in the cauldron of the Estádio da Luz for the first leg in early November 1960. It was as if all Guttmann's anger at what he had to endure in Újpest sixteen years before had been channelled into positive energy, and transmitted to his players.

After just twenty-eight minutes, Újpesti Dózsa were a remarkable five goals down, with Águas, José Augusto, Coluna and Santana all wreaking havoc. This was not blitzkrieg, but footballing slaughter. 'Not even Real Madrid could survive here,' reported a breathless Augusti Pujol, UEFA's delegate at the match.

Although Benfica took their foot off the gas in the second half, the final 6–2 scoreline meant that the tie was virtually secure. There was to be no triumphant return to Újpest for Guttmann, however. It was decided that it would be imprudent for him to travel to Hungary when there was a risk that the Communist regime wouldn't let the émigré out again. He listened to the game on a radio in Vienna, with Benfica securing a comfortable victory on the aggregate score despite a 2–1 defeat.

Perhaps even more significant in Guttmann's quest to capture the European Cup was the result that emerged from Spain a week earlier. More than 200,000 fans had watched the two legs of the tie in which Real Madrid, European champions for each of the five seasons since the tournament had been inaugurated, went out to bitter rivals Barcelona. There would be a new name engraved on the trophy this year, and Pujol's controversial assessment would have to wait another year to be tested.

In the domestic sphere, meanwhile, the team nicknamed *Las Águias* (The Eagles) were flying high. Benfica won fourteen of their first fifteen matches, drawing the other. Only Sporting were anywhere near them, but the gap already looked impregnable by the time Guttmann's team took to the field for their European Cup quarter-final tie against Aarhus of Denmark in March 1961.

The margin of victory in the first leg in Lisbon, 3–1 to Benfica, gave Aarhus hope that they could overturn the deficit when the collection of Portuguese and Africans ventured to the unfamiliar bitter cold of northern Europe in late winter. But the Danes were simply torn apart by a rampant Benfica, who were three ahead by half-time, counter-attacking with electrifying pace.

If the Újpest tie took Guttmann down memory lane, the semi-final was to be no different. Benfica were paired with Rapid Vienna, the team Guttmann faced in his last ever game as a player, at the Prater stadium in 1933. Rapid had won the Austrian championship by a canter the previous season, in a league full of teams recognisable from the 1920s, with the glaring exception of Hakoah.

After hearing of the Újpest demolition job, you could hardly blame Rapid for coming to Lisbon for the first leg with a highly defensive game plan. But despite virtually all their men being packed behind the ball, the rearguard collapsed under an irresistible force. In a typically blistering start, Coluna and Águas bagged early goals. Rapid recovered after the break, but the imperious Germano snuffed out the main Austrian threat, centre-forward Robert Dienst. On the hour mark, Cavém smashed in a spectacular volley to end the first leg at 3–0.

Benfica had a league game sandwiched in between the two legs of the semi-final, which were eight days apart. Interestingly, eight of the players who played in the first match against Rapid were rested for this league game, away to Porto. In other words, decades before squad rotation was an accepted principle as a means to keep players fresh and free from injury before important games, Guttmann was putting the very same concept into practice. He knew, with two league games against weaker opposition to go after the Porto match, and with only one more point needed to clinch the title, that a safety-first policy was in order. Benfica lost 3–2 to their rivals, but it simply didn't matter. The Porto fans, still angered by Guttmann's departure, must have been driven to distraction by his conspicuous disregard for the fixture.

Benfica were confronted by an intimidating wall of noise at the Prater stadium for the return leg of the semi-final in early May, with the Rapid supporters worked up into a frenzy by the still op-timistic local media. They believed history was on their side. Their

comeback from 3–0 down against Schalke to win the 1941 German Football Championship in front of 95,000 spectators in Berlin was etched into the club's folklore. Clearly, the reality of a Nazi German title won in the heart of Nazi Germany at the height of Nazi Germany's power had done little to prevent Rapid's supporters from remembering the game with misty eyes.

In general, the European Cup had fired the imagination of the continent's mass footballing public in recent years, with matches played in packed stadiums under recently installed floodlights, creating a unique and unprecedented atmosphere. Representatives of France, West Germany and Italy had been beaten by Real in the five finals to date. Now Portugal and Austria had their chance, and this time there was no Real to block their progress to the trophy. Portuguese teams had previously never even got past the first round, and the excitement back home in Lisbon was intense.

Missed chances and resolute Benfica defending kept the game goalless until Águas broke the deadlock mid-way through the second half. But Rapid equalised three minutes later, and the crowd believed again as their team launched wave after wave of attack. With two minutes to go, Dienst looked to be fouled by Cruz in the penalty area. The crowd bayed for a penalty, only for their entreaties to be rejected by the English referee, Reg Leafe.

Cue pandemonium. Cruz was knocked to the ground by a Rapid player, and the furious crowd stormed the playing area. The police had a job protecting Leafe and the Benfica players, and escorting them from the pitch. With the abandoned match duly awarded to Benfica, the team had to wait in their dressing rooms for several hours until the coast was clear.*

* Rapid Vienna's working-class fan base had a reputation for anti-Semitism, dating from before the war. The sight of a Jewish coach defeating their heroes, one whom many of the older fans will have remembered from his Hakoah days, can't have helped to calm the waters.

The following week, Benfica claimed the title with an 8–0 massacre of Sporting da Covilhã at the Estádio da Luz. The team had scored ninety-two goals in their twenty-six league games, at an average of more than 3.5 per game: a stunning record. Águas had notched twenty-seven of them, and José Augusto twenty-four.

But could Guttmann drive his team to the ultimate achievement, a victory in the European Cup Final on 31 May, with the whole of the continent watching? Lying in wait for them at the Wankdorf stadium in Bern were Barcelona, the conquerors of Real Madrid, and strong favourites to keep the cup in Spain.

• • •

The defeat of Real Madrid was not the only reason Barcelona were favourites. They boasted a fearsome forward line, with which Guttmann was all too well acquainted. He had coached Zoltán Czibor and Sándor Kocsis at Honvéd. He had come up against another Hungarian émigré, László Kubala, back in the late 1940s, before he had become a goalscoring legend at Barcelona. The Brazilian Evaristo had notched several goals for Flamengo against Guttmann's Honvéd in 1957. And the last member of the strike force was no pushover either. Luis Suárez had won the title of European Footballer of the Year just a few months before.

The first half an hour of the final followed a predictable course. Kocsis headed in a Suárez cross after twenty minutes. Germano cleared off the line from Czibor, as a hungry Barcelona looked to finish the game off.

But the character of the Benfica team reflected its battle-hardened coach. They weren't going to give up in a hurry. Two mistakes by the Barcelona goalkeeper and captain Antoni Ramallets handed the initiative to the Portuguese. On the half hour, he rashly raced from his line to cut out a cross from Domiciano Cavém. He missed it, and José Águas put the ball into the empty net.

One minute later, Benfica were ahead. A Barcelona defensive header looped towards their own goal. Ramallets was slow to react, and could only palm the ball onto the post. The ball trickled across the goal-line, and the Swiss referee adjudged that it had gone over.

Mário Coluna had broken his nose early on in the game. Too nervous of his injury to want to head the ball, he lingered outside the penalty area as Cavém crossed from the left ten minutes after half-time. The ball rebounded out to Coluna, who smashed a volley into the corner of the net with his unfavoured right foot to make it 3–1.

Barcelona were staring defeat in the face, and surged forward in desperation. But providence was on the side of Guttmann and his team. The great Kocsis, unbelievably, headed against the post while one metre from the goal-line, and with the goalkeeper Costa Pereira nowhere to be seen. Kubala hit a shot from outside the area that bounced off one post onto another and into the grateful clutches of the goalkeeper.

But then, the third Hungarian, Czibor, scored with a spectacular long-range volley to halve the deficit. There were fifteen minutes left on the clock. There was still time for Czibor to hit the Benfica post yet again, before the referee blew his whistle to trigger wildly disparate emotions.

Czibor and Kocsis, who suffered a shock defeat to West Germany on the same Bern pitch in the World Cup Final seven years previously, had to experience a similar fate. They left the ground in tears.

Amid the outpouring of raw emotion and the unrestrained jubilation of Benfica fans streaming onto the pitch, the 42-year-old club president Vieira de Brito suffered a minor heart attack. And what must the Holocaust survivor Béla Guttmann have been thinking as he looked to the heavens, the newly crowned king of European football?

CHAPTER 10

RETENTION

In his speech to the nation on Israel's Independence Day on 21 April 1961, Prime Minister David Ben-Gurion dwelt on the lessons of the Adolf Eichmann trial, which had started in Jerusalem just a few days before:

> *Here, for the first time in Jewish history, historical justice is being done by the sovereign Jewish people. For many generations, it was we who suffered, who were tortured, were killed – and were judged ... For the first time, Israel is judging the murderers of the Jewish people ... And let us bear in mind that only the independence of Israel could create the conditions for this historical act of justice.*

Eichmann, living under the pseudonym Ricardo Klement, had been identified and captured by Israeli secret service agents in Argentina the previous year, and secretly transported to Israel.

The Mossad operation provoked wildly differing responses. Argentina lodged an official complaint with the United Nations Security Council, claiming that Eichmann's abduction was 'typical of the methods used by a regime completely and universally condemned'. Some Western news outlets were similarly critical. The Washington Post *decried Israel's*

'jungle law' applied 'in the name of some imaginary Jewish identity',
while the New York Times *labelled Israel's behaviour as 'immoral*
and illegal'.

But for Israelis, the news was greeted with a mixture of wide-eyed
disbelief and unbridled joy. When Ben-Gurion had originally broken
the news of Eichmann's capture to his cabinet the previous May, the re-
action of Minister for Transport Yitzhak Ben-Aharon typified the sense
of shock, of a world turned upside down. Ben-Aharon, born Yitzhak
Nussenbaum in what is now Romania, sat stupefied, muttering in his
native Yiddish, 'Ve macht man das?' (How does one do that?)

The trial itself lasted four months, with television pictures beamed
throughout the world. The prosecution countered Eichmann's claims that
he was an impotent bureaucrat carrying out orders from above, arguing
instead that he was actually possessed by a burning passion to kill Jews.
As part of this strategy, the prosecution laid out the case that Eichmann
had eagerly murdered a Jewish boy named 'Salomon'. The boy had been
accused of stealing cherries from the orchard outside the Budapest villa
where Eichmann lived in 1944, the villa that belonged to Lipót Aschner,
Béla Guttmann's boss.

Salomon was allegedly taken to the garden tool shed to be interrogated
by Eichmann and his orderly, Franz Slawik. 'The door closed,' said the
witness, Avraham Gordon, who had worked with Salomon and several
other Jewish teenagers at the villa:

> *After that I heard terrible screams, beatings, blows and crying ... These screams*
> *lasted about 10 to 15 minutes ... Suddenly there was silence. And then I didn't*
> *hear the shouting any more, the door opened and Eichmann came out. I saw*
> *him, his clothing was dishevelled, he looked wild, his shirt was sticking out. I*
> *noticed stains on his shirt and I thought that these were bloodstains.*

On 29 May 1962, Eichmann wrote a letter to the president of Israel,
Yitzhak Ben-Zvi, appealing against the death sentence that had been

handed down by the court. Ben–Zvi dismissed the request, scrawling a biblical verse on the letter: 'As your sword made women childless, so shall your mother be childless among women.'

Two days later, the man who meticulously planned the murder of Béla Guttmann's family was dead.

• • •

Win a major sporting trophy once, and the naysayers will dismiss the success as random luck. Win it twice, and the same people are forced to eat their words. The season 1961/62 was when Béla Guttmann wrote his own name in the pantheon of coaching greats.

A chance meeting in the unlikely venue of a barber's shop, several months before the first European Cup victory, had paved the way for further success. Guttmann bumped into José Carlos Bauer, a former Brazilian international, who was now coaching Ferroviária in his native country, and whom he rated as a shrewd judge of the game.

'He greeted me happily, saying they were on a tour (in Lisbon) and they'd soon go to Africa,' recalled Guttmann:

> I told him: 'Listen to me, old man, if you see a talented player for me, someone who was born in Portugal, keep his name in mind.' A month after this conversation, I was at the barber's again, and as if I was telling you a joke, Bauer came in again. 'What's up? Have you found anyone for me?' 'Oh,' he said, 'I saw a black lad in Mozambique … I wanted to get him for myself … but those fools are asking for twenty thousand dollars for him!' 'What's the lad called?' His face was being lathered as he blurted out: 'Eusébio!'

Eusébio da Silva Ferreira had been playing for Sporting de Lourenço Marques. Sporting Lisbon regarded their namesake in Mozambique's capital as their feeder club, and went berserk when

they found out that Guttmann had usurped their supposed rights, signing the highly promising striker for their bitter rivals instead.

A Sporting director turned up at Eusébio's door and offered him 500,000 escudos, a huge sum of money for an eighteen-year-old, to change his mind. 'He put the money on the table and told me that it was mine if I signed for Sporting,' Eusébio recalled. 'I told him that it was a low thing to do, that I wasn't mad and I wasn't going to sign two contracts.'

Guttmann had stolen a march, and not by sheer luck either. The master networker had spent decades building up his contacts, and one of them had led him to this future star.

He tenaciously held on to his advantage. Eusébio was hidden in Lagos in the Algarve for twelve days for fear that Sporting would try to swoop again. 'I sent three bodyguards to hang around him and I told them my orders,' said Guttmann. 'Eusébio cannot be left alone, not for a minute, and he can only stay at the Benfica house.'

When Eusébio did emerge for his first Benfica training session in early 1961, Guttmann stood on the sidelines, purring with pleasure at his sly capture, transfixed by Eusébio's devastating acceleration, explosive shot and ability to glide past opponents. Unable to contain himself, he eventually turned to his assistant Fernando Caiado, shouting '*O menino é ouro!*' (The boy is gold!).

Ineligible, as a recent signing, for the European Cup, Eusébio made his debut in a domestic friendly match the week before the Bern triumph, scoring a hat-trick. He scored again on his league debut a couple of weeks later, before being named as a substitute against Pelé's Santos in a close season international tournament in Paris in June 1961.

With his tired team 4–0 down at half-time, Guttmann looked to the bench and called for his new gem. 'I sent him on and he scored three goals, all of them from a 20–25 metre distance,' he said. The next day, the French sports newspaper *L'Équipe* ignored the

result of the match, instead running the headline 'Eusébio 3 Pelé 2'.
Guttmann now had his passport to footballing immortality.

• • •

Before the next league and European Cup campaign could get
underway, Benfica found themselves up against South American
champions Peñarol in the Intercontinental Cup, a competition
launched the previous year as a showdown between the two great
footballing continents.

Mário Coluna grabbed the solitary goal in the first encounter in
Lisbon, before the team made the long trek to Montevideo for the
return leg two weeks later. Exhausted and unacclimatised, Benfica
were thrashed 5–0.

According to the rules, however, the aggregate score was irrele-
vant and both teams were awarded two points for their victory. The
tie therefore went to a play-off, to be staged, rather unfairly, in the
Estadio Centenario in Montevideo, just two days later.

It called for emergency measures, and Guttmann duly obliged.
He immediately summoned two replacements to be flown from
Lisbon straight after they had played a reserve game. He brought
over his new signing Eusébio, who had not appeared in the first
two matches. Once again showing his courage as a coach, and his
belief that youth was no barrier to success, he also gave a debut
to a seventeen-year-old left-winger. Guttmann had spotted the
tricky and diminutive António Simões the previous season. 'He
told his assistant Caiado that this young lad has to play next season
with the big lads,' Simões reminisced. 'He needs to play with
Costa Pereira, Coluna and Águas, because he has nothing else to
learn here.'

Guttmann's additions improved the performance drastically, de-
spite them just walking off a long flight. Eusébio scored with another

trademark long-range effort, but Benfica still went down 2–1, a result that left their coach still smarting many years later. 'I'm telling you, the referee was bribed,' he fumed. 'Later, I was told by insiders that it really was so ... I wanted to make them change the refereeing [for the third match], but all I got was the referee and linesman swapping over. We lost because of a penalty.'

Six weeks later, after a bye in the preliminary round, Benfica's defence of their European Cup got underway. Just six months after the poisonous Rapid semi-final, Guttmann was back in Vienna, this time up against FK Austria. Once again, the city was beside itself with excitement, with people clamouring for tickets to witness another match in this intoxicating tournament. A crowd of almost 80,000 turned up at the Prater stadium, still the record for any match in Austria involving a club side.

Although the stadium was packed, the atmosphere was somewhat less intimidating this time round. The whole feel of FK Austria Vienna, whom Guttmann briefly went on to manage more than a decade later, was altogether different from that of their local rivals. 'If Rapid stood for proletarian toughness and the suburb, then "Austria" stood for the city, coffeehouse, and the liberal Jewish middle class,' summarises the sociologist Roman Horak, a pre-war generalisation that still held good, apart from the Jewish bit.*

The first leg ended 1–1, but any Austrian hope of an unlikely victory was left in tatters by another whirlwind in Lisbon. Now switching Coluna to a deeper role to accommodate Eusébio, Guttmann masterminded a 5–1 victory, as the Austrians were pulverised. The traditional Portuguese kick-off time of 11 p.m. added to their sense of disorientation, as they trudged from the field wondering what day of the week it was.

* FK Austria Vienna had been known as Wiener Amateur-SV when Guttmann was playing for Hakoah. There was some antipathy between the assimilated Jewish supporters of Wiener Amateur/Austria Vienna and their Zionist rivals.

Guttmann had transformed the Estádio da Luz into an impregnable fortress, and his team into a force that inspired fear throughout the continent of Europe. 'Benfica,' Guttmann once said, 'have their own brand of mystique, an inexplicable atmosphere all of their own.'

They certainly did at that moment in time, and it was thanks to him.

• • •

Despite their progress in the European Cup, Benfica had stuttered badly at the start of the league campaign. The team won only one of six games between mid-October and the beginning of December, virtually ruling out another domestic championship at an early stage. Whether the team had lost its will for the bread and butter of league football after their European triumph, or whether a newly refashioned team was experiencing teething problems, Guttmann sensed that all was not well in the ranks.

He later claimed to have adopted his usual tactic in response, rounding on a star player to enforce team discipline. Going back to the dressing room after one match, he saw that his captain José Águas was looking particularly downcast:

'What's the matter?' I asked him. He didn't answer me but Costa Pereira whispered in my ear: 'His pass was bad and Eusébio told him off really badly!' Eusébio was just coming back from the shower, but I didn't say a word, I didn't want to make the situation worse. However, in the first training I gathered all the boys and said to him: 'Listen to me Eusébio, you can be the biggest star here, but if you don't show respect to any of your fellow players in the future, I will kick you in the butt and you can fly straight back to Mozambique!' He never forgot this lesson!

Eusébio was injured for the first leg of the quarter-final in early February 1962 in Nuremberg. FC Nürnberg, not Bayern Munich,

were then the masters of Bavarian and German football, having won
the league a record eight times in their history. Known in Germany
simply as *Der Club* (The Club), their star player and captain was
Max Morlock, now a veteran at thirty-six, but a World Cup winner
and the man who pulled the strings for Nürnberg's potent attack.

If the prospect of taking on Germany's finest without their star
player wasn't daunting enough, the pitch was covered in snow,
conditions previously unseen by the Portuguese. Guttmann, who
played much of his own career on similar surfaces, tried to reassure
the troops. 'Snow is only a problem if it's more than half a metre in
height,' he joked.*

His attempt to bolster spirits achieved little. An early lead
through Cavém was quickly overturned, and Benfica returned
home contemplating a 3–1 deficit, their crown in real danger of
being snatched away.

But if the players sensed any threat to their supremacy, they had a
funny way of showing it. In the second leg in Lisbon, Nürnberg took
their turn to be destroyed by a blitzkrieg special. Two goals down
within four minutes of the start, another one after twenty, the Ger-
mans were eventually thrashed 6–0, with Eusébio and José Augusto
both notching two. Like punch-drunk heavyweights, Nürnberg were
battered, dazed and deafened. 'In this place,' Morlock said through
gritted teeth, 'you can only play with cotton wool in your ears.'

• • •

If the route to the 1961 final had been relatively straightforward,
the hurdles this time round continued to get steeper. Next up was
Tottenham Hotspur, who had the previous season become the first

* The match was played at the Städtisches Stadion, the setting for several Nazi Party
 rallies and sports days for the Hitler Youth.

team in the twentieth century to win the English League and FA Cup double, and who had already taken apart Poland's Górnik Zabrze and Czechoslovakia's Dukla Prague on their route to this semi-final clash.

Spurs boasted several top-class players – their inspirational captain and veteran Northern Irish midfielder, Danny Blanchflower; Dave Mackay, the tough-tackling and determined Scot; the gifted inside forward and great passer of the ball, John White, also from Scotland; the Welshman Cliff Jones, one of the best wingers in the world; and up front, the big English centre-forward Bobby Smith and the recently signed young goalscorer, Jimmy Greaves, a future legend of English football, who was to make his European debut in this semi-final.

The North London team also had the minor advantage of playing in Lisbon first, thus playing in front of their own crowd at the denouement, and avoiding the intense second-leg passion of the Estádio da Luz that had reduced FK Austria and Nürnberg to rubble.

Guttmann knew he had to be at his absolute best to get his team through, and he didn't disappoint. The eventual outcome of the tie between these two great sides, a narrow victory for Benfica, owed much to the box of wily tricks he had assembled during thirty long years as a coach throughout the world. His adversary, the relatively inexperienced Bill Nicholson, lost out in the battle of the small details, a fatal defeat in such an evenly matched confrontation.

Despite witnessing the Nürnberg demolition, Nicholson failed to prepare his team psychologically for the inevitable early onslaught in Lisbon. Goals by Simões and José Augusto put Benfica two up within twenty minutes, before Spurs had even settled into the game. Even though Spurs dominated the second half and Smith got one back, another goal from the inspired José Augusto meant that Benfica were to bring a 3–1 lead to London for the second leg.

A good lead, but one that Guttmann knew could evaporate in just a few minutes of frenzied action at a packed and raucous White Hart Lane, with the home fans electrified by the possibility of their team becoming the first English representative in a European Cup Final.

He did everything in his power to stop that happening. His main weapon was the media. 'When I go to the press conference before the game,' José Mourinho once said, 'in my mind the game has already started.' 'At a press conference you need to come out as the winner,' agrees Alex Ferguson. Football analysts routinely point to such comments as evidence of these coaches' acute awareness, their ability to sense the subtle influence of media messages on the psychology of players. Béla Guttmann was doing exactly the same thing more than fifty years ago.

A large English press pack were camped at his team's base at the Park Lane Hotel to cover a game that had captured more public attention in England than any against a foreign team since Hungary's visit in 1953. To allow his tense players to rest and relax in private, Guttmann's opening move was to shift the spotlight to himself. He reiterated his intention, first hinted at a few months before, to leave Benfica at the end of the season. As usual, he was less than fully honest about the reasons, which would become apparent only later, claiming that he had taken the team as far as he could and craved a fresh challenge.

Next, he sought to sway the course of the game more directly. He worried that his Portuguese players were insufficiently accustomed to the typically British physicality of players such as Mackay and Smith. 'I told the journalists that I expected a bloodbath and they, in turn, went to Poulsen, the Danish referee, and told him Guttmann did not think he was strong enough to handle the match,' he later recounted. 'It was an old ploy, but it worked. Poulsen kept a close check on those players, and we got more than our share of free kicks.'

In those days, the two teams would come out for the start of the game separately. Whereas Guttmann allowed Spurs to come out first in Lisbon, where they were made to wait for their opponents amid the din like gladiators in the colosseum, he made sure his own team would not suffer the same fate in London. 'On the night of the match, I was concerned about the effect the Spurs crowd might have on the nerves of my players,' he said. 'They are much closer on English grounds than on the continent. So I locked the dressing-room door and only let Benfica go out at the last minute, with the referee and linesmen. The game started before the crowd got at us.'

Whereas Spurs conceded two goals in the opening few minutes in the Estádio da Luz, Benfica actually went one up after fifteen minutes at White Hart Lane, with Águas converting a cross from Simões. Smith levelled the score before half-time, and Blanchflower converted a penalty early in the second half. Spurs were just one behind on aggregate, and the crowd scented blood.

The Benfica team, however, were to show the same resolve that had got them through in Bern against Barcelona. With Costa Pereira making save after save, and Germano once again a rock in the centre of defence, they reached the final by the skin of their teeth, owing a considerable debt of gratitude to their maestro, their soon-departing coach.

• • •

Guttmann had decided to leave because of money. Having brought Benfica and Portuguese football unprecedented glory, he believed that the directors of the club should be bending over backwards to keep him, not quibbling over salary demands and minor expenses.

He asked for a salary increase of 65 per cent if Benfica were to win the European Cup a second time, only to be met by a non-committal

response. As time drifted on, he was further irritated by an incident after the quarter-final in Nuremberg. Mariann had gone with him and the team to Germany – a rare occurrence. Back in Lisbon a few days after the game, Guttmann received a bill from the club – for half the cost of his hotel room. He regarded this behaviour as similar to the demand of the Portuguese Football Association that he fork out for a fine when he wasn't even getting paid to do the job.

In spite of his clear brilliance, it seemed that old attitudes were not shifting easily. The club hierarchy still couldn't quite believe that a coach could be so important, and their penny-pinching reflected a foolish insouciance. 'I am the most expensive coach in the world, but looking at my achievements, I'm actually cheap,' Guttmann said a couple of years later. With hindsight, given the prize money and ticket sales the team was earning, it is hard to disagree with that assessment. The Benfica board, with the mind-set of the footballing establishment of 1962, somehow contrived to do so.

Just as there was a push factor for him leaving, there was also a pull. 'Not long after the World Club Final, a certain gentleman visited me, a representative of the winners Peñarol,' he said. There was clearly an attractive offer on the table from Uruguay, his next port of call.

By stubbornly insisting on his value, we can say that Guttmann set in motion an upward ratchet in coaching pay that is still continuing to this day. The deals did not come as easily as they would for a top international coach now, and the amounts were insignificant by comparison, but the fact remains that he left Porto for Benfica after being offered more money, and Benfica for Peñarol for the same reason. And, unlike modern coaches, he conducted these protracted negotiations all by himself, without the aid of an agent.

But before his eventual departure from Lisbon, he was to face the biggest single game and greatest challenge of his coaching career. On 2 May 1962, in the Olympic stadium in Amsterdam, Benfica took on the mighty Real Madrid in the European Cup Final.

This was to be a conclusive battle for supremacy, for the right to be viewed as the dominant force in European football. Real Madrid were back where they thought they belonged after a one-year hiatus. Was that one year just a blip, or could Benfica consign them to the status of also-rans and has-beens, while assuming the throne themselves?

Again, Guttmann's team were underdogs. Real had won the Spanish league, while their opponents had eventually finished a distant third in Portugal. They had annihilated Standard Liège in the semi-final. And their team contained the ageing but still brilliant duo – Ferenc Puskás and the Argentinean-born forward Alfredo Di Stéfano.

Who wouldn't be intimidated by such names, by a team with such a record in the European Cup? Guttmann's mastery of human psychology was evident once more. Everything he said before and during the final was calculated to counter this inevitable fear, with one message to the fore: they are history, you are the present, you will win. 'Straight after the semi-final against Tottenham, he was building us up, telling us, "we are going to be champions again",' recalls António Simões.

In the dressing room just before the kick-off, he sat his team down, and told them about his experiences at the 1924 Olympics. 'I had the opportunity to meet some well-known celebrities, including the Finnish idol, Paavo Nurmi,' he said. 'He ran the 5,000 metres in what was regarded then as a superhuman time, 14:31. In the 1960 Olympics, an unknown New Zealander [Murray Halberg] beat his time by almost a minute.' In sport, he was at pains to convey, time does not stand still.

Benfica needed all the self-belief they could muster. Just like the previous year, they were down early on, only this time by two goals, both scored by Puskás. Again, they rallied. Águas got a goal back after Eusébio's free kick hit a post. Then Cavém rifled a long-distance

shot into the top corner. A frenetic half of football ended with the deadly left foot of Puskás restoring Real's lead. 3–2 at half-time, and already the great Hungarian had scored a hat-trick.

There was work to do in the dressing room. Guttmann may be best known for his teams' attacking talents, but he was no slouch in defensive organisation either. In order to isolate Puskás and deprive him of service, he told the versatile Cavém to stick closely to Di Stéfano. 'He always had the technical knowledge to know how to single out the threats in the opponent's team and stop them playing,' remembers José Augusto.

With tactics out of the way, and less than fifteen minutes to play with at the interval, he moved to the mind. He had told his players before the kick-off that they would win against their older opponents if they were only two down at half-time. Now, it turned out, the deficit was only one.

'Guttmann said to us, "Gentlemen, we're going to win, we're stronger than Real Madrid!"' recalls Augusto. 'The important thing about those words was the belief and conviction with which he said them, and that conviction transferred to us. He gave so much strength because he spoke with such force. It was as if a divine force had entered us!'

Simões echoes his former teammate's recollections:

We really had the belief we could win the game. I remember Gutt-mann in his own special language, a sort of mix of Portuguese and Italian, telling us: 'Mister, sit down, mister, sit down, Real Madrid tired, Real Madrid tired, Real Madrid old, old, old, they cannot win, Real Madrid cannot run, Di Stéfano dead.' That moment really struck us.

After five minutes of the second half, it was 3–3. For the second European Cup Final in succession, Coluna had scored a spectacular

goal with his weaker right foot. From that moment on, it was to be the Eusébio Show, as irrepressible youth triumphed over ageing experience. Running from his own half past tiring defenders, the so-called Black Pearl waltzed into the Real area and was brought down. Leo Horn, the Jewish referee, pointed to the spot, and Eusébio himself calmly dispatched the penalty.*

Five minutes later, it was all over. Eusébio's deflected shot ended up in the corner of the net to make it 5–3. Real Madrid knew they were beaten. They were gone – tired, old and dead.

The scenes at Bern were repeated, as the crowd stormed the pitch at the final whistle, unable to contain their joy. Eusébio, symbolically, exchanged shirts with Di Stéfano, and Guttmann was carried off the pitch by his players.

The European Cup Final traditionally brings together the great and the good of football for this annual showpiece event. At the winners' banquet that night, Guttmann was in his element, sharing memories at a Hungarian-speaking table. How satisfied and content he must have felt, the 63-year-old two-time European Cup winner, chatting the night away with friends and colleagues from his now illustrious career. Aside from Puskás, there was Emil Östreicher, general manager of the Honvéd tour and now performing a similar role at Real Madrid; Gyula Mándi, former teammate with MTK and Hungary, now coach of the Israeli national team, the third of Guttmann's past teammates to assume this position; Lajos Czeizler, the much-travelled coach with whom Guttmann had fallen out in spectacular fashion in a Milan restaurant; and Dezső Solti, Guttmann's partner-in-crime, and now general manager, for want

* Horn had been a hero of the Dutch resistance in the war under the alias 'Doctor van Dongen', carrying out daring raids and helping to hide other Jews. After the war, he became a successful businessman in the textile industry as well as a top-flight referee, taking charge of the 1953 Hungary defeat of England at Wembley. His elder brother, Edgar Horn, was murdered at Sobibór in April 1943.

of a less polite term, of Inter Milan. A group of Jews, somehow still alive, with one of the greatest footballers ever to walk the planet.

Some guests at the banquet approached Guttmann and begged him to stay in Lisbon. But angered by the directors' intransigence and parsimony, and with the world at his feet, he was having none of it. With a wave and a curse, he was gone.

FADING OUT

Approximately one thousand Jews were crammed into a police station in the Leopoldstadt district of Vienna, just a few minutes' walk from the Hakoah stadium. It was Kristallnacht, *the Night of the Broken Glass, a devastating pogrom that raged throughout Nazi Germany and Austria on 9 and 10 November 1938.*

'The Jews were being handled by people who were acting like mad animals,' reported one witness at the time:

> *They were forced to roll around on the ground without their shoes touching the ground. [They received] blow after blow, because it is not easy to do that. Then hopping, jumping, squats – always accompanied by blows, then the people had to spit on each other, slap each other round the face, and if they did not punch with full force the partners were given extra blows. Others had to stand against the wall and were then threatened with execution, but even better – they were beaten while accompanied by the words 'You Jewish pig', 'You traitor against the people'.*

Ninety-three synagogues in Vienna were partially or totally destroyed by fire in one night of terror. Only one, the Stadttempel, remained intact, saved by the fact that it couldn't be burned down without ruining

*neighbouring buildings. 'It was "only" totally wrecked and stripped out,'
recounted another witness:*

> *On this occasion numerous Jews had the torn-up Torah scrolls tied to their
> backs, they had to put on* kittels *[ceremonial robes] and* talleisim *[prayer
> shawls] stolen from the Tempel and were chased through the streets of the
> Innere Stadt, the centre of Vienna, with the* lulav *[palm branch] in their
> hands. In individual districts of Vienna, especially in Leopoldstadt, the
> 'Jewish district', the prayer implements and prayer books were publicly
> burned and this medieval spectacle rapturously cheered by the crowd.*

Ten years to the day after Kristallnacht, *9 November 1948, the post-war
Austrian cabinet met to discuss a proposal to create a fund for returning,
impoverished Jews.*

*'I do not know why, at this particular time, one race should receive
special privileges,' said Minister for Agriculture, Joseph Kraus. 'Others
who did not leave get no such support, but the Jews should?'*

*'The injustice that was inflicted on the Jews was not inflicted by
Austria,' chimed in Minister of Trade, Ernst Kolb. 'I see Jews growing
their influence everywhere, for example in medicine and in commerce,
particularly in Vienna,' said Minister for the Interior, Oskar Helmer,
seemingly oblivious to the fact that the Jewish population of Vienna had
decreased by 191,000 from its inter-war high of 200,000. '...One cannot
put through a special process ... The Nazis also had everything taken
from them in 1945.'*

*'The application [to set up a returning migrants' fund] will not be
approved by the Council of Ministers,' concluded Chancellor Leopold
Figl, who had been elected as Austrian leader in the first free elections in
more than a decade. 'A difficult position in relation to National Socialists
would have been created.'*

• • •

would like to be able to continue in the same vein as in the previous three chapters, to describe the next stage in the Greatest Comeback. I would like to, but I can't. The parallel with the wider Jewish story ends here. The final stages of Béla Guttmann's life were characterised by bitterness, demeaning work, waning abilities, racism, constant accusations of greed (racism), gambling addiction and financial difficulties.

Back in 1962, he was of course on top of the world, or certainly on top of Europe, and vowed to continue working. He had received a shock in January of that year when his close friend from his MTK days, György Orth, two years his junior, collapsed and died of heart failure while coach of FC Porto. Fearing that the stresses of the job would consign him to the same fate, Guttmann took the opportunity to visit a recommended medical specialist while Benfica were in Nuremberg preparing for their quarter-final. 'Don't give up!' came the doctor's considered verdict. 'Inactivity would be more dangerous for someone like you.'

We know of two firm offers for his services as he was leaving Benfica, both from teams whose names began with a 'P'. There was Peñarol, the best club team in the world, reigning champions of Uruguay and South America and holders of the Intercontinental Cup, who wanted Guttmann to help them retain all three titles. And there was Port Vale, having just finished twelfth in the third division of the English league, who sent a representative to speak with Guttmann after the final against Real Madrid in Amsterdam.

Such was the parochialism of English football that this is the only recorded approach by any English club to this great manager, a man who spoke decent English after six years spent in the United States. It wasn't as if he was averse to the idea of a big job in England either. On the day of the Spurs semi-final in London, he told the *Evening Standard* that 'it would be a great honour to coach in the country which gave football to the world'. It was to be almost

another three decades before any top-flight team in England were to appoint a foreign coach.

Given that Peñarol were offering him a very substantial increase on his Benfica salary, plus a three-roomed suite at a top hotel, the club from Stoke-on-Trent couldn't have been too shocked to see Guttmann board a flight for Montevideo.

Despite losing with Benfica to Peñarol the previous year in the Intercontinental Cup Final, he had clearly impressed the powers that be at one of the two leading clubs in Uruguay, who were in the hunt for a top coach after Roberto Scarone had gone off to manage the national team at the World Cup in Chile. Hopes were high that Guttmann could emulate the successes of Imre (Emérico) Hirschl, the kosher butcher of Budapest and 'big con man', who had led the club to two championships a decade earlier.

The appointment was certainly fitting for a man who had enjoyed such great triumphs in recent years. The country he was travelling to may have been small in population and size, but it punched well above its weight in footballing terms, winning two of the first four World Cups. And Peñarol, of course, were riding high.

• • •

Guttmann's first major challenge came soon after his arrival, in July 1962. Peñarol had been drawn against the other leading Uruguayan club, Nacional, in the semi-final of the Copa Libertadores, the international club cup competition in South America. To add further spice to the two-legged tie, the two teams would be fighting for local pride in one of the oldest and most intense derby fixtures in world football.

Nothing could separate the fierce Montevideo rivals on this occasion. Nacional won the first leg 2–1, and Peñarol won the second 3–1. In front of passionate full houses at the Estadio Centenario,

both matches were marred by foul play and fighting, with five players sent off over the two games, including three for Peñarol. Even after the third match, a play-off, the teams were still deadlocked after a 1–1 draw. With penalty shoot-outs yet to be introduced in world football, Peñarol were awarded the tie based on their better goal difference in the first two games.

Santos of Brazil were to be their next opponents in a two-legged tie to commence just a few days later, less than three months after Benfica's victory in Amsterdam. Major finals were coming thick and fast for Guttmann.

All was not well in the Peñarol camp, however. Unlike at São Paulo five years previously, Guttmann was coming into a highly successful team. This time, his foreign perspective was viewed not so much as a welcome breath of fresh air, but as superfluous interference. 'He wanted to us to make those cross-field passes typical of European players, but we were used to another style, to defending our area and launching a counter-attack,' reflected Peñarol goalkeeper Luis Maidana many years later.

Guttmann also antagonised players by switching their positions. He had done this to great effect in the second European Cup-winning season at Benfica, moving Domiciano Cavém and Mário Coluna from their accustomed roles, but by that stage his team would have agreed to walk through a brick wall for him. At Peñarol, on the other hand, he was merely met by puzzled expressions, as the Spanish-speaking players wondered whether they had correctly understood their coach's unique blend of Portuguese and Italian.

Guttmann would have to wait to resume his acquaintance with the great Pelé, who had been injured in the recent World Cup. The Santos team were nevertheless full of stars from the Brazil squad which had successfully retained their crown just six weeks earlier, including the captain Mauro Ramos who had so admired Guttmann while playing for him at São Paulo.

The Brazilians' quality showed through in the first leg in Montevideo, running out 2–1 winners. Guttmann now knew that he would have to win away at the Estádio Vila Belmiro in Santos, scene of one of his greatest ever victories back in 1957, to take the tie into a play-off.

He did so, but the result of the football match was almost incidental. Guttmann had seen plenty of violence in football grounds, such as at Hakoah and in Benfica's semi-final at Rapid Vienna, but perhaps nothing quite like this.

Just after half-time, Peñarol scored two goals in as many minutes to go 3–2 up. Seeing the tie slip away from their heroes, the Santos crowd went berserk. A bottle struck the Chilean referee, Carlos Robles, and he fell unconscious. He came round in the dressing room some minutes later, whereupon he resolved to abandon the game, while recommending that the current scoreline should stand.

The Santos officials were apoplectic, placing huge pressure on a groggy Robles to resume the match. The referee even claimed to have been threatened with a gun. Rather unsurprisingly, the game restarted, but only after a fifty-minute delay.

Santos scored to give the apparent scoreline of 3–3, at which point a linesman was hit by another bottle. When Robles blew the final whistle, the Brazilian crowd were in ecstasy, saluting their team as champions.

However, the South American Football Confederation had other ideas. They accepted the suggestion from Robles in his post-match report, presumably written in the safety of his home in Chile, that the official final score should be 3–2 to Peñarol, as per his original intention.

The resulting play-off was scheduled to take place in Buenos Aires in mid-August, but there was a slight hitch. Santos didn't show up, ostensibly in protest against the confederation's decision, but possibly also because Pelé was still struggling to regain full

fitness. After some political toing and froing, the match was actually played two weeks later than originally planned.

The authorities pulled out all the stops to avert potential disorder this time, summoning a European referee to officiate, an unusual move. And if they wanted someone tough, who else could they choose but Leo Horn, Holocaust survivor and hero of the Dutch resistance?

The match passed without incident under Horn's intimidating glare, but unfortunately for Guttmann and Peñarol, Pelé was back and champing at the bit. He scored two goals as Santos cruised to a 3–0 victory, and Guttmann's dream of winning the premier competitions in both major footballing continents in the same year was shattered.

The end came in customary fashion soon afterwards. On returning to Montevideo after an away fixture, Guttmann insisted that his players stay together and then travel the following day to an out-of-town camp to prepare for a forthcoming league game against Nacional. 'They tried to convince me that it was a custom to go home, and twenty-four hours didn't count, but I didn't care, I worked according to my own ideas and that was it!' he said. When the players defied him, he went to see the president and treated him to a well-practised refrain. 'Players can never say no to a coach,' he told him. 'If they dare to do it, that coach must take his hat and say goodbye!'

Guttmann agreed to stay on for the Nacional match in October 1962, which Peñarol won 4–1, virtually securing the national championship. But, believing his authority to be undermined, he returned to Europe before he could add the Uruguayan Primera División to his long list of titles.

● ● ●

Still basking in the glory of his double European Cup triumphs, Guttmann remained in no mood to sell himself short. Largely through his own efforts, the realisation was dawning in football

club boardrooms throughout the world that the coach is a major determinant of team success. And Guttmann was still the most celebrated coach in the game. Angered that he had not got his proper financial reward for what he achieved at Benfica, he was determined to cash in before age finally caught up with him.

Guttmann had been in Uruguay for only a couple of months when Benfica came running, hoping to lure him back before the European season got underway again in the autumn. The bewildered, if not furious, reaction of players and fans to his departure, particularly in light of the victory against Real, would have elicited the intended reaction from the Benfica directors. Their competitive instinct was no doubt also roused. The board may have originally assumed that Guttmann was all talk, that he would never actually leave the European champions when it came to the crunch. But now here he was, in Montevideo, at a team that had proven the previous year to be even better.

Benfica's target was in two minds. 'I still saw the potential in the team led by Eusébio, but I really wanted to make Peñarol the champion of South America,' Guttmann said. '...I said I would only go back to Lisbon if Peñarol let me out of the contract with no hard feelings.'

Guttmann said that the clubs held negotiations for three days, eventually agreeing a long-term interest-free loan to Peñarol, plus two friendly games between the two clubs, for which the Uruguayan club would take the majority of the proceeds. But Benfica still refused to match the monthly salary that Guttmann was receiving from Peñarol. The club's stubborn approach to his financial demands added fuel to an already raging fire.

'Who changes for a less favourable contract, right?' he later asked:

The directors at Benfica resented that amount. They were OK with the 50,000-dollar loan and giving up revenue from the friendly game,

but they didn't want to spend on me, they didn't want to give me what was due. What's more, it looked like they went to complain to a newspaper, because I was reading the next day that I was a hard case, who overestimated his skills and took Benfica for a bunch of fools! The article said that 'Guttmann wants five litres of blood per day.'

When he did eventually return to Europe after the Santos defeat, it was Peñarol's turn to chase after the bloodsucking Jew. In April 1963, the club's vice-president flew to visit Guttmann in Rome, where he was on vacation with Mariann. He agreed to pay Guttmann the same salary as the previous year to return to Montevideo, with two months upfront, plus the same luxurious accommodation.

Same money, same outcome. After crushing Everest of Ecuador in the first round, Peñarol crashed out to Boca Juniors in the semi-final of the Copa Libertadores, losing narrowly both at home and in Buenos Aires in another ill-tempered tie that eventually descended into a mass brawl. Guttmann soon left Montevideo and South America for the final time.

Benfica came sniffing again in the summer of 1963. The Portuguese club had failed to win their third successive European Cup, losing in the final to AC Milan at Wembley. 'We would have won in 1963 if Guttmann had been in charge,' laments José Augusto more than half a century later. '[New coach Fernando] Riera just didn't have the experience.' Moreover, there were some rumblings in the ranks that the style of football played under the Chilean Riera paled in comparison with the dashing verve of the Guttmann era.

But their former coach had no intention of playing ball. Revenge was in the air. It was they who had let him go; now he would make them pay. Guttmann wanted a substantial increase on his previous salary at the club, a 100 per cent bonus in the event he won the European Cup, paid vacations in Austria, free accommodation in an upmarket area, and use of a chauffeured car. Again, the Benfica board

baulked at the demands. To raise his hackles further, the club turned instead to Lajos Czeizler, now almost seventy, against whom Guttmann harboured a particular grudge.

An offer also came in from Sporting Lisbon. Guttmann claimed that he couldn't find it in his heart to work for Benfica's local adversaries, and turned the proposal down. But given that he was spitting feathers at the latest rebuff at the hands of his former employers, we can suppose that Sporting wouldn't meet his demands either.

He did eventually reach a satisfactory agreement, but with an unlikely partner. The Austrian Football Association had apparently banished the 'frictions' that had prevented his appointment in 1958. So, in March 1964, Béla Guttmann assumed his third coaching role for a national team, but his first with full responsibility for selection and tactics. It was also his first job in Austria since, as coach of Hakoah, he had fled the approaching Nazis in 1938.

• • •

Guttmann was to work in tandem with Joschi Walter, a former player and now football administrator, who would be responsible for the root-and-branch restructuring of Austrian professional football. He apparently formed an agreement with Walter on their division of responsibilities over a game of cards, an increasingly frequent pastime for a man with more time on his hands now, and some money to burn.

Austria had failed to make it to the 1962 World Cup Finals, and had gone out in the first round of the qualifying tournament for the 1964 European Championships. Indeed, the six matches before Guttmann took over had resulted in five defeats. For a nation whose collective footballing memory harked back to the days of Hugo Meisl and the 'Wunderteam', such performances were unacceptable.

Given these circumstances, Guttmann's record in his five friendly

games at the helm was worthy of considerable praise. His team recorded home victories against Hungary and the Soviet Union, both of whom reached the last four of the European Championships in 1964, and lost only once, to Uruguay. The *Kurier* newspaper gushed that 'the position of a coach such as Béla Guttmann has risen to the importance of diplomats and generals'. Guttmann even received a telegram from Heinrich Drimmel, the country's Education Secretary, with the words 'Please stay in Austria!'

For a while, at least, Guttmann seemed to be enjoying himself, treating his players to his distinctive perspective on the importance of shooting: 'You can't go on dribbling and passing the ball so much in front of the opponent's goal,' he reportedly told his players:

> You must shoot immediately, shoot, shoot and shoot again! It's just like when you are with your wife or your girlfriend and you keep on kissing and kissing and making small talk. You have to score a goal for them too in the end. It's only then that satisfaction will show on everybody's face.

But it was only a matter of time before the powerful, but covert, anti-Semitism of post-war Austria would venture out into the open. Guttmann sensed it from the Football Association, from the team and from the press. He both heard and read remarks that he was a fraud, that he was acting like a 'Wonder Rabbi' (*Wunderrabbiner*) in training sessions.

Walter was also disillusioned that his radical proposals for Austrian football were facing insurmountable opposition from the footballing establishment. In October 1964, just seven months into their reign, the two managers handed in a joint resignation.

In an uncharacteristically frank broadside against racism, Guttmann opened up to the weekly newspaper *WiWo* (*Wiener Wochenblatt*). Here is the relevant excerpt in full:

Certain circles, allegedly, and one newspaper in particular, have tried to make the life of the internationally famous coach Guttmann miserable, on whose birth certificate the word 'Israelite' is written, by means of multiple provocative accusations and teasing until Guttmann took his hat and left. The energetic Béla Guttmann discussed this in his interview with *WiWo* in his Hungarian-accented German: 'Do I have to like it if somebody writes and says about me that I walk around in training like a "wonder rabbi", or things like that?' He also points out that the term 'wonder rabbi' wasn't used by accident. There is a purpose behind it – a purpose to portray him as somebody racially inferior. 'Look'– he developed the habit to start all his sentences with this expression – 'I always thought that it doesn't matter at all in sport if somebody is Catholic, Protestant or Jewish. But now, when I have to endure the exact opposite, I am really sad.'

Of course, even as his outrage led him to speak his mind about anti-Semitism for the first and only time on record, Guttmann was holding an enormous amount in reserve. He implies that this was the first time racism had interfered with his football career. He doesn't mention that he fled from Hungary in both 1920 and 1922, in large part to avoid the White Terror against the Jews. He doesn't mention that his international playing career came to an abrupt halt amid barely concealed establishment anti-Semitism. He doesn't mention that he endured horrific abuse as a Hakoah player. He doesn't mention that he was the last coach of a club that was liquidated by Jew hatred. He doesn't mention that he was forced to step down as coach of Újpest because of anti-Jewish laws immediately after winning the league and Mitropa Cup. He doesn't mention that his Jewishness barred him from working in an official job in football from 1939 to 1945, robbing him of what should have been his peak years as coach. And that rather lengthy list excludes all the snide insinuations, the constant anti-Semitic mood music,

with which he would undoubtedly have had to contend throughout his career.

Once again, he was barely scratching the surface.

• • •

Although Benfica had won the Portuguese League and Cup double in 1963/64 under Lajos Czeizler, such was the example set by Béla Guttmann that this was now regarded as a failure. The team had crashed out of the European Cup in humiliating fashion in the first round, losing 5–0 away to Borussia Dortmund.

At the beginning of the following season, Guttmann himself was unavailable as a potential replacement, having recently taken the Austria job. Benfica turned instead to Elek Schwartz, a Romanian Jew, who had started his playing career in the 1920s at one of several Zionist clubs in his native country at the time, Kadima Timişoara. He moved to France, lying low in the war years, before making his name as the studious and longstanding coach of the Netherlands, well before that country had emerged as a footballing power.*

Having resigned from the Austria job, Guttmann decided to spend the 1964 Christmas holiday season in Lisbon. For old time's sake, he stayed at the Hotel Tivoli, his favourite retreat in the city. Once ensconced there, he wasn't shy about telling the sports newspaper *A Bola* exactly what was on his mind. The interview lays bare the acrimony and envy that had built up inside him since leaving Benfica two and a half years before.

'When I won the national league with Benfica, I received 150,000

* The Dutch Jewish footballer Bennie Muller made his debut for the national team under Schwartz. Many years later, Muller asked him: 'Mr Schwartz, I've always wondered. Are you Jewish?' Schwartz replied, 'Of course I am, Bennie. But there are so many crazy people that I don't shout about it.' About such brief and seemingly jocular comments it would be possible to write long and very serious books.

escudos, but Czeizler got 250,000 and was put in a hotel costing 8,000 a month,' he said:

> As Benfica were earning a lot of money from football after what I achieved, I wanted to eat what I had cooked. But instead others came to eat what I had cooked. I won the European Cup with players like Neto, Saraiva, Serra, Artur Santos and Mário João. Serafim alone [signed from Porto, a year after Guttmann's departure] cost more than all my signings: Eusébio, Torres, Germano, José Augusto. And Serafim has hardly played! And I am supposed to be the expensive coach!

Six months later, under huge pressure from the club's supporters, the Benfica board finally submitted to Guttmann's logic, acceding to all his costly demands and sky-high bonus provisions. Schwartz's team may have won the Portuguese league for the third year in succession, but they had lost by a single goal to Inter Milan in the 1965 European Cup Final, cementing the impression that only Guttmann had the charisma and imagination to lead Benfica to ultimate glory.

It was Inter's second European Cup in succession, emulating Benfica's feat from three years before. Their coach was Helenio Herrera, an Argentinean who had by now assumed Guttmann's mantle as the hottest coaching property in world football. Benfica's ageing Messiah flew into Lisbon airport once more, greeted by a huge and exuberant crowd, and set about reclaiming his throne.

• • •

Early reverses, away to Porto and a comprehensive 4–2 home defeat to Sporting Lisbon, spelt trouble ahead. Sporting were now led by Otto Glória, whom Guttmann had deposed as Benfica coach back in 1959, a clear indication that the world had moved on. The

unfancied Levski Sofia also gave the team an almighty fright in the first round of the European Cup. A 2–2 draw in Bulgaria was followed by a narrow 3–2 victory for Benfica in the Estádio da Luz.

Manchester United and their veteran manager, Matt Busby, awaited them in the quarter-final. History portrays the Busby of the 1960s as a wise old man determined to capture the European Cup denied to his young team of 1958, who had tragically died in the Munich Air Crash. But it is worthwhile noting that he was fully ten years younger than Guttmann, a man desperately struggling to recapture the Midas touch of his halcyon years.

When Guttmann had left Benfica in that glorious spring of 1962, he was in total control of his players. They were eating out of his hands, taking in everything he told them. We know also that this managerial authority was central to Guttmann's entire philosophy. But when he came back, he sensed that something was amiss, that the players had turned arrogant, that they had lost their hunger for success. Neither would they have been so wide-eyed and deferential when he spoke, having since worked under another three highly regarded coaches and reached two European Cup finals in the process.

'In 1962, four or five players had a car,' says António Simões. 'In 1965, when he came back, he sees that everyone has a car. I remember him turning to his assistant Caiado, saying "the players are rich. I don't like this."' He was furious that his three successors in the intervening period had not only profited financially from his work, but had also spoilt 'his' players, leaving him to tidy up the mess. Those imbeciles didn't know what they were doing! Players and coaches had just been getting drunk on the successes *he* had created! And what had *he* got? Nothing!

In yet another striking similarity to José Mourinho, the self-proclaimed 'Special One', Guttmann did not take kindly to his now near-perfect reputation being called into question, either by

the press or by team members. In a suicidal move for any coach, he deflected any perceived criticism on to his players, triggering a downward spiral.

Before the first leg in Manchester, he told some journalists of his concern that the team was over the hill, and lacking in motivation. The players got wind of his comments, and angrily called for an emergency meeting with their coach. Guttmann defended himself, saying that this was all part of his psychological warfare, designed to throw Busby off course and make United overconfident. But whereas his mind games used to be cunningly deployed to establish his control, or relax his players and build their confidence, now it just seemed that personal bitterness was distorting his managerial judgement. Bill Nicholson may have been outfoxed before the White Hart Lane semi-final in 1962, but Busby was probably left thinking that his opposite number was just shooting himself in the foot.

Benfica nevertheless remained very much in the tie after a magnificent exhibition of European Cup football at a packed and noisy Old Trafford. With Eusébio outstanding as usual, Guttmann's team came away with a narrow 3–2 defeat, making them favourites for the second leg. After all, they had still never lost a European Cup match at the Estádio da Luz. 'One goal in the bank perhaps may not be enough for Manchester United,' wrote Geoffrey Green in *The Times*. 'But at least this night cannot be taken away. It was something to remember.'

The club authorities, meanwhile, had got wind of the squad's displeasure at Guttmann's carping. The directors may have regarded his idiosyncratic outbursts as displays of genius when things were going swimmingly a few years before. Now they had started to interpret similar behaviour merely as evidence of desperation and cluelessness.

They told him to stop talking to the press, humiliating him and removing one of his favoured coaching props. 'For the first time in

my entire life I have been forbidden from speaking,' he said, adding indignantly that he intended to leave Benfica for good at the end of the season. But a Guttmann in his prime would have walked out there and then, whether there was a European Cup to play for or not.

By the time the second leg came around, Benfica had actually climbed ahead of Sporting to the top of the Portuguese league. But their progress was built on flimsy foundations. As Guttmann himself said until he was blue in the face, when the coach is neutered and there is mutiny in the air, there is no hope either for him or the team.

Someone just needed to topple the house of cards, and finish Guttmann off once and for all. That someone was George Best, showing the full extent of his greatness on the European stage for the first time. In the return leg at the Estádio da Luz, the nineteen-year-old Best was unstoppable, himself scoring two goals in the first fifteen minutes. The Benfica faithful may have been accustomed to such a blitzkrieg, but not from the opposition. 'We put a stop to their damn firecrackers and rockets,' recalled Best in one of his books. 'They had been masters of Europe but we showed them how to play the game.' The final score was a crushing 5–1 victory to United, a humiliating way for Guttmann to bow out of this great competition for good.

The collapse gathered pace. Benfica lost to Vitória de Guimarães and drew with lowly Sporting Braga, effectively surrendering the Portuguese title to Sporting. Yet more indignities were heaped on Guttmann. Training responsibilities were removed from his remit, and awarded to youth team coach Fernando Cabrita. His trusted assistant Fernando Caiado was asked to leave the club. Then a rudderless Benfica crashed out of the Taça de Portugal in a two-legged quarter-final to Braga.

Guttmann couldn't contain his anger. In the couple of days after the last league game at the beginning of May, and before leaving Lisbon for the last time, he gave an explosive interview to the

newspaper *Diário Popular*. He lashed out at 'a total failure of management', and 'stars who wield direct and damaging influence on members of the management'. He called Gastão Silva, the Director of Football, 'a sinister figure'. His worst was reserved for the greatest Benfica hero of them all. 'Eusébio has an unhealthy lifestyle ... his indiscipline makes him let himself go, [and] his body suffers. He stopped scoring, he couldn't run, he was out of breath ... It is sad to watch the end of a great footballer.' (Guttmann's fury was again clouding his judgement. Eusébio was the top scorer in the 1966 World Cup Finals, held in England two months later.)

But possibly regretting what was, even for him, a highly undiplomatic outburst, he gave another interview on the same day to *A Bola*, contradicting what he had just said. He called the players 'respectful and polite', Eusébio 'a boy with a pure heart', and refuted the idea that players were running the club.

The journalists at *Diário Popular* were outraged, following him to the south of France, where Guttmann was taking a vacation with Mariann. Cornered, he admitted that his original, defamatory words were correctly represented. No sooner had *Diário Popular* published their triumphant confirmation than another newspaper, *Mundo Desportivo*, interviewed him again. 'It is untrue that he has attacked any individual Benfica player,' assured the newspaper. 'Many of my words were twisted,' said Guttmann. 'Here in Nice, I was once more betrayed by a Portuguese daily newspaper.'

Meanwhile, many of the players that once lionised him were now in uproar. 'Is a good coach someone who is aware of the unhealthy lifestyle of the player and only mentions this when he's already got one foot on the departing plane?' asked Eusébio. *Diário Popular* weren't finished either, now attacking a scheming individual 'who goes back on what he's said according to how he feels at the time', ending the article with the words: 'Béla Guttmann: Requiescat in pace!'

In this grubby way, Béla Guttmann's once glorious association with Benfica arrived at its rather tragic conclusion. 'These eyes, Sir, that haven't known tears for ages, shed tears over a few nights,' he told one journalist. 'If ever you have had a great love,' he warned another, 'do not ever dare to go back.'

This was a lesson that has been learned the hard way in recent years by the likes of Kenny Dalglish, José Mourinho and Kevin Keegan in British football. Their initially triumphant returns to Liverpool, Chelsea and Newcastle United respectively all ended in similar tears. As usual, Guttmann was ahead of everyone else.

What about the curse, the words for which Béla Guttmann is now most famous? Little attention was paid to the alleged mal ediction in the years immediately following Guttmann's two spells at the club. It seems that the first explicit mention of the curse in the Portuguese press didn't actually appear until May 1988 (in *A Bola*), seven years after Guttmann's death, when Benfica lost in a penalty shoot-out in the European Cup Final to PSV Eindhoven. But as defeat followed defeat in European competition, the original disregard slowly evolved into something of an obsession.

But did he actually ever utter the following sentence, or something similar, in his inimitable Esperanto? *'Nos próximos 100 anos, o Benfica não voltará a ser campeão europeu'* (For the next 100 years, Benfica will never be European champions). And if so, when and to whom did he say it?

Unfortunately for researchers such as myself, there is absolutely no written evidence that he articulated the phrase that now gets talked about far and wide every time Benfica come anywhere near a European final. The nearest approximation in print is a comment he made to *Mundo Desportivo*, published on 4 May 1966, after his final game as coach of the club: 'Nobody will take away from me the two European titles that I helped to win and nobody else has won, and never will win.'

Unsurprisingly, given the enormity of what he achieved there, Guttmann's most popular nicknames at Benfica evoked mystical or Machiavellian powers: *o feiticeiro* (the sorcerer), *o mago* (the magician), *o velha raposa* (the old fox). In the years that followed his departure, there certainly seems to have been a growing, if unarticulated, sense that the former coach was wishing the club harm in some supernatural way. (Indeed, I have just an inkling that the fixation with the curse may be somehow related to the deep-rooted perception of the demonic Jew.)

In an interview published in *A Bola* on 3 December 1970, when he was in semi-retirement, Guttmann was asked whether Benfica could win another European title. He replied: 'Was there any other manager, in Portugal, besides Guttmann, that was able to do that?' The article continued: 'And the "old magician" … bade farewell with a loud laugh which seemed, to us, to be filled with irony.'

Ângelo Martins, who played as a defender in Guttmann's European Cup-winning seasons, insists that Guttmann made a 'prophecy' that Benfica would win another European Cup only after a hundred years. Others merely dismiss the curse as a rumour that has only gained traction due to Benfica's repeated European failures.

But if you were to ask me whether – at some point between 1962 and the end of his life – Béla Guttmann damned Benfica to a barren century in European football, I would wager rather a lot that he did. If truth be told, I would wager rather a lot that he said something similar on several occasions, and far worse to boot. Such was his sustained rage, I would actually be rather surprised if he limited himself to one hundred years.

• • •

His second departure from Benfica really should have been it. Guttmann knew exactly, during that match at the Prater stadium in

1933, when he had to retire as a player. But it seems that he couldn't be equally ruthless with himself as a coach. He hobbled on, taking four more short-lived and somewhat pointless jobs.

Conventional wisdom has it that he spent the war years in Switzerland. As we now know, that story is false. The first time he did eventually live in Switzerland was in the autumn of 1966, a few months after his second departure from Benfica, when he was appointed as coach of Servette FC in Geneva. He had spent much of his career in the various nerve centres of world football. Now he found himself in a backwater, in a country that, to this day, has never sent a team to a European final.

He guided Servette through to the quarter-finals of the European Cup Winners' Cup, one of the two less prestigious European club competitions at the time. But a 3–0 defeat in Bulgaria in early March 1967 to Slavia Sofia put paid to this adventure, and to his job.

A few months later, he again tasted defeat in the same competition. By September 1967, he was in Athens as coach of Panathinaikos. Drawn against Bayern Munich in the first round of the Cup Winners' Cup, his team was routed 5–0 in Germany, and once again, any hopes of a glorious comeback had been quashed. He soon departed, with familiar allegations of greed ringing in his ears. 'Lakis Petropoulos was my assistant coach,' he recalled. 'He later became the manager of the Greek national team. After I left, he told the *Kurier* [a Viennese newspaper]: "Guttmann wasn't impressed by the drachma!"' Different country, same script.

Guttmann returned to Vienna, and for six years that seemed to be that. But in March 1973, he was coaxed out of retirement to take on the role of technical director of FK Austria Vienna, overseeing football operations at the club for a few months until the end of the season.

His final destination was the club he deserted amid great acrimony in 1959, just after winning the league. Perhaps feeling cheated

out of his best years, FC Porto swallowed their pride and appointed Guttmann, now a pale imitation of his former self, for the 1973/74 season. In a largely forgettable venture, Porto finished a distant fourth. Guttmann did, however, manage one last notable victory, a 2–1 win at the Estádio das Antas in March 1974 against a Benfica team that still contained Eusébio and António Simões. The winning goal was scored by the Peruvian Teófilo Cubillas, later to terrorise Scotland at the 1978 World Cup in Argentina.

Guttmann's last season was also marked by a tragic incident. Porto midfielder Pavão, aged twenty-six, collapsed during a home game against Setúbal, and was rushed off to hospital. At the end of the game, the public address system announced to the departing fans that Pavão had died, apparently from a congenital heart condition. 'I loved him very much, as if he had been my son,' said Guttmann. 'His death gave me such a shock that I turned my back on football.'

About time, too. By the time he left Porto, he was seventy-five years old, four years older than the supposedly ancient Alex Ferguson and Bobby Robson when they finally left the stage. Besides, the comparatively late retirement of those two elder statesmen of British football made sense. They had simply continued as much-loved coaches of Manchester United and Newcastle United respectively until the time was right to bow out. Guttmann, for his part, spent his final years in football doing jobs that just didn't really add up.

So the question is this: why did he cling on to football for so long, blemishing a reputation he had so painstakingly built up?

The first point to understand is that Guttmann will only have started bringing in good money when he took on the Milan job in 1953, by which time he was already in his mid-fifties. Prior to that, a few years after the Holocaust, he will have had next to nothing to his name. At the peak of his earning power just ten years later, he will have felt the urge to make up for lost time when others in his position would have been pottering about in retirement.

Perhaps, too, he just couldn't abandon the thrill of football, the adrenaline of winning. He kept wanting one final glorious moment. Of course, he and Mariann had no children or grandchildren to focus on in their advancing years. Boredom, therefore, probably played some role in prolonging his career.

But I think there was another reason as well.

• • •

One beautiful summer's morning in 2016, I took a taxi from my hotel in central Vienna to the Zentralfriedhof (Central Cemetery) in the city's outskirts, one of the largest cemeteries in the world, and the final resting place for many of the great and the good. But I didn't walk with the other tourists to visit the graves of Beethoven, Brahms or Schubert. I wanted to see where Béla and Mariann Guttmann were buried.

For Béla Guttmann's grave, I walked to the Jewish section of the cemetery. In the serene and leafy surroundings, in the same spot where Eusébio is said to have prayed for Benfica's absolution, I took a few moments to contemplate a life that now occupied most of my waking thoughts. The idea struck me that no immediate relative would have been alive to say *kaddish* for him at his funeral or thereafter. Alone, I uttered the traditional and emotional Jewish prayer, recited over many centuries during periods of mourning for loved ones, praising God's name at the height of personal grief.

Armed with the details of the whereabouts of Mariann's grave, supplied to me by the Viennese city administration, I then walked half an hour or so to the main Christian section. With the aid of a map, I eventually managed to find the place I was looking for – Group 75A, Row 3, Number 29. I paced up and down the row, checking and checking again. I asked a passing gardener to check with me. But there was no sign of Mariann Guttmann's gravestone.

I went in to enquire at the main office of the cemetery, handing them the grave coordinates on my sheet of paper. It must be wrong, I said. They checked on their computer system. The details I had were absolutely correct. After Mariann died aged eighty-seven in 2000, nineteen years after Béla, no stone had been erected on her burial plot, just a small wooden cross. Within a few years, exposed to the elements, the cross would have gradually disintegrated. Mariann Guttmann is buried in an unmarked grave.

Things started to piece together in my head. When she died, whoever cleared out her residence will have found two cardboard boxes and a leather suitcase, all containing a collection of memorabilia from Béla's career – photographs, medals, books and many other souvenirs. With seemingly no family or friends around to claim the items, they found their way to the Viennese city authorities, and hence to four antique shops, before someone finally grasped the collection's historical and financial value. An auctioneer of sports memorabilia, based in Kassel, Germany, eventually sold the items to an unnamed buyer in June 2001.

My curiosity awakened, I contacted the Viennese city department responsible for wills and estates. Despite repeated requests, the central district that held Béla's details refused to divulge his testament to any non-relative. But, happily for me, the suburban district office with information on Mariann (who was identified by the original name on her birth certificate, Maria, in all official documents) imposed no such restrictions.

What they eventually sent to me revealed her dire financial straits when she died. By that time, she had moved from the apartment in central Vienna which she shared with Béla to an old age care home on the outskirts of the city, in the district of Hietzing. The cash in her bank account amounted to just 10,542 Schilling (worth approximately £450 at the time), insufficient to pay for a basic funeral (13,485 Schilling).

Outstanding debts to her care home, totalling 341,682 Schilling (approximately £15,000), dwarfed her assets. Although the state must have paid the shortfall in her funeral costs, there was certainly no money in her estate to pay for a gravestone, and nobody else evidently felt duty-bound to stump up the necessary expense.

Her nephew Pál Moldoványi says that Mariann had visited his family in Germany a couple of years after Béla died in 1981. He never saw her again, although his mother (Mariann's sister-in-law) did stay in telephone contact. 'I only heard of her a few times,' he remembers. 'She was out of the picture.' She most probably died lonely, as well as poor.

Where did the money go? For the answer to that, we have to go back to Imre Guttmann's comments about his uncle Béla's gambling successes in Las Vegas in the 1920s. 'From that moment on he was past help,' Imre says. 'Wherever he travelled, he had to play. He worked hard, he earned a lot, but he squandered at least half of his income.' Imre saw him in action just once, accompanying him to a casino in Portugal soon after the European Cup Final in 1962, but insists that his uncle 'lost millions in different kinds of casinos'.

Moldoványi's evidence confirms that Guttmann's addiction to gambling dated back several decades. 'My father (Pál Moldován) told me that he and Béla regularly went to casinos and often played cards and pool together,' he said. 'It is true that Béla was a big gambler.'

If he or she is lucky, an addict will have a spouse or supportive family desperately trying to help them overcome a self-destructive habit. But it seems that Mariann was no better herself. 'My father and Mariann loved playing, too,' says Moldoványi. 'Somehow it was in the family, it was something they shared. Once when Mariann visited us, she complained that she had financial difficulties because she would lose 300 Marks on bridge every night and that was a bit too much. She loved to squander money.'

Although José Augusto says he and other players knew that Guttmann gambled, António Simões claims to have been unaware. His coach was no doubt mindful that the truth would have severely undermined his constant exhortations to the players about their own lifestyle, and tried his best to keep his big weakness a secret. However, Simões did say, without prompting, that 'his [Guttmann's] wife liked to go to the casino'.

Singing the praises of Lisbon in his interview with Tibor Hámori, Guttmann remarked that 'the most beautiful holiday resort, Estoril, was also located near the Portuguese capital', adding 'we often made a trip there'. No wonder! The largest casino in Europe can be found there, and Simões confirms that Mariann was a regular visitor.

Mariann also shared Guttmann's liking for the high life. 'She lived for her family, was a housewife but also got on well with the higher echelons of society,' says Augusto. All that keeping up with the privileged European elites can play havoc with a bank account.

So Béla and Mariann just egged each other on, throwing hard-earned money down the drain, with no parental conscience about an offspring's financial future to hold them back. 'They talked about how much, millions in Marks, they had lost in the 1970s when the dollar depreciated,' Moldoványi remembers. One suspects that this remark is a case of addict denial, that the real cause of their financial loss was staring right back at them from their bedroom mirror. It is very likely that Béla and Mariann together wasted most of their money before he died, and Mariann soon lost the remainder all by herself. The ultimate net financial result of all Béla's demands and negotiations was less than zero.

With this background information to hand, it becomes a little easier to understand why the great football coach Béla Guttmann didn't finally retire until the age of seventy-five, working in jobs well below his station.

• • •

Around noon every day, an elderly Béla Guttmann would leave his apartment on Walfischgasse in the old town of Vienna, and slowly stroll the five minutes or so to Café Europa on Kärntnerstrasse. He was just a few kilometres from the scene of Hakoah's triumphs all those years ago, when young Jewish men in the summer of their lives would take on the world, and win. How the city had changed since then!

He described how he would hold court in the café, with eager listeners hanging on his words. "'What's up, Uncle Béla? What did you think of the match? Haven't you changed your mind? Did you finish for good?" Why should I deny it? Time has passed me by.'

There is no reason to doubt the degree of awe in which he was held. He was, and still is, one of the giants of football history. A 2013 poll by *World Soccer* magazine asked seventy-three international football experts to name the greatest football coach of all time. Guttmann came in at number nine. I would have put him higher, but still, pretty good, all things considered. I did scour the life histories of the top eight, but as far as I could make out, not one was hunted down by the Nazis, had their family murdered or escaped from a forced labour camp. Moreover, the top eight all came after him. It was he who blazed the trail for the others to follow.

He talked of travelling around Europe during his final years (why would anyone think he would stay in the same place for very long?), seeing various blasts from the past. 'When I last visited Pest, Bonzó [István] Balogh [scorer of the final goal for Újpest in the Mitropa Cup Final of 1939] came to see me at the Béke Hotel. We were so happy to see each other. Just imagine, I hadn't seen him for thirty-three years!'

Journalists and footballing organisations might occasionally seek him out for his opinion on developments in the game. In their book

on the history of the European Cup, John Motson and John Row-linson describe Guttmann's speech at an event in Vienna to mark the competition's twenty-fifth anniversary, in 1980. His reported words, spoken in the wake of a couple of dreary and defensive finals won by Liverpool and Nottingham Forest, reveal some degree of disillusionment: "'Please let us remember,' he implored, hands held out in a solemn gesture, his eyes moving anxiously behind his dark glasses, "the European Cup stands for great teams. And it should be about great players.'"

He may have been sorry to see his beloved sport depart from his romantic ideal of breathless entertainment, but was he otherwise happy and content in his final years? During his detailed discussion with Hámori shortly before his death, there was no reference what-soever to his second stint at Benfica, an indication that bitterness still lingered within his soul. Or perhaps he was just embarrassed, and didn't want to dwell on this blot on the copybook.

Did he ruminate on the more serious events in his life, from the Holocaust period? Did tragic thoughts stop him in his tracks? In a person's last years, as life's pace slows down for even energetic high achievers like Béla Guttmann, dark thoughts cannot so easily be banished by constant activity. Could we even suggest that the extreme anger that burst forth in his later dealings with Benfica can be attributed, at least in part, to past suffering and a great sense of loss? Just as with someone who returns from a bad day at work to take it out on his family, perhaps this was just diverted rage?

When I think of these questions, the words of António Simões enter my head: 'He would always talk about the importance of family, that one of the pillars in our lives is the family. If you have got a good family, he would say, that is half the way to success.'

One wonders what images paraded before Guttmann's eyes when he said these words. The sort of man who goes out of his way to tell young, high-spirited footballers about the importance

of their family is also likely to think constantly about the tragedy that befell his own, whatever his public diffidence about the subject. As glorious European football nights receded in the rearview mirror, sorrowful reflection then had the chance to dominate an emptying mind.

I would like to think, too, that he frequently pondered, with a great sense of shame, the effects of his reckless actions on the family of Giuliano Brene, the seventeen-year-old boy whose young life he snuffed out on the streets of Milan in 1955. Did he experience flashbacks of that awful scene of panic, blood and death, a scene from which he fled in order to save his own skin? We may speculate that the excitement generated from feeding his gambling addiction may have served to block out the memory of events that many of us are lucky enough never to experience.

Did he share his innermost and darkest thoughts with Mariann, his partner for more than four decades? Their close bond was sealed in the most desperate of circumstances, and what they managed to withstand together in 1944 must surely have stiffened their determination to overcome the more typical ups and downs of married life. Her frequent visits back to Vienna during his career certainly suggest that his preferred lifestyle was not always to her taste.

Hints at marital difficulties and infidelity did surface in the Portuguese newspapers at the time of Guttmann's final departure from Benfica in 1966. The fact that he had several enemies in Lisbon by this stage does give rise to some scepticism about the validity of these rumours, although we do nevertheless have to pay attention to the words of Pál Moldoványi: 'Mariann escorted Béla everywhere in the world, she was always by his side. She did have to watch him, since Béla was very susceptible to women. He was an excellent dancer and a great flatterer.'

On the issue of their childlessness, we cannot know whether this was at any stage a source of deep sadness for Mariann or Béla. Nor

can we know whether one or both decided against starting a family early on in their marriage, or whether they were simply unable to have children. Guttmann's views on family, recounted by Simões, make this latter explanation the more convincing for me. (He also declared in his autobiography that he 'loves' and 'idolises' children.) For her generation, Mariann was not young (thirty-three) when she finally had the opportunity to marry, after the war had ended. Perhaps, indeed, this was just one further layer of tragedy in their lives.

What was Guttmann's attitude, in his last years, to his Jewishness? He was certainly never interested in attending synagogue. Revealingly, Pál Moldoványi believed that it was '[his] origin and not religion that was important to him'. As he reflected on his family and friends, his adolescence and playing career, and the persecutions and prejudice that marred his life, his Jewish identity would have seemed to him an undeniable fact. It is perhaps worth noting that he chose to be buried in an Orthodox Jewish cemetery, when he will have known full well that the love of his life, the woman whose family risked everything to save him, could never, as a non-Jew, be buried alongside him. When push came to shove, and despite all his earlier dissembling, I think the elderly Béla Guttmann knew exactly who he was.

• • •

Béla Guttmann died from a heart attack in Lainz Hospital in Vienna on Thursday 27 August 1981. He was eighty-two.

Two days later, as he lay in the mortuary, Jews leaving a barmitzvah ceremony at the Stadttempel, the only synagogue in the city to survive *Kristallnacht*, were attacked by terrorists from the Abu Nidal Organization. Two of them, Nathan Fried and Sarah Kohut, were murdered, and eighteen wounded. The Jew hatred that formed the backdrop to Guttmann's life had already started to assume a deadly new guise.

Guttmann was buried the day after the attack. The funeral, attended by a delegation from Benfica, was presided over by Rabbi Akiba Eisenberg, born and brought up in Vác, a Hungarian town just north of Budapest. Rabbi Eisenberg had survived the almost total annihilation of the Jews of the town by hiding in the surrounding countryside. He may well have been unaware of the bitter coincidence that Béla Guttmann, according to his own testimony, himself spent some time in a forced labour camp in Vác in 1944. Six months after Guttmann's funeral, a bomb exploded outside Eisenberg's Vienna apartment while he was on holiday.

On Guttmann's gravestone is inscribed his Hebrew name – *Baruch ben* (son of) *Moshe Avraham*. Jewish sages have suggested that the name parents choose for their child will reflect their unique essence, personality and path in life. The meaning of the word *baruch* – blessed – certainly seems apt for Béla Guttmann. He was blessed, above all, with the survival denied to the overwhelming majority of his fellow Jews in Europe. He was blessed with an iron will, a stubborn resolve to overcome the most appalling personal tragedy and hardship. And he was blessed with that extremely rare, precious and undervalued talent to coax young people to live up to their full potential, and fulfil their dreams.

Béla Guttmann was the Jew who conquered Europe. Not just, using the favoured phraseology of sports headline writers, because he led an unfancied team from a hitherto small footballing nation to successive triumphs in Europe's most prestigious competition, but also because he conquered the demons and tribulations that have confronted Jews ever since they first set foot in that often venomous continent. His all-consuming passion for football drove him, incredibly, to return to the terrifying Europe of 1938 as other Jews clamoured desperately to leave it. Yet, equally incredibly, he not only survived, but prospered.

Also on the gravestone, by the way, is Guttmann's date of birth.

Stated as 26 January 1899, this is one day before the date on his birth certificate, and more than a year before many other references, including the date of birth inscribed on his statue at the Estádio da Luz.

With Béla Guttmann, things were never quite what they seemed. And the truth, as far as I can make out, is even more remarkable than the legend. It is time to place the achievements of this great man in their proper perspective.

CONCLUSION

REFLECTIONS

'In truth, football has never been quite the same [since Guttmann left Benfica in 1962],' writes Jonathan Wilson in *Inverting the Pyramid*:

> Guttmann, more than anyone since [Herbert] Chapman, had defined the cult of the manager. The man who would take on his mantle was Helenio Herrera [the coach of Inter Milan], whose conception of the game could hardly have been more different. Out went all romantic notions of scoring one more than the opposition, and in came cynicism and *catenaccio* and the theory of conceding one fewer.

Guttmann's significance in footballing history is well recognised by a small breed of highly knowledgeable writers such as Wilson, as indeed his all-time ranking in the survey of world experts suggests. He also emerged as the greatest Hungarian-born coach in a 2014 survey of leading football journalists in that country, pipping Golden Team boss Gusztáv Sebes. But among the general population of football fans, even among those who take some interest in the history of the game, Guttmann's renown is patchy, to say the least. It is only in Portugal that his name regularly crops up outside

the quasi-academic realm of football historians or light-hearted articles about the curse.

It could be that the very fact of Guttmann's originality not only denied him what he considered his rightful financial recompense, but a prominent international legacy as well. Whereas the likes of Pelé and Puskás were, and still are, known the world over, coaches were not then accorded the same status reserved today for house-hold names such as Mourinho and Guardiola.

My own unscientific survey, based on limited conversations with Hungarian football fans and on discussions with Hungarian con-tacts who know the Guttmann story well, is that he is little known among the broader public even in the country of his birth. And this despite the fact that he is the only Hungarian-born coach to lift the European Cup.

Iván Balog, a sociologist and historian, attributes his relative an-onymity in Hungary to the fact that he spent so little time there. 'Guttmann was only active in Hungarian football as a player and coach for around seven years overall, with huge gaps in between some of his spells,' says Balog. 'This period of time appears to me too short to establish him as a cult figure in Hungarian collective football memory.'

We also have to bear in mind that Guttmann left Hungary in early 1949, just before the Communist system was firmly estab-lished. Communist countries made much of the achievements of their sports stars, painting them as muscular and imposing products of a superior system. On the other hand, the history of both Hun-garian sport before Communism and the success of Hungarian émigrés were accorded much less, if any, attention.

Indeed, the Hungarian government extracted great propaganda value from the Golden Team of the 1950s, whose history is there-fore deeply embedded in the national psyche. Given the country's mournful preoccupation with the defeat to West Germany in the

1954 World Cup Final, it is easy to forget that Hungary did also reach the final of the same competition in the pre-Communism days of 1938. Similarly, as Guttmann had defected to the West, his exploits did not serve the interests of the government. His Jewishness, it could be argued, may also have counted against him. Was he sufficiently 'Hungarian' to invoke national pride?

The Jews themselves would perhaps be the most obvious constituency to claim Guttmann as their own and promote his name far and wide. He is certainly the only Jewish coach to win the European Cup. In fact, he is by some distance the most successful Jewish figure in the history of the world's most popular sport.

But for various reasons, Guttmann is little known in Jewish circles, save perhaps in the now tiny community of Vienna. The overwhelming reason, needless to say, is the Holocaust, which almost erased European Jewry, scattered the few survivors, and left their collective memory, identity and self-confidence in ruins. The central and eastern European Jews who did stay in the region, and who may have particularly identified with Guttmann, were subject to the same Communist influences as the general population.

The vast majority of the world's Jews now reside in either the United States or Israel. The American Jews may have taken great pride in the feats of sports stars such as the baseball player Hank Greenberg or the swimmer Mark Spitz, but the accomplishments of a European Jew in the foreign sport of soccer were never going to register. It is a long time since New York's Jews were entranced by the visit of Hakoah Vienna. The newly established State of Israel, for its part, was perhaps too busy building its own national folklore and identity to pay much attention to the achievements of a diaspora Jew.

I can maybe talk with most knowledge about Britain. I have been an ardent follower of football since I can remember. In my earliest adult years, I also developed a very strong interest in Jewish history.

But the stories of Béla Guttmann and Hakoah Vienna entered into my consciousness only around my mid-thirties.

One reason, as perhaps with the United States and Israel, is the overriding focus on the exploits of British Jews. For example, in late 2013 and early 2014, the Jewish Museum in London staged an exhibition that promised to tell 'the untold story of Jews and football'. With all due respect to the likes of Mark Lazarus, who scored the winning goal in the 1967 League Cup Final for Queens Park Rangers, and David Dein, the former vice-chairman of Arsenal, I think the story remained untold. Where were Guttmann, Braun, Meisl, Kohn, Kürschner, Erbstein, Weisz, Hertzka and Hirschl, to name just a few Jewish footballing greats off the top of my head? Where were the stories about Hakoah Vienna, in my view the most romantic, gripping, heroic and tragic tale of *any* football team in history, let alone a Jewish one?

I appreciate that the mission of the museum is 'to surprise, delight and engage all people, irrespective of background or faith, in the history, identity and culture of Jews in Britain'. But the story of the Jews necessarily cuts across international borders. Confining the perspective in this way risks the big picture being completely missed.

Jewish historians' lack of interest in football, perhaps even snobbishness, further explains why Guttmann's name is not as prominent as it should be. The *Encyclopedia Judaica*, a thoroughly comprehensive resource first published in the early 1970s (just a decade after Guttmann's main triumphs), contained more than 25,000 articles on a wide range of Jewish subjects and personalities. Guttmann and Hakoah are given passing mentions in a general article about sport. But, remarkably, neither was awarded an individual article, an honour nevertheless accorded to Béla's namesakes Michael Guttmann, a Talmudic scholar from the Hungarian provinces, and Robert Guttmann, an artist from Prague.

This neglect inevitably leads to distortion and untruth. A tongue-in-cheek editorial in the London-based *Jewish Chronicle* (the *JC*), published in early 2016, referred to the participation of a young, local Jewish player in the England cricket team's practice before a big game. 'It is rare for the *JC* to be able to hail the role of a Jewish sportsman,' the article tells us:

> ...Perhaps now is the time to reveal some previously hidden examples. The tailor who sewed the elastic band on Pele's trousers; the accountant who checked how many clubs were in Jack Nicklaus's golf bag; the doctor who put a plaster on Lasse Viren's arm after his transfusion. And, of course, the Bloom's [kosher restaurant] waiter who served Mohammed Ali before his fight with Joe Frazier.

If this book achieves anything, I want it to help put a stop to this kind of drivel. To say that the Jews of pre-Holocaust Europe played a part in the development of football is an understatement. Central European Jews moulded its current form; they were pivotal in introducing thought and strategy into the sport. Their restless wanderlust predated, and very possibly accelerated, its eventual globalisation. Guttmann, the survivor, continued that tradition long after a considerable number of similarly advanced or just burgeoning football brains were turned to ashes. And as with so many aspects of modern life, we can only guess what course football might have taken if the Holocaust had never happened.

Europe's Jews do not have much of a role in football now. That's because, for the most part, they are either dead or gone. We have a responsibility, however, to tell the truth about the lives that were wiped out. Football may not be top of the list when it comes to remembering the great Jewish communities of Europe, but the stories of Hakoah's tours make plain that the sport was a real passion for many who were murdered.

'Six million of our people live on in our hearts,' said Shimon Peres, the then President of Israel, at the 2011 opening ceremony for Yom Hashoah, the annual Holocaust remembrance day in Israel. 'We are their eyes that remember. We are their voice that cries out.'

• • •

'In the 1990s there are still come clans in Kaifeng [in China] who are vaguely conscious of Jewish ancestry,' writes Bernard Wasserstein in his book *Vanishing Diaspora*, published in 1996. 'Some even claim [when meeting foreign Jewish tourists] to recall that their grandparents abstained from eating pork or lit candles on Friday … The Jews of Europe now face a similar destiny. Slowly but surely, they are fading away. Soon nothing will be left save a disembodied memory.'

In January 1925, Béla Guttmann scored for Hakoah Vienna in an 11–2 victory over Maccabi Tel Aviv. When this game took place, there were more Jews in Vienna (200,000) than in the whole of Palestine. Today, there are more than six million Jews in Israel, and fewer than ten thousand in Vienna. The respective fortunes of Maccabi Tel Aviv and Hakoah Vienna reflect this astonishing demographic sea change. The former are regular participants in the UEFA Champions League, whereas Hakoah didn't get past the Anschluss.*

Guttmann hailed from a vibrant Jewish Europe that no longer exists. In 1939, there were 9.5 million Jews in the continent. Now there are only 1.4 million, constituting just 10 per cent of the

* In 2002, as part of a restitution agreement between the Viennese Jewish community and the local and national government, the land Hakoah was forced to vacate more than sixty years earlier was returned to the community. In 2008, a new and state-of-the-art Hakoah sports club was reopened, amid great emotion. A Jewish school was also built on the site. There is no Hakoah football team, however. The Jewish football club is Maccabi Wien.

world's Jews, and 0.2 per cent of Europe's total population. (Even that number was bolstered in the post-war years by the 300,000 Jews who fled from north Africa to France, now the country with the largest Jewish population in Europe. In recent years, thousands of French Jews have been leaving every year for Israel to escape the growing hostility towards them.)

The Jews may have largely gone, but the anti-Semitism that plagued Guttmann's life has not disappeared with them. A 2014 global survey by the Anti-Defamation League sought to establish people's attitudes to Jews by asking them whether they agreed with eleven stereotypes, such as 'Jews have too much power in international financial markets', 'Jews have too much control over global affairs', 'Jews still talk too much about what happened to them in the Holocaust', or 'Jews think they are better than other people'.

If the respondent was sufficiently brazen to admit to a stranger that they agreed with six or more of these eleven statements, he or she would be said to harbour anti-Semitic attitudes. Seven decades after the gas chambers were closed, the percentages meeting this rather charitable threshold are still substantial in Guttmann's various domiciles: 41 per cent in Hungary, 28 per cent in Austria, 21 per cent in Portugal, and 20 per cent in Italy.

In this survey, the Anti-Defamation League sought to measure traditional Jew hatred, a powerful impulse rendered less socially acceptable in some countries, at least temporarily, by the Holocaust. But the animus simply had to find a more respectable and convenient outlet, soon to be located in the country that Fritz Löhner-Beda, Hakoah's co-founder, could only dream about as he was being pummelled to death in Auschwitz. It is the country that Natan Sharansky, the former Soviet dissident turned Israeli politician, likes to call 'the world's Jew'. According to a 2014 survey by the BBC Monitoring Service, overwhelming majorities in the United Kingdom, France, Spain and Germany (the four European

countries polled) possess 'mainly negative' attitudes to Israel, with the relevant percentages nearing the levels of those who express antipathy to North Korea and Iran.

'Anti-Semitism is a virus that survives by mutating,' writes Jonathan Sacks, the former Chief Rabbi of the United Kingdom. 'In the Middle Ages, Jews were hated because of their religion. In the nineteenth and twentieth centuries, they were hated because of their race. Today they are hated because of their nation state.'

There is, it seems, no end to it. But things, it is worth remembering, are seldom black and white. The Guttmann story would probably never have come to pass without the extremely courageous actions of a Hungarian non-Jew, Pál Moldován. If Guttmann deserves a lot more recognition, then this unknown hero most certainly does. I would like this book to end with his name to the fore.

TIMELINE AND ACHIEVEMENTS

TIMELINE

Born 27 January 1899 in Budapest
Died 27 August 1981 in Vienna

PLAYER
1917–1920: Törekvés
1921–1922: MTK Budapest
1922–1926: Hakoah Vienna
1926–1928: New York Giants
1928–1929: New York Hakoah
1929–1930: Hakoah All-Stars
1930: New York Soccer Club
1931–1932: Hakoah All-Stars
1932–1933: Hakoah Vienna

COACH
1933–1935: Hakoah Vienna

1935–1937: Enschede

1938–1939: Újpest

1945–1946: Vasas

1946–1947: Ciocanul Bucharest

1947: Újpest

1948: Kispest

1949–1950: Padova

1950–1951: Triestina

1953: Quilmes

1953: Apoel Nicosia

1953–1955: Milan

1955–1956: Vicenza

1956–1957: Honvéd

1957–1958: São Paulo

1958–1959: Porto

1959–1962: Benfica

1962: Peñarol

1963: Peñarol

1964: Austria

1965–1966: Benfica

1966–1967: Servette

1967: Panathinaikos

1973: Austria Vienna

1973–1974: Porto

ACHIEVEMENTS

PLAYER

Hungarian league championship: 1920/21
Austrian league championship: 1924/25
United States Open Cup: 1929
4 international caps for Hungary (vs Germany in June 1921, and vs
Switzerland, Poland and Egypt, all in May 1924)

COACH

European Cup: 1960/61, 1961/62
Mitropa Cup: 1939
Hungarian league championship: 1938/39, 1946/47
Portuguese league championship: 1958/59, 1959/60, 1960/61
Campeonato Paulista: 1957

ACKNOWLEDGEMENTS

I couldn't have written this book without the help of some exceptional people. It may be a cliché, but it is also a fact. Almost all of the important sources of information about Béla Guttmann are in languages I don't speak. A very talented team of translators helped to shine a torch on his life – Hajnalka (Hajni) Deák from Hungarian; Andrea Rimaszombati from German; Rob Lindsay from Portuguese; and Paola Garbini from Italian.

Hajni also tirelessly tracked down Hungarian sources for information and photographs that I would otherwise never have known about. Her brother, László Harri Németh (Harri), joined Hajni and me for a tour around the various sites of Guttmann interest in Budapest. Standing in the spot where he hid in 1944, or in Eichmann's garden – this was a day I shall never forget.

Zsolt Gulyás has a fascination with Guttmann that matches my own. His interview with Pál Moldoványi unlocked the remaining mystery of Guttmann's Holocaust experience. Zsolt also provided me with other invaluable information and some photographs, either taken by him or belonging to Pál Moldoványi.

I owe a great debt to Tamás Kárpáti, whose treasure trove of Hungarian sports publications and newspapers from the interwar

period allowed me to piece together Guttmann's early playing days, and to clarify the careers of other Hungarian Jewish football personalities from that era.

Without the help of Imre Guttmann, Béla's nephew who lives in Brazil, I may never have discovered the missing pieces of the Guttmann family jigsaw. Speaking in person to Béla's closest living relative was a very emotional moment for me.

Robert Friedman of Steps to the Past Genealogical Research, and Kinga Frojimovics, Director of the Hungarian Section at Yad Vashem Archives, gave me some very useful advice on how to discover what happened to the Guttmann family. Etz Hachaim, a company that specialises in Hungarian Jewish family research, carried out invaluable fact-finding on Guttmann's parents and siblings. Gavriel Bar Shaked of Yad Vashem also gave me the benefit of his expertise. The Újpest Local History Collection provided a detailed map of the Jewish ghetto in Újpest in 1944. The Miskolc Jewish community supplied a photograph of Ármin Guttmann's grave, and information on his post-Holocaust life.

Gunnar Persson shared his intimate knowledge of Hakoah Vienna, revealed some illuminating details about Guttmann's time at the club, and helped me to solve one or two puzzles about his pre-war career.

Laurie Sudwarts was a key point of contact for me in Vienna. He went out of his way to introduce me to several leading figures in this small but very active Jewish community. It was a pleasure, in particular, to spend time talking with Paul Haber, the president of the modern-day Hakoah sports club.

On my behalf, George Sternschein pursued information on Mariann Guttmann's testament from the relevant Viennese authorities and then translated the resulting document. He also translated the minutes of an Austrian cabinet meeting in 1948.

The Viennese City Archives provided extensive information on

Béla and Mariann – their movements in and out of the country, residences, burial locations, and details of Béla's application for Austrian citizenship in 1956, which itself contained some important biographical material. The Israelitische Kultusgemeinde Wien (the Jewish Community of Vienna) supplied information on Guttmann's burial in 1981.

The United States Citizenship and Immigration Services (USCIS) sent me the relevant information on Guttmann's 1938 visa application for permanent residence in the United States.

The staff at Benfica were helpful beyond the call of duty. Rita Costa, of the Documentation and Information Centre at the club, provided me with photographs, and her team compiled a thorough research document on the story of the Guttmann curse. Thanks also to Ricardo Maia and Luís Filipe for their hospitality at the Estádio da Luz.

It was a wonderful privilege to be able to meet in person with the former Benfica player António Simões. Another member of the European Cup-winning team, José Augusto, had to pull out of our scheduled meeting in Lisbon due to unforeseen circumstances. However, he later very kindly made himself available for a lengthy telephone call with Rob Lindsay, who conducted the interview in Portuguese on my behalf. The insights of these two great legends from the Guttmann era were like gold dust to me.

Other football clubs were also very accommodating. Marco Amato at AC Milan, Michael Serra at São Paulo, Massimo Candotti at Padova, and Mariangela Blouna at Panathinaikos contributed photographs and information.

Thanks also to the following institutions for giving their permission to use photographs: the Joseph Yekutieli Maccabi Sports Archive in Ramat Gan, Israel; the Hungarian Olympic and Sport Museum; the Jewish Museum of Vienna; and AGON SportsWorld in Germany, the company that auctioned Guttmann's memorabilia after Mariann's death.

There were many others who pointed me in the right direction in terms of my research, put me in contact with other people, or gave me the benefit of their own expertise. I fear there will be names missed out on this list (for which I apologise profusely) but I would like to mention Dominic Bliss, Gábor Sisák, Miklós Hadas, Iván Balog, Mátyás Szeli, György Újlaki, Péter Ráckövesi, Inacio Steinhardt, Colin Jose, Ari Muzicant, Ben Segenreich, Pierre Lopper, Michael Brooks, Michael John, Róbert Vago Wallenstein, Rui Costa, Deborah Harris, Jo Rosenfelder, Ruth Tarlo, Neil Blair, Frank Praverman and Barry Wilson.

I was working on this book for a considerable period before finding a willing publisher. I just couldn't stop researching and writing. How could I turn my back on this extraordinary story? And how could I not learn a lesson in persistence from the master himself, Béla Guttmann? I knew I would eventually find someone of like mind, and I did. Jeremy Robson, my publisher at Biteback, immediately understood what I was trying to accomplish with the book, and responded with enthusiasm within a few minutes of my initial email. My gratitude also to Olivia Beattie, Laurie De Decker and the rest of the team at Biteback Publishing for their hard work and professionalism.

My friends Paul Lewis, Jim Poyser, Will Rosen and Robin Shepherd read the draft of the book and gave me welcome encouragement and useful suggestions.

Béla Guttmann said that family is an indispensable pillar in our lives. I couldn't agree more.

The constant love and support from my wife Janie is a great source of strength for me. Our children Yael, Joe and Tali bring so much joy. My love for them all is bigger than the sky. I hope that one day they will read this book and understand why their father spent so much time writing about 'that Jewish football guy'. As I did, I hope also that they take lessons from the story. Never ever give up!

My phone conversations with my brothers Richard, Jeremy and Alan give me a lift every single day. They and their families mean the world to me.

My mother Eve died shortly after I started working on this book. She encouraged me in this endeavour, as she always did. None of our lives are the same without her. Although my father Anthony died so many long years ago, I still miss him terribly. He would have loved this story.

I would also like to mention my father's great friend, the late Aubrey Jaffe, who indulged a boy's passion for football by taking me to Old Trafford throughout my youth. The image of Aubrey and my father laughing like schoolboys will always stay with me.

I dedicate this book to the memory of my parents, Eve and Anthony Bolchover, and my grandparents, Dinah and Elio Sampson, and Rosie and Jonas Bolchover. They somehow managed to instil in me a passion and fascination for our Jewish heritage. Of all the gifts they gave to me, this was their greatest.

People asked me whether I was enjoying writing this book. I have certainly been highly engaged by it, to the point of obsession. And I absolutely loved the football element of the book. But I did not enjoy spending my days reading story after story about the murder, torture, imprisonment, expulsion and humiliation of Jews just like me, of Jewish families just like mine, of beautiful Jewish children just like mine. At the end of this long adventure, it is a great release for me to write the following words. *Am yisrael chai.* The Jewish nation lives.

David Bolchover
London
December 2016

SELECT BIBLIOGRAPHY

Péter Apor (2013), *The Lost Deportations and the Lost People of Kunmadaras: A Pogrom in Hungary, 1946*, in *Hungarian Historical Review*.

Yitzhak Arad (1987), *Belzec, Sobibor, Treblinka: The Operation Reinhard Death Camps*. Indiana University Press.

Arthur Baar (1959), *50 Jahre Hakoah 1909–1959*. Tel Aviv.

Arthur Baar (1974), *Fußballgeschichten – Ernstes und Heiteres: Hakoah Wien*. Tel Aviv.

Susana Bastos Mateus & Paulo Mendes Pinto (2014), *The Massacre of the Jews: Lisbon, April 19 1506*. Alêtheia Editores.

Eric Batty (1961), *The Coach Who Never Stays Put*, in *World Soccer* magazine.

Eric Batty (1965), *Interview with Bela Guttmann*, in *World Soccer* magazine.

Susanne Helene Betz, Monika Loescher and Pia Schoelnberger (ed.) (2009), *Mehr als ein Sportverein: 100 Jahre Hakoah Wien 1909–2009*. Studien Verlag.

Ervin Birnbaum (2009), *Evian: The Most Fateful Conference of All Times in Jewish History* in *Nativ Journal*.

Dominic Bliss (2014), *Erbstein: The Triumph and Tragedy of Football's Forgotten Pioneer*. Blizzard Books.

Bela Bodo (2011), *Pál Prónay: Paramilitary Violence and Anti-Semitism in Hungary, 1919–1921*, in *Russian & East European Studies*.

William Bowman (2011), *Hakoah Vienna and the International Nature of Interwar Austrian Sports*. Gettysburg College.

Randolph Braham (1981), *The Politics of Genocide: The Holocaust in Hungary*, Colombia University Press.

Michael Brenner & Gideon Reuveni (ed.) (2006) *Emancipation through Muscles: Jews and Sports in Europe*. University of Nebraska Press

John Bunzl (1987), *Hoppauf Hakoah: Jüdischer Sport in Österreich von den Anfängen bis in die Gegenwart*. Junius.

Luis Catarino (2012), *The Flight of the Eagles*, in *The Blizzard* football magazine.

Andy Clark (2012), *Great Expectations: The Story of the Hungarian Football Team at the 1912 and 1924 Olympic Games*, in the *Hungarian Review*.

Detlev Claussen (2006), *Béla Guttmann. Weltgeschichte des Fußballs in einer Person*. Berenberg Verlag, Berlin.

Detlev Claussen (2015), *Guttmann Béla: A Világfutball Edzőlegendája*, Akadémiai Kiadó.

Conor Cruise O'Brien (1986), *The Siege: The Story of Israel and Zionism*. Simon & Schuster.

Jenő Csaknády (1964), *Die Béla Guttmann Story: Hinter den Kulissen des Weltfußballs*, Bintz-Dohany.

Tamás Dénes, Mihály Sándor & Éva B. Bába (2016), *A Magyar Labdarúgás Története, Volumes 1–3*. Alexandra Kiadó.

Oswald Dutch (1938), *Thus Died Austria*, Arnold Books.

Encyclopaedia Judaica (1972), Keter Publishing.

Francois Fejtö (1971), *A History of the People's Democracies*. Pall Mall Press.

Franklin Foer (2006), *How Football Explains the World.* Arrow.

Franklin Foer and Marc Tracy (ed.) (2012), *Jewish Jocks: An Unorthodox Hall of Fame.* Twelve.

Norman Fox (2003), *Prophet or Traitor? The Jimmy Hogan Story.* Parrs Wood Press.

Tibor Frank (2009), *Double Exile: Migrations of Jewish–Hungarian Professionals through Germany to the United States, 1919–1945.* Oxford: Peter Lang.

Kinga Frojimovics et al (1999), *Jewish Budapest: Monuments, Rites and History.* Central European University Press.

Martin Gilbert (1987), *The Holocaust: The Jewish Tragedy.* Fontana.

Brian Glanville (1991), *Champions of Europe: The History, Romance and Intrigue of the European Cup.* Guinness Publishing.

Arthur Goldman (1963), *Stars of David.* South African Maccabi Council.

Hardy Grune (alias R. Keifu) (2001), *Die Trainerlegende. Auf den Spuren Bela Guttmanns.* Agon Sportverlag.

Miklós Hadas (2000), *Football and Social Identity: The Case of Hungary in the Twentieth Century*, in the *Sports Historian* journal.

Tibor Hámori (1984), *Régi Gólok, Edzösorsok.* Lapkiadó Vállalat.

Andrew Handler (1985), *From the Ghetto to the Games: Jewish Athletes in Hungary.* Eastern European Monographs.

William B Helmreich (1995), *Against All Odds: Holocaust Survivors and the Successful Lives They Made in America.* Transaction Publishers.

Moshe Herczl (1995), *Christianity and the Holocaust of Hungarian Jewry.* New York University Press.

Raul Hilberg (1961), *The Destruction of the European Jews.* Yale University.

Benjamin Horowitz (1976), *Hakoah in New York: A New Dimension for American Jewry*, in *Judaism.*

Michael John (2006), *Bela Guttmann. Ballzauberer und Erfolgstrainer*,

in Matthias Marschik/Georg Spitaler (ed.), *Helden und Idole. Sportstars in Österreich*. Studien Verlag.

Colin Jose (2013), *The American Soccer League: The Golden Years of American Soccer 1921–1931*. Scarecrow Press.

Géza Kadlecovits (2014), *Zsidósors 1944. Újpest*. Újpest Önkormányzat.

Ilse Josepha Lazaroms (2014), *Marked by Violence: Hungarian Jewish Histories in the Wake of the White Terror, 1919–1922*, in *Perspectives on Jewish Culture*.

Deborah Lipstadt (2011), *The Eichmann Trial*. Schocken.

John Lukacs (1994), *Budapest 1900: A Historical Portrait of a City and its Culture*. Avalon Travel Publishing.

Roger MacDonald (1968), *Britain versus Europe*. Pelham Books.

David Meek & Tom Tyrrell (2002), *Manchester United in Europe*. Coronet Books.

Willy Meisl (1956), *Soccer Revolution*. Sportsmans Book Club.

Peter Meyer et al (1953), *The Jews in Soviet Satellite States*. Syracuse University Press.

John Motson & John Rowlinson (1980), *European Cup, 1955–80: A History of Europe's Premier Football Club Competition*. Queen Anne Press.

Zsuzsanna Ozsváth (2008), *From Country to Country: My Search for Home*, in *The Writer Uprooted: Contemporary Jewish Exile Literature*. Indiana University Press.

Raphael Patai (1988), *Apprentice in Budapest: Memories of a World That Is No More*. University of Utah Press.

Raphael Patai (1995), *The Jews of Hungary: History, Culture, Psychology*. Wayne State University Press.

Gunnar Persson (2004), *Stjärnor På Flykt: Historien om Hakoah Wien*. Norstedts.

Vera B. Profit (2014), *The Devil Next Door: Toward a Literary and Psychological Definition of Human Evil*. Rodopi.

Karl Heinz Schwind (1994), *Geschichten aus Einem Fußball-Jahrhundert.* Ueberreuter.

Rory Smith (2016), *Mister: The Men Who Gave the World the Game.* Simon & Schuster.

Rogan Taylor and Klara Jamrich (ed.) (1997), *Puskas on Puskas: The Life and Times of a Footballing Legend.* Robson Books.

Ludwig Tegelbeckers (2003), *Béla Guttmann. Weltenwanderer ohne Kompromiss*, in Dietrich Schulze-Marmeling, *Davidstern und Lederball*, Verlag Die Werkstatt.

Ariel Toaff (2007), *Passovers of Blood: The Jews of Europe and Ritual Murders.* Lulu.com.

Krisztián Ungváry (2002), *The Siege of Budapest: 100 Days in World War II.* Yale University Press.

Bernard Wasserstein (1996), *Vanishing Diaspora: The Jews in Europe since 1945.* Penguin Books.

Bernard Wasserstein (2012), *On The Eve: The Jews of Europe before the Second World War.* Profile Books.

Beth S. Wenger (1996), *New York Jews and the Great Depression: Uncertain Promise.* Yale University Press.

Jonathan Wilson (2008), *Inverting the Pyramid.* Orion.

ONLINE RESOURCES

www.degob.org – Witness accounts by 5,000 Hungarian Holocaust survivors, recorded in 1945 and 1946

www.ushmm.org – United States Holocaust Memorial Survivors and Victims Database

www.wienerlibrarycollections.co.uk – Pogrom November 1938: testimonies from Kristallnacht

www.yadvashem.org – Shoah victims' names database at Yad Vashem museum, Jerusalem

www.yivoencyclopedia.org – The YIVO Encyclopedia of Jews in Eastern Europe

www.familysearch.org – Genealogical archives

www.austriasoccer.at – Austrian football statistics

www.foradejogo.net – Portuguese football statistics

www.nela.hu – Hungarian football statistics

www.rsssf.com – The Rec.Sport.Soccer Statistics Foundation (RSSSF) is an international organisation dedicated to collecting statistics about association football

INDEX

Headings in italics are a book, newspaper or magazine.

2-3-5 formation (tactics) 30
4-2-4 formation (tactics) 18, 180–1, 193

Aarhus, Denmark (football club) 198
Abu Nidal Organisation 248
AC Milan (football club) ix–x, 147–52, 158, 165, 175, 177, 191, 227, 260
Admira, Austria (football club) 34
Against All Odds (book) 115
Agar, Nathan 47, 49, 52
Águas, José 196, 197–201, 207, 209, 213, 215
Ajax Amsterdam, Netherlands (football club) 71–2
All-Stars (Hakoah), United States (football club) 58–61, 67, 108, 145–6, 259
Amaury 183
Ambrosiana Inter, Italy (football club) temporary name for Inter Milan 80
American Soccer League (ASL) 42, 47, 50–3, 58, 60–1, 76
 see also United States
Amsterdam, Netherlands 114
Angola 192, 196
Anne Frank Huis, Amsterdam 114
Anschluss (1938) 24, 65, 74, 162
Anti-Defamation League 257
anti-Semitism 112–14, 257–8

Austria 27, 33–5, 63, 66, 109, 126, 187, 200, 219–20, 229–30, 257
 France 257–8
 Germany 257–8
 Hungary 1–3, 19–21, 77–8, 85–9, 92–4, 100, 126, 257
 Italy 137–8, 257
 Poland 38–9
 Portugal 185–6, 257
 Romania 129–30, 163
 Russia 125, 163
 Spain 185, 257–8
 United Kingdom 257–8
 United States 46
 see also Holocaust
Antonescu, Ion 129–30
Antunes, José Maria 194
Apoel Nicosia, Cyprus (football club) 147, 260
Argentina 64, 109, 203
 football xv, 58–9, 77, 146, 240
 players 141, 149, 215, 232
Arrow Cross party 87–8, 97, 98, 100, 106, 167
Arsenal (football club) x, 122, 254
AS Roma, Italy (football club) 140, 141, 143
Aschner, Lipót 81–3, 92–3, 204
Assicurazioni Generali 143
Association of Hungarian Coaches 134
Athletic Bilbao, Spain (football club) 165–8

Atlantic Coast League (United States) 58
Atlético Lisbon, Portugal (football club)
 196
Atlético Madrid, Spain (football club) 166,
 169
Attila Miskolc, Hungary (football club)
 105
Augusto, José 3, 192–4, 197–8, 201, 210,
 211, 216, 227, 232, 244
Auschwitz concentration camp xiii, 88,
 103, 121, 154–5
 victims 14, 24–6, 43, 86, 90, 101–3, 105,
 139, 148, 257
Australia 64
Austria xv
 anti-Semitism 27, 33–5, 63, 66, 109,
 126, 187, 200, 219–20, 229–30, 257
 Austrian parliament 65
 Austrofascism 65–6
 national team 15, 68, 69, 109, 187,
 228–30, 260
Austria Vienna FK, Austria (football club)
 formerly Wiener Amateur-SV 208,
 211, 239, 260
Austrian Football Association 68, 163, 187,
 228, 229
Austrian League 10, 29, 68–9, 139
 championship xi–xii, 35, 199–200, 261
Austrian Olympic Committee 28
Austro-Hungarian Empire 2, 4, 8–9, 24

Baar, Arthur 30–1, 32, 34, 42–3
Bahir, Moshe 161
Ba'ir Hahariga (poem) 27
Balkan and Central European
 Championship 133
Balmazújváros, Hungary 154
Balog, Iván 252
Balogh, Bonzó (István) 245
Balzac, Honoré de 159
Bank of the United States 45–6
Barcelona FC, Spain (football club) xv, 73,
 166, 170, 198, 201–2
Bárczy, István 9
Barreirense FC, Portugal (football club)
 188, 192
Barreiro CUF, Portugal (football club) 189
Batty, Eric 111–12
Bauer, José Carlos 205
Baumgarten, József 1–2
Baumgarten, Zsigmond 1–2

Bayern Munich, Germany (football club)
 72–3, 239
BBC 110, 257
Beckenbauer, Franz 47
Bécsi Magyar Újság (newspaper) 21
Béla Guttmann Story, Die (book) 108
Belenenses, Portugal (football club) 187, 188
Belgium 64, 167–8
Ben-Aharon, Yitzhak (Yitzhak
 Nussenbaum) 204
Benfica, Portugal (football club) 140, 187,
 188–9, 226–8, 231–5, 240
 BG as coach ix–xi, 122, 123, 171–6,
 178, 190–202, 205–18, 223, 232–8,
 246, 260
 European Cup xv, 174–5, 195–202,
 208–18, 237, 261
Ben-Gurion, David 203
Ben-Zvi, Yitzhak 204–5
Beogradski, Serbia (football club) 80
Berengaria (RMS) 114
Bergen-Belsen concentration camp 111, 114
Beria, Lavrentiy 163
Berlin, Germany 20, 33
Best, George 47, 235
Bethlehem Steel, United States (football
 club) 52, 53
Bialik, Chaim 27
Bilbao Athletic, Spain (football club)
 165–8
Birtles, Garry 177–8
Blanchflower, Danny 211, 213
Blatt, Thomas 160
Blickensdörfer, Hans 175
blitzkrieg football strategy 193–4, 198,
 210, 235
Bloom, Leopold 143
Blum, Zoltán 19
Boca Juniors, Argentina (football club)
 146, 227
Bocskai, Hungary (football club) 154
Bola, A (newspaper) 178, 231, 236, 237,
 238
Bolton Wanderers (football club) 15, 32
Borussia Dortmund, Germany (football
 club) 231
Boston Wonder Workers, United States
 (football club) 47
Botafogo, Brazil (football club) 170
Bozsik, József (Cucu) 132, 165, 169, 173,
 176

Braun, József 16, 254
Brazil 64, 101, 109, 159, 161
 football xv, 18, 179–82, 193, 224
 football tours 58–9, 168–70
 players 188, 201, 205
 World Cup tournaments 148, 170, 181,
 184, 223
Brene, Giuliano 153–7, 247
Brianzoli, Graziella 153
Britain 64
 English football 165, 211, 221, 254
 Jewish communities 253–4, 257–8
 Scottish football 14–19, 69
Brooklyn Hakoah, United States (football
 club) 58
Brooklyn Wanderers, United States
 (football club) 42, 47, 50, 52
Brown, Davey 49, 54
Brüll, Alfréd 14, 16
Brunner, Leo 144
Bucharest, Romania 128–31
Buchenwald concentration camp 24, 104
Budai, László 168
Budakalász Deportation Centre, Hungary
 86
Budapest, Hungary xi, 2, 11, 83, 90, 259
 anti-Semitism 85–9, 100
 Jewish communities 1–3, 4–7, 8
Budapest Institute of Sciences, Hungary 3
Bulgaria 233
Burgess, Herbert 20
Burnley (football club) 15
Busby, Matt 16, 122, 233, 234
Busini, Antonio 147, 148

Cabrita, Fernando 235
Caiado, Fernando 206, 207, 233, 235
Calabote, Inocêncio 189
Campeonato Paulista tournament, Brazil
 179, 184, 261
Canhoteiro 183
Capello, Fabio 123
catenaccio (tactics) 148, 251
Cavém, Domiciano 178, 189, 199, 201–2,
 210, 215–16, 223
Chapman, Herbert x, 70, 251
Chelsea (football club) 237
China 256
Christian Social Party, Austria 65
Church of São Domingos, Lisbon,
 Portugal 186

Ciocanul Bucharest, Romania (football
 club) formerly Maccabi Bucharest, later
 Dinamo Bucharest 111, 128–31, 260
Circle of Hungarian Fitness Activists 12
 see also MTK (Magyar Testgyakorlók
 Köre) Budapest, Hungary (football
 club)
Claussen, Detlev 91
Clemence, Ray 177
Clough, Brian 177–8
CNN.com 89
coaching x–xi, 122–4, 214
 Jewish coaches 17–18, 128–9, 139, 145,
 147, 217–18
 style of BG 17, 30–1, 55–7, 121–7,
 148–50, 171–84, 188, 215, 223, 234
Colonia, Giacobbe da 137–8
Colonia, Servadio da 137–8
Coluna, Mário 196, 198, 199, 202, 207–8,
 216–17, 223
Communists
 Austria 65
 Hungary 101, 134–5, 139, 162–4, 252
Conceição, Pedro da 194
concentration camps 24–5, 53, 83, 111,
 143, 160–1, 217
 Auschwitz xiii, 3, 88, 103, 121, 154–5
 Auschwitz victims 14, 24–6, 43, 86, 90,
 101–2, 103, 105, 139, 148, 257
 see also Holocaust
Coolidge, Calvin 41
Copa Libertadores de América 222–3, 227
Corinthians, Brazil (football club) 179,
 181, 183
Costa Pereira, Alberto da 172, 174, 196,
 202, 207, 209, 213
Coughlin, Charles 46
Cruyff, Johan 47
Cruz, Fernando 192, 200
Csaknády, Jenö 56, 108
Csatay, Lajos 96–7
Csurgó, Hungary 2
Cubillas, Teófilo 240
CUF Barreiro, Portugal (football club) 189
curse of BG ix–x, 218, 237–8, 252
Curti, José 141
Cyprus xv, 147, 260
Czechoslovakia 69
Czeizler, Lajos 145, 147–8, 151–2, 217,
 228, 231–2
Czibor, Zoltán 165, 168, 170, 201–2

Dachau concentration camp 24
Daily Mail 32–3
Dalglish, Kenny 237
dance schools
 Hungary 8, 9, 10–11, 105
 United States 48, 61
 Vienna, Austria 38
Danziger Vorposten (newspaper) 64
De Kuip stadium, Rotterdam, Netherlands 73
Dein, David 254
deportations xiii, 63, 85–6, 88, 97, 103, 109, 148, 154, 163
 individual victims 25, 43, 106
 return from 119–21, 220
Destruction of the European Jews, The (book) 24–5
Deutsch, Judith 28
Dexter Park, New York, United States 54–5
Di Stéphano, Alfredo 215–17
Diário Popular (newspaper) 236
Dickens, Charles 159
Dienst, Robert 199, 200
Dimbleby, Jonathan 111
Dimbleby, Richard 110–11
Dinamo Bucharest, Romania (football club) formerly Ciocanul Bucharest and Maccabi Bucharest 130
Diszel, Hungary 2
Dittrich, Vinzenz 67
Dizengoff, Meir 40
Dollfuss, Engelbert 65–6
Donato (servant) 138
Dostoyevsky, Fyodor 159
Double Exile, The (book) 20
Dowie, Iain xiv
Drancy Internment Camp, France 43
Drei Masters (Three Masters) (book) 159
Dreyfus Affair, France 26
Drimmel, Heinrich 229
Drucker, Leo 42, 50, 52, 66, 67
Duarte, Carlos 188
Dukla Prague, Czechoslovakia (football club) 211
Dutch football and Jewish communities *see* Netherlands
Dwa Grosze (newspaper) 38–9

East German national team 194
Eastern League (United States) 52, 58

Egypt 37, 39, 261
Eichmann, Adolf (Ricardo Klement) xv, 83, 100, 203–5
Eindhoven PSV, Netherlands (football club) 71, 237
Eisenberg, Akiba 249
Eisenberger, Benjamin (Gábor Péter) 164
Eisenhoffer, József 36, 39, 42, 50, 52, 54, 66, 67
Encyclopedia Judaica 254
England national team 165
English FA Cup 211
English Football Association 18
English Football League 211, 221
English League Cup 177–8, 254
Enschede Sportclub (SC), Netherlands (football club) now Twente 70–3, 140, 191–2, 260
Équipe, L' (newspaper) 206–7
Erbstein, Ernő Egri 98–9, 138–40, 145, 254
Estadio Centenario, Montevideo, Uruguay 207, 222–3
Estádio da Luz, Lisbon, Portugal x, 193, 197, 201, 209, 211, 213, 233, 234–5, 250
Estádio das Antas, Porto, Portugal 188, 190, 240
Estádio Vila Belmiro, Santos, Brazil 224
Estaus Palace, Lisbon, Portugal 185–6
Etz Hachaim 102, 103
European Championship 194–5
European Cup (later UEFA Champions League) xvi, 32, 69, 81, 153, 246
 Benfica 122, 171, 227, 261
 Benfica (1959/60) 191–3
 Benfica (1960/1) xv, 195–202
 Benfica (1961/2) ix–x, 208–18
 Benfica (1964/5) 232–5
 Benfica (1987/8) 237
 Honvéd, Budapest (football club) formerly Kispest 165–8
 Real Madrid 132
European Cup Winners Cup 239
European Footballer of the Year 201
European Wrestling Championships (1932) 28
Eusébio ix–x, 205–10, 215, 217, 226, 232, 234, 236, 240, 241
Evaristo 201
Evening Standard 64, 221

Everest, Ecuador (football club) 227
Évian conference on Jewish Refugees
 (1938) 63–5, 75

Fabian, Alexander 29–30, 36, 50, 53
Faragó, Lajos 168
Farben, I. G. 24
FC Barcelona, Spain (football club) xv, 73,
 166, 170, 198, 201–2
FC Barreirense, Portugal (football club)
 188, 192
FC Nürnberg (Der Club), Germany
 (football club) 209–10, 211, 214
Feldmann, Gyula 16, 139
Feola, Vicente 181, 184, 193
Ferencváros, Hungary (football club) 9,
 12–14, 17, 37, 39, 80, 164
 players 19, 36, 79, 145
Ferguson, Alex 16, 122, 124, 212, 240
Ferreira, Eusébio da Silva ix–x, 205–10,
 215, 217, 226, 232, 234, 236, 240, 241
Ferroviária, Brazil (football club) 205
Feyenoord, Netherlands (football club)
 71–2, 73
FIFA (Fédération Internationale de
 Football Association) 42, 168, 170, 194
Figl, Leopold 220
Figueiredo, Germano de 196, 199, 201,
 213, 232
Fiorentina, Italy (football club) 157
First Vienna, Austria (football club) 31
First World War 2, 8–9, 24, 77
Fischer, Lajos 42, 50, 53
FK Austria Vienna, Austria (football club)
 formerly Wiener Amateur-SV 208,
 211, 239
Flamengo, Brazil (football club) 18, 167,
 170, 181–2, 201
Folha de São Paulo (newspaper) 180
Football
 Jewish coaches 17–18, 128–9, 139, 145,
 147
 Jewish influence xi, 81, 253–5, 255
 Jewish players xi–xiii, 9, 12–20, 25,
 28–35, 38–42, 50, 53–4, 231
 tactics 14–19, 30, 69, 148, 180–1,
 193–4, 198, 210, 251
Football Association (England) 18, 211
Ford, Henry 46
4-2-4 formation (tactics) 18, 180–1, 193
Fradi see Ferencváros, Hungary (football club)

France 26, 43, 66, 67, 74, 113, 236, 257
Frank, Anne 70–1, 113–14
Frank, Hans 130
Frank, Otto 113–14
Frank, Tibor 20
French Ligue 1 66
Freud, Sigmund 74
Fried, Nathan 248
Fußball (newspaper) 33

Gál, Sanyi 99
Gallowich, Tibor 132
gambling 56–7, 127, 221, 243–4, 247
Garrincha 18, 170
Gemmill, Archie 177–8
Germano de Figueiredo see de Figueiredo,
 Germano
Germany
 football 69, 165, 194, 200, 202, 253, 261
 Football Championship (1941) 200
 German League 210
 see also Nazis
Gerő, Ernő 163
ghettos 8, 39, 85, 88, 90, 94, 100, 103,
 105–6, 109
Gimnasia, Argentina (football club) 146
Glanville, Brian 153
Glasgow Celtic, Scotland (football club) 61
Glória, Otto 195, 232
Glover, Teddy 54
Góis, Damião de 186
Gold, Max 50
Goldman, Arthur 112
Goldner, Lucie 28
Gömbös, Gyula 37, 78
Gordon, Avraham 204
Górnik Zabrze, Poland (football club) 211
Great Depression, America 45–6
Greaves, Jimmy 211
Greece xv, 147, 239, 260
 national team 239
Green, Geoffrey 181, 234
Greenberg, Hank 253
Greenock Morton, Scotland (football club)
 47
Grüne, Hardy (R. Keifu) 90, 91, 125
Grünwald, Max 29, 31, 36, 42, 48, 53, 55
Gschwindt, Ernő 37
Guardiola, Pep x, 73, 252
Gulyás, Zsolt 102
Guttman, Irén 105

Guttmann, Abrahám (father) xi, xiii, 7, 8, 101–2, 103
Guttmann, Ármin (brother) 7, 10, 104–5, 112, 117
Guttmann, Béla xiii, 74–6, 163, 254, 259–61
 character xiii–xiv, 27–8, 31, 37, 123, 125
 coaching career Benfica x–xi, xv, 191–202, 205–18, 231–8
 coaching career Europe xiii, 67–8, 70–5, 78–81, 92–3, 127–34, 139–53, 157–8, 165–71, 186–202, 228–30, 239–40, 260–1
 coaching career South America 146–7, 169–71, 179–84, 221–7, 260–1
 coaching style 17–18, 30–1, 55–7, 121–7, 148–50, 171–84, 188, 215, 223, 234
 curse of ix–x, 218, 237–8, 252
 dance instructor 9, 10–11, 38, 48, 61
 death and burial ix, 241–2, 248–50
 family xi, 4, 7–9, 90, 101–7, 241
 finances ix–x, 56–7, 213–14, 221, 226–7, 240
 gambling 56–7, 127, 221, 243–4, 247
 Jewish identity 110–11, 114, 126, 248, 253
 manslaughter charges 153–7, 170, 247
 marriage 90, 92, 125, 128, 247–8
 playing career xi–xiii, 9–12, 16–19, 21, 25, 29–43, 46–56, 58–62, 66–7, 259, 261
 retirement 125, 221, 245–8
 wartime experiences xiii, 89–117
Guttmann, Emil 92
Guttmann, Ernő (brother) 7, 56, 93, 101, 102, 105, 106, 107
Guttmann, Ervin (nephew) 101, 102, 103, 105
Guttmann, Eszter (née Szántó, mother) xi, 7, 8, 101
Guttmann, Imre (nephew) 56, 93, 101, 104–6, 107, 115, 126, 183, 243
Guttmann, Irén 105
Guttmann, Margit 93, 106, 107
Guttmann, Mariann (née Moldován) 108, 125, 128, 241–4, 247–8
 health 142, 184, 190
 travel with BG 140, 145, 146–7, 161, 214, 227, 236
 wartime experiences 90–1, 93, 94–5, 99, 100, 105–6

Guttmann, Michael 254
Guttmann, Robert 254
Guttmann, Szerén (sister) xiii, 7, 101, 102–3, 104
Györ, Hungary 133

Haaretz (newspaper) 40
Hadas, Miklós 13
Hagibor Cluj, Romania (football club) 11
Hakoah All-Stars, United States (football club) 58–61, 67, 145–6, 259
Hakoah New York, United States (football club) 52–4, 58, 76–7, 108, 259
Hakoah Vienna, Austria (football club) xii–xiii, 23–35, 44, 67–8, 74, 114, 199, 224
 BG xi–xiii, 12, 20–1, 108, 190, 230, 256, 259, 260
 ex-players xiii, 52–3
 tours xii, 32–3, 35–43, 47, 50–1, 66, 253, 254
Hakoah Vienna, Austria (sports club) xiii, 28–9
Halberg, Murray 215
Hámori, Tibor 66–7, 91, 93, 94, 108, 115–16, 244, 246
Häusler, Moritz 29, 42, 48, 50, 53, 55, 67
Heart of Midlothian, Scotland (football club) 197
Hegedüs, András 162
Hegedüs, Mihály 106
Helmer, Oskar 220
Helmreich, William 115
Herd, Billy 49
Hernâni 188
Herrera, Helenio 232, 251
Hertha Vienna, Austria (football club) 31
Hertzka, Lippo 73, 194, 254
Herzl, Theodor 6, 26
Hess, Lajos 42
Heysel Stadium, Brussels, Belgium 168
Hidegkuti, Nándor 133
Hilberg, Raul 24–5, 129
Himmler, Heinrich 88
Hirschl, Imre (Emérico) 145–6, 222, 254
Hirschl, Mickey 28
Hirzer, Férénc 37–8
Hitler, Adolf 27, 46, 62–3
Hofmann, Leopold 31
Hogan, Jimmy 15–19, 20, 32, 68, 69, 173, 176

Holocaust xv, 43, 87, 102–16, 119–21, 129–30, 255, 256–7
 BG xiii, xiv, 102–9, 112, 171, 246, 253
 records 39, 102
 survivors xiv, 85, 98, 110–15, 225, 256
 see also anti-Semitism; concentration camps
Honvéd, Hungary (football club) formerly Kispest 152, 165–71, 183, 201, 217, 260
Horak, Roman 208
Horn, Edgar 217
Horn, Leo 217, 225
Horowitz, Benjamin 53, 55, 58, 61
Horthy, Miklós 2–3, 77–8, 88, 97, 130
Howe, Irving 45–6
Hudal, Alois 161
Huddersfield Town (football club) x
Hungária *see* MTK (Magyar Testgyakorlók Köre) Budapest, Hungary (football club)
Hungarian Football Association 11, 116, 167
Hungarian League (Nemzeti Bajnokság) 9, 10, 43, 92–3
 championship 16, 79, 165, 197, 261
Hungarianisation 4–7, 13, 77, 114
Hungary xiii, 4, 11, 69, 110, 127–8, 139, 257
 anti-Semitism 1–3, 19–21, 77–8, 85–9, 92–4, 100, 126, 257
 Brazilian tour 169–71
 football xv, 139, 164–70
 Hungarian Parliament 3
 Hungarian Revolution (1956) 163–4, 166
 Jewish communities 4–7, 8
 national team xi, 16–17, 19, 36–8, 132, 164–5, 261
 national team (golden team, Aranycsapat) 17, 133, 169, 180, 251, 252
 national team players 53, 76, 77, 79, 131
 Soviet occupation 101, 134–5, 139, 162–4
Hunter, Billy 32
Hyman, Paula 113

I. G. Farben 24
Iaşi, Romania 129–30
IFK Norrköping, Sweden (football club) 148

Indiana Flooring, United States (football club) later New York Nationals 51, 52
Inter Bratislava, Slovakia (football club) 191
Inter Milan, Italy (football club) 139, 141, 147, 149, 153, 218, 232, 251
Intercontinental Cup 207–8, 221, 222
internment camps
 France 43
 Switzerland 89–90, 107
Inverting the Pyramid (book) 15, 89, 251
Ireland 64, 194
Israel xv, 39–40, 203–5, 253–4, 256
 see also Jewish State, Palestine; Palestine
Israeli national team 42, 217
Israelite Congregation of Pest, Hungary 3
Italian football association 144
Italian League 141, 148, 149
Italy 109, 155–7, 166, 257
 football xv, 80, 82, 99, 131, 139–53, 157–8, 161, 175, 177
 national team 70, 148, 157
 World Cups 49, 70, 79
 see also Milan, Italy; Rome, Italy

Jabotinsky, Vladimir 41
Jacobson, Howard 18
Jairzinho 18
Jelgava, Latvia (Mitau) 36
Jewish Chronicle 255
Jewish communities xii, xvi, 253–4, 256
 Britain 253–4
 Budapest, Hungary 4–7, 8, 85–9
 central Europe xi, 110, 255
 ghettos 8, 39, 85, 88, 90, 94, 100, 103, 105–6, 109
 Italy 143, 148
 Netherlands 70–1
 New York 45–6, 47–8, 61
 Portugal 185–6
 Újpest, Hungary 85–6
 Vienna, Austria 20–1, 23–4, 63, 256
Jewish laws, Hungary 78, 82, 91–2
Jewish Legal Aid Office 1
Jewish Museum, London 254
Jewish State, Palestine 5–6
 see also Israel; Palestine
Jewish Telegraphic Agency 39, 55
Jews 137–8
 deportation xiii, 25, 43, 63, 85–6, 88, 97, 103, 106, 109, 148, 154, 163

Jews *cont.*
 football coaches 17–18, 81, 128–9, 139,
 145, 147, 217–18
 football players 19–20, 129, 231, 253–5
 football teams xi–xii, 9, 12–18, 23–43,
 50, 52–4, 128–31, 255
 massacres 100, 129–30, 143, 160–1, 185–6
 migration 7, 20, 63–5, 74–5, 125–6
 refugees 63–5, 70–1, 75, 107
 return from deportation 119–21, 220
 violence against 1–3, 26–7, 119–21,
 137–8, 219–20
Jews of France, The (book) 113
João, Mário 232
Jones, Cliff 211
Jose, Colin 47
Joyce, James 143
Jungreisz 120
Juventus, Italy (football club) 141, 143,
 149, 153

Kadima (Zionist student organisation) 23
Kadima Timişoara, Romania (football
 club) 231
Kaifeng, China 256
Kárpáti, Tamás 147
Kaufmann, Pista 130–1
Kay, George 33
Kecskémet, Hungary 2
Keegan, Kevin 237
Keifu, R. (Hardy Grüne) 90, 91, 125
Kertész, Adolf 16
Kertész, Vilmos 16
Khrushchev, Nikita 162–3
Kielce, Poland 120–1
Kishinev pogrom, Moldova 26–7
Kispest, Hungary 86
Kispest, Hungary (football club) later
 Honvéd 132–4, 165, 173, 260
Klement, Ricardo (pseudonym of Adolf
 Eichmann) xv, 83, 100, 203–5
Kocsis, Sándor 165, 170, 201–2
Kohn, Richard (Dombi) 72–3, 254
Kohut, Sarah 248
Kolb, Ernst 220
Konrád, Jenő 16
Konrád, Kálmán 16
Körner, Ignaz Hermann 25–6, 34, 41, 51
Kraus, Joseph 220
Kristallnacht (Night of Broken Glass)
 (1938) 219–20, 248

Kubala, László 201–2
Kun, Béla 2
Kunmadaras, Hungary 119–20
Künsztler, József 145, 147
Kurier (newspaper) 229, 239
Kürschner, Izidor (Dori) 18, 181–2, 254
Kuti 120

labour camps 16, 90, 96–8, 105
Lagos, Portugal 206
Landauer, Kurt 73
Langer, Ruth 28
Las Vegas, United States 56, 243
Lazarus, Mark 254
Lazio, Italy (football club) 141–2, 158
Leafe, Reg 200
League Cup Final, England 177–8, 254
Leixões, Portugal (football club) 194
Levski Sofia, Bulgaria (football club) 233
Libero International (magazine) 125
Liedholm, Nils 148
Lipschitz, Lipót 5
Lisbon, Portugal 185–6, 231, 244, 247
 Atlético Lisbon (football club) 196
Liverpool (football club) 122, 177, 237, 246
Löhner-Beda, Evamaria 25
Löhner-Beda, Fritz (Bedřich Löwy) 23–5,
 40, 257
Löhner-Beda, Helene 25
Löhner-Beda, Liselotte 25
Lombardi, Vince 50
Löwy, Bedřich (Fritz Löhner-Beda) 23–5,
 40, 257
Löwy, Izsák 79
Ludwigshafen, Germany 194
Lueger, Karl 27
Lukacs, John 9
Lutz, Carl 89, 90
Lutz, Lajos 93
Lynch, Ronald 183

Maccabi Bucharest, Romania (football
 club) later Ciocanul Bucharest and
 Dinamo Bucharest 128
Maccabi Tel Aviv, Israel (football club)
 40, 256
Maccabi Wein, Austria (football club) 256
Mackay, Dave 211–12
McNab, Alex 47, 48
Madrid (Atlético), Spain (football club)
 166, 169

Magyarisation 4–7, 13, 77, 114
Mahrer, Pavel 53
Maidana, Luis 223
Mailander 120
Maldini, Cesare 149
Maldini, Paolo 149
management, football *see* coaching
Manchester City (football club) 20
Manchester United (football club) 16, 20, 122, 124, 233–5, 240
Mándi, Gyula 17, 217
Manuel I, King of Portugal 185
Maracanã Stadium, Rio de Janeiro, Brazil 170
Marcali, Hungary 2
Marcus, Joseph 46
Markowitz, Arthur 35–6
Martins, Ângelo 238
massacres of Jews x, 100, 129–30, 143, 160–1, 185–6
Maurinho 183
Mauro (Ramos) 183, 184, 223
Mauthausen concentration camp 83
Megyeri úti stadium, Úpest, Hungary 85
Meir, Golda 65
Meisl, Hugo 15, 20, 68–70, 145, 228, 254
Meisl, Willy 68
Mendel, Günther (pseudonym of Gustav Wagner) 159, 160–1
Mengele, Josef 154–5
Metz, France (football club) 66
Milan, Italy 166–7
 AC Milan (football club) ix–x, 147–52, 158, 165, 175, 177, 191, 227, 260
 Inter Milan 139, 141, 147, 149, 153, 218, 232, 251
Milejkowski, Reuven 39
Miskolc, Hungary 102–3, 105, 117, 120
Mitau, Latvia (Jelgava) 36
Mitropa Cup 69, 79–81, 85, 117, 127, 131, 166, 230, 245, 261
Moldován, Pál 93–6, 99–100, 105–6, 243, 258
Moldoványi, Pál 91–6, 99–100, 102, 114, 243–4, 247
Molnár, György 16, 50
Monowitz work camp, Auschwitz 24
Monsider, Zvonko 141–2
Moorhouse, George 49, 54
Morlock, Max 210
Morpurgo, Giuseppe Lazzaro 143

Mossad 203
Motson, John 246
Mourinho, José x–xi, 69, 90, 122–3, 173–4, 212, 233, 237, 252
Mozambique 192, 196, 205
MTK (Magyar Testgyakorlók Köre) Budapest, Hungary (football club) xi, 9, 11–21, 32, 79, 164, 169, 197, 259
 ex-players 50, 72, 148, 181, 217, 221
Muhammad Ali 255
Muller, Bennie 231
Mundo Desportivo (newspaper) 236, 237
Munich Air Crash (1958) 233
Mussolini, Benito 80, 99

Nacional, Uruguay (football club) 222–3, 225
Nagy, Imre 162–4
Nagyvárad, Hungary (now Oradea, Romania) 94
Napier, Charlie 61
National Army, Hungary 2
National Committee for Attending Deportees, Hungary 85
National Soccer Hall of Fame, USA 42, 54
nationalisation, Hungarian football 164–5
Nazis 64, 78, 109, 159, 200, 210, 220
 Austria 24, 63, 65, 66, 74, 162
 Hungary 80, 83, 103
 opposition 28–9
Nemes, Sándor (Alexander Neufeld) 36, 42, 50, 52
Netanyahu, Binyamin 39
Netherlands xv, 114, 217
 football 69, 70–3, 231
 Jewish communities 70–1
 see also Enschede Sportclub (SC), Netherlands (football club)
Neto 232
Neue Freie Presse (newspaper) 31
Neufeld, Alexander (Sándor Nemes) 36, 42, 50, 52
New York, Jewish communities 45–6, 47–8, 61
New York All Stars Select XI, United States (football team) 41
New York Cosmos, United States (football club) 41
New York Giants, United States (baseball team) 51

New York Giants, United States (football club) later New York Soccer Club 42, 46–50, 52, 54, 60, 99, 259
New York Hakoah, United States (football club) 52–4, 58, 76–7, 108, 259
New York Jews and the Great Depression (book) 46
New York Metropolitan Oval, United States 48
New York Nationals, United States (football club) formerly Indiana Flooring 51, 52
New York Soccer Club, United States (football club) formerly New York Giants 60, 259
New York State Superintendent of Banks 45
New York Times (newspaper) 33, 49, 54, 89, 204
New Zealand 215
Newark Portuguese, United States (football club) 52, 54
Newcastle United (football club) 237, 240
Nicholson, Bill 211, 234
Nicklaus, Jack 255
Nickolsburger, Rudolph 53
Noé 188–9
Nordahl, Gunnar 148
Nordau, Max xii, 26
Northern Ireland football team 194
Nottingham Forest (football club) 177–8, 246
Novara, Italy (football club) 143
Novello, Sebastiano 138
Novi Sad, Serbia (formerly Újvidék, Hungary) 10–11, 71, 104
numerus clausus law (1920), Hungary 3
Nurmi, Paavo 215
Nürnberg, Germany 221
Nürnberg FC, Germany (football club) 209–10, 211, 214
Nussenbaum, Yitzhak (Yitzhak Ben-Aharon) 204
Nyúl, Ferenc 11, 20

Obitz, Gábor 37–8
O'Brien, Shamus 54
Old goals, the fate of coaches (Régi gólok, edzősorsok) (book) 91
Old Trafford, Manchester 234

Olympic games
 1924 Paris 19, 37–8, 78, 215
 1932 Los Angeles 28
 1936 Berlin 28
 1960 Rome 215
Olympic Stadium, Amsterdam, Netherlands ix, 214
Olympique de Marseille, France (football club) 67
Oradea, Romania (formerly Nagyvárad, Hungary) 94
Orlando, Gino 183
Orth, György 16, 181, 221
Orthodox Intermediary Office 5
Ostmark Vienna, Austria (football club) 34
Östreicher, Emil 167–8, 170, 217
Ozsváth, Zsuzsanna 87

Pacaembu stadium, São Paulo, Brazil 183
Padova, Italy (football club) 140, 141–2, 152, 175, 260
Paes de Almeida, Raymundo Manoel 171, 184
Paisley, Bob 122
Palestine 25, 39–40, 41, 64, 65, 121, 256
 see also Israel; Jewish State, Palestine
Palestine Maccabees (football club) 99
Palmeiras, Brazil (football club) 179
Panathinaikos, Greece (football club) 147, 239, 260
Paris, France 19, 37–8
Patai, Raphael 4, 110
Patyi, Mihály 134
Pavão 240
Pécs, Hungary 11
Pécsi MFC, Hungary (football club) 11, 21
Pedroto, José Maria 188, 191
Pelé 18, 41, 47, 179, 182, 206, 223–5, 252, 255
Peñarol, Uruguay (football club) 60, 146, 149, 207–8, 214, 221–7, 260
Peres, Shimon 256
Persson, Gunnar 114
Pesti Napló (newspaper) 76
Pestszentrerzébet, Hungary 86
Péter, Gábor 164
Petropoulos, Lakis 239
player fitness 17, 123–4, 149, 171–80, 188
pogroms 6, 26–7, 119–21, 129–30, 219
Poland xii, 38–9, 162, 261
Pollack, Egon 42, 48

Polo Grounds, New York, United States
41, 50, 61
Polonia Warsaw, Poland (football club)
38–9
Port Vale (football club) 221
Porto, Portugal (football club) 186–91,
192, 199, 214, 221, 232, 240, 260
Portobuffolé, Italy 137–8
Portugal x, xv, 251
anti-Semitism 185–6
football 172, 186–202
national team 194–5
see also Benfica, Portugal (football club);
Lisbon, Portugal
Portuguese Football Association 194–5,
214
Portuguese League (Primeira Divisão)
187–8, 192, 199–200, 206, 209, 231–2
championship 189, 191, 194, 201, 235,
261
Postavy Ghetto, Belarus 39
Potok, Edith 103
Poulsen, Aage 212
Poy 183
Poznán, Poland 162
Pozzo, Vittorio 70
Prater Stadium, Vienna, Austria ix, 66,
199, 208, 238
Prohibition era, United States 56–7
Prónay, Pál 2
PSV Eindhoven, Netherlands (football
club) 71, 237
Pujol, Augusti 198
Puricelli, Ettore 152, 191
Puskás, Ferenc 132–4, 152, 165–6, 168,
170, 215–17, 252
Puskás, Ferenc, Senior 133
Putnik, János 1–2
pyramid formation (tactics) 30

Queens Park Rangers (football club) 254
Quilmes, Argentina (football club) 146–7,
260

Raab, Esther 160
Rákosi, Mátyás 139, 162–3
Rákospalota, Hungary 86
Ramallets, Antoni 201–2
Ramos, Mauro 183, 184, 223
Rapid Vienna, Austria (football club) 66,
199–200, 208, 224

Real Madrid, Spain (football club) ix, 73,
132, 166, 170, 192, 194, 198, 200, 201,
214–17
Red Star Belgrade, Serbia (football club)
197
refugees 70–1, 107
Évian conference on Jewish Refugees
(1938) 63–5, 75
Régi gólok, edzősorsok (Old goals, the fate of
coaches) (book) 91
Reich, Walter 114
Riberto 183
Ricagni, Eduardo 149, 150
Riera, Fernando 227
Riga, Latvia 36
Rimet, Jules 69
Risiera di San Sabba, La, concentration
camp 143
River Plate, Argentina (football club) 146
Rizzoli, Andrea 149, 150, 151
Roberto, Luís 188
Robertson, John Tait (Jacky) 14–15
Robles, Carlos 224
Robson, Bobby 240
Romania xv, 110, 128–31, 133, 163
Rome, Italy 227
AS Roma (football club) 140, 141, 143
Roosevelt, Franklin D. 63
Rosenfeld, Majer 102–3
Rosinger 119
Rosten, Leo 145
Rothschild, Henri de 41
Rotling, Béla 1
Rowlinson, John 246
Russia, anti-Semitism 163

Sacchi, Arrigo 69
Sacks, Jonathan 258
St Louis Madison Kennel, United States
(football club) 54
Salgótarján, Hungary (football club) 92
Salomon (Jewish boy) 204
Sampdoria, Italy (football club) 151, 158
San Lorenzo, Argentina (football club)
146
San Mámes Stadium, Bilbao, Spain 166
San Siro Stadium, Milan, Italy 141, 147,
151
Santana, Joaquim 196, 198
Santiago Bernebau Stadium, Madrid,
Spain 166

Santos, Artur 196–7, 232
Santos, Brazil (football club) 179, 182–3, 206, 223–5
São Paulo, Brazil 101, 145, 161
São Paulo, Brazil (football club) 18, 60, 171, 179–84, 193, 223, 260
Saraiva 232
Sarará 183
Sas, Ferenc (Ferenc Sohn) 77
Scarone, Roberto 222
Schalke, Germany (football club) 200
Scheuer, Max 43
Schiaffino, Juan Alberto 149, 151
Schlosser, Imre 16
Schönfeld, Heinrich 42, 50
Schuschnigg, Kurt 66
Schwarcz, Ernő 30, 42, 48, 53, 55
Schwarcz, Sándor 154
Schwartz, Elek 231, 232
Schweigsame Frau, Die (The Silent Woman) (opera) 159
Scottish football 14–19, 47, 69
scudetto (Italian league championship) 149
Seattle Sounders, United States (football club) 55
Sebes, Gusztáv 17, 133, 164–5, 167–9, 169, 251
Sebestyén, Béla 16
Serafim 232
Serantoni, Pietro 142
Serbia 11
Serie A (Italian League) 141, 148, 149
Serra 232
Servette FC, Geneva, Switzerland (football club) 239, 260
Setúbal, Portugal (football club) 240
Shankly, Bill 122, 177–8
Sharansky, Natan 257
Silent Woman, The (Die Schweigsame Frau) (opera) 159
Silva, Gastão 236
Simões, António xi, 174–8, 207, 211, 213, 215–16, 233, 240, 244, 246, 248
Sindelar, Matthias 69
Slavia Prague, Czech Republic (football club) xii, 36, 80
Slavia Sofia, Bulgaria (football club) 239
Slawik, Franz 204
Smith, Bobby 211–13
Smith, Gordon 197
Sobibór Death Camp, Poland 160, 217

Soccer Wars, United States 51–2, 58
Sohn, Ferenc (Ferenc Sas) 77
Solti, Desző (Desző Steinberger) 153–7, 217–18
Sordi, de 183
Sørensen, Jørgen 148, 150
South American football 207–8
 see also Argentina; Brazil; Uruguay
South American Football Confederation 224
Southampton (football club) 177–8
Soviet occupation, Hungary 101, 134–5, 139, 163–4
Spain 165
 anti-Semitism 185
 football 69, 165–6
 players 36
 Spanish league 73, 194, 215
 see also Real Madrid, Spain (football club)
Spitz, Mark 253
Sport Lisboa e Benfica see Benfica, Portugal (football club)
Sportclub (SC) Enschede, Netherlands (football club) now Twente 70–3, 140, 191–2, 260
Sporthirlap (newspaper) 81, 82–3
Sporting Braga, Portugal (football club) 235
Sporting da Covilhã, Portugal (football club) 201
Sporting de Lourenço Marques, Mozambique (football club) 205–6
Sporting Lisbon, Portugal (football club) 187, 192, 193, 198, 205–6, 228, 232, 235
Städtisches Stadion, Nürnberg, Germany 210
Stadttempel, Vienna, Austria 219–20, 248
Stalin, Joseph 125, 162
Stampa, La (newspaper) 151–2, 155, 157, 166–7
Standard Liège, Belgium (football club) 215
Stars of David (book) 112
Stéfano, Alfredi di 166
Steinberger, Desző (Desző Solti) 153–7, 217–18
Sternberg, László 53, 76–7, 79
Stoneham, Charles 51, 52
Straus, Nathan 40–1

Strauss, Richard 159
Stricker, Robert xii, 26
Stunde, Die (newspaper) 48
Suárez, Luis 201
Sunday Times, the (newspaper) 153
Svevo, Italo 143
Sweden 88, 148, 181, 187
Swinna, Slovakia 120
Switzerland xiii, xv, 64, 88, 89, 107, 165,
 239, 261
Syria 161
Szalai, András 135
Szilágyi, Gyula 128
Szőnyi, Tibor 135
Szusza, Ferenc 131, 169

Taça de Portugal 189, 235
tactics 18, 30, 69, 180–1
 2-3-5 formation 30
 4-2-4 formation 18, 180, 193
 blitzkrieg 193–4, 198, 210, 235
 catenaccio 148, 251
 pyramid formation 30
 W-M formation 18, 180, 193
Tegelbeckers, W. Ludwig 125
Teixeira, António 188–9
Tel Aviv, Israel 39–40
Theresienstadt concentration camp 53
Three Masters (Drei Masters) (book) 159
Tichy, Lajos 169
tika-taka (tactics) 69
Times, The (newspaper)181, 234
Topol'čany, Slovakia 120
Törekvés, Hungary (football club) 9–10,
 104, 139, 259
Torino, Italy (football club) 99, 140, 141,
 143, 144
Torres 232
Total Football system 69
Tottenham Hotspur (Spurs) (football club)
 210–13, 234
Trainerlegende, Die (book) 90
Treviso, Mose da 137–8
Trianon, Treaty of (1920) 77, 78
Triestina, Italy (football club) 142–4, 149,
 152, 175, 260
Tunsgram Factory, Újpest, Hungary 100
Twente, Netherlands (football club)
 formerly Sportclub (SC) Enschede
 70–3, 140, 191–2, 260
2-3-5 formation (tactics) 30

UEFA 165, 198
UEFA Champions League (formerly
 European Cup) 32, 256
Új Élet (newspaper) 119–20
Újpest, Hungary 85–6, 89, 90, 93, 97
Újpest, Hungary (football club) 9, 197–9,
 245
 BG as coach 74, 76, 79–81, 93, 108,
 131–2, 172, 176, 230, 260
 ex-players 53, 169
Újpesti Dózsa (formerly Újpest, football
 club) 197–9
Újvidék, Hungary (now Novi Sad, Serbia)
 10–11, 71
Ukraine 7, 88, 129, 167
Ulysses (book) 143
União Torreense, Portugal (football club)
 188, 189
Unione Triestina, Italy (football club)
 142–4, 149, 152, 175, 260
United Nations 121, 203
United States xv, 20, 64, 74–7, 99, 253–4
 football 46–56
 Hakoah Vienna tour xii, 40–3, 47, 50–1
 national team 42
 see also American Soccer League
 (ASL); New York clubs
United States Citizenship and
 Immigration Services 75, 107
United States Football Associaton (USFA)
 51–2
United States Holocaust Memorial
 Museum 114
United States Open Cup 51–2, 53–5,
 76–7, 261
Upton Park, London 36
Uruguay xv, 58–9, 98, 214, 221, 222, 225
 players 149

Vác, Hungary 90, 98, 249
Vandeweghe, Maurice 47, 49, 52–3
Vándor, Kálmán 133
Vanishing Diaspora (book) 256
Vasas, Hungary (football club) 127–8, 260
Venezia, Italy (football club) 141
Venezuela 170
Venice, Italy 137–8
Verga, Solomon ibn 186
Vicenza, Italy (football club) 155, 157–8,
 175, 260
Vicini, Azeglio 157

Vieira de Brito, Maurício 191–2, 202
Vienna, Austria 65, 125, 140, 161–2, 175,
 186–7, 198, 239, 241–2, 245, 259
 anti-Semitism 33–5, 74, 219–20
 football xii, 20–1, 23–9
 Jewish communities 256
Viennese Soccer Association Club (WAF)
 34
violence at football matches 31, 33–5, 190,
 224, 227
Viren, Lasse 255
Vitali, Giancarlo 141
Vítor 183
Vitória de Guimarães, Portugal (football
 club) 235

WAF (Viennese Soccer Association Club)
 34
Wagner, Gustav (Günther Mendel) 159,
 160–1
Walker, Jimmy 41, 61
Wall Street Crash 45, 57–8, 126
Wallenberg, Raoul 89, 90, 100
Wallenstein, Róbert Vago 104
Walter, Joschi 228, 229
Wankdorf Stadium, Bern, Switzerland 201
Warsaw, Poland 38–9
Washington Post (newspaper) 203–4
Wasserstein, Bernard 256
Weisz, Árpád 139, 254
Weisz, Clara 139
Weisz, Elena 139
Weisz, Roberto 139
*Welt von Gestern, Die (The World of
 Yesterday)* (book) 159
Wembley Stadium, London 32–3, 165
Wenger, Arsène 122
Wenger, Beth S. 46
West German national team 165, 194, 202,
 252–3
West Ham United (football club) xii, 32–3,
 36, 42–3
Wetzer, Rudolf 129
whirl (tactics) 69
White, John 211
White Hart Lane, London 212–13, 234
White Terror, Hungary xi, 1–3, 4, 10, 19,
 20, 36, 77, 104, 230
Wiener Amateur-SV, Austria (football
 club) later FK Austria Vienna 208
Wiener Morgenzeitung (newspaper) 31, 34

Wiener Sport-Club, Austria (football club)
 29
Wiesel Commission 129
Wiesenthal, Simon 161
Wilson, Jonathan 15, 18, 89, 181, 251
WiWo (Wiener Wochenblatt) (newspaper)
 229–30
W-M formation (tactics) 18, 180, 193
World Cup 18, 37, 129, 193, 222
 Finals (1930) 59
 Finals (1934) 31, 49, 53, 69–70, 139
 Finals (1938) 70, 77, 79, 139, 142
 Finals (1954) 148, 165, 169, 202, 253
 Finals (1958) 148, 181, 184, 187
 Finals (1962) 184, 222
 Finals (1966) 236
 Finals (1978) 240
 Finals (1990) 157
World of Yesterday, The (Die Welt von Gestern)
 (book) 159
World Soccer Magazine 89, 111, 123, 245
World War I 8–9, 24, 77
World Zionist Conference, Vienna,
 Austria (1925) 35
World Zionist Organisation 26
Wortmann, Siegfried 36, 51, 52, 54

Yad Vashem Holocaust museum, Jerusalem
 39, 102, 103
Yom Hashoah (Holocaust remembrance
 day), Israel 256
Yugoslavia xv, 69, 194–5

Zamora 36
Zauber, Samuel 129
Zentralfriedhof (Central Cemetery)
 Vienna, Austria ix, 241–2
Zionism xi–xii, 6, 23, 26, 35, 163
 sports clubs 23–9
Zionist Congress, Basel, Switzerland
 (1897) 5
Zionist Jewish National Party 26
Zizinho 182–3
Zsengellér, Gyula 79, 80, 131, 172–3
Zweig, Lotte 160
Zweig, Stefan 159–60